Fyodor Dostoevsky

CRIME AND PUNISHMENT

[Edited with Summary and Analysis, Study Questions and Criticism]

Mansi Sachdeva
B.A. English (Hons), Delhi University;
M.A., M. Phil. (English), IGNOU

ANMOL PUBLICATIONS PVT. LTD.
NEW DELHI - 110 002 (INDIA)

ANMOL PUBLICATIONS PVT. LTD.
H.O.: 4374/4B, Ansari Road, Daryaganj,
New Delhi-110 002 (India)
Ph.: 23278000, 23261597
B.O.: No. 1015, Ist Main Road, BSK IIIrd Stage
IIIrd Phase, IIIrd Block,
Bangalore - 560 085 (India)
Visit us at: www.anmolpublications.com

Crime and Punishment

First Published, 2009

PRINTED IN INDIA

Printed at Mehra Offset Press, Delhi.

Contents

Preface

Dostoevsky was not only a chronicler of the exact physical surrounding, he was also writing subjects of modern concern. During the time that Dostoevsky was writing and publishing, the American public was reading about the romantic adventures of Hiawatha and Evangeline by Longfellow, stories that were set in some unrealistic and romantic distant past, or else the bizarre stories of Edgar Allen Poe. Dostoevsky established one of the precepts of modern realism was to present life as it actually was lived. This is exactly what Dostoevsky did from his earliest novels to his final masterpiece *The Brothers Karamazov*.

Dostoevsky was a prodigious reader and was well informed about the newest ideas and the most recent philosophical concepts of his time. His characters are driven by inner emotions that were just being investigated towards the end of his life. Sigmund Freud's investigations of the psychological states of one's mind were being published only after Dostoevsky had written many of his studies of the mental forces that drive a person to commit certain acts. Porfiry's investigations into the motives behind a crime and of the mental state of the criminal would not become an acceptable manner of investigation until sometime in the twentieth century. As a psychologist, Dostoevsky was well ahead of Freud. His descriptions of the inner emotions are psychologically realistic and true. Some are based on fact: for example, due to his involvement with writing and printing censored material, and subsequently, being condemned to death, Dostoevsky would often write about man's absolute despair.

And the book is an attempt to capture the similar images and make it a critical read.

Author

Chapter 1

Introduction

Personal Information: Personal: (Name also transliterated as Fedor, Feodor; also Mikhailovich; also Dostoevski, Dostoievsky, Dostoevskii, Dostoevsky, Dostoiewsky, Dostoiefski, Dostoievski, Dostoyevskiy, Dostoieffski) Russian novelist and short story writer. Born October 30, 1821, in Moscow, Russia; died after suffering a hemorrhage in his throat, January 29, 1881, in St. Petersburg, Russia; buried in the Alexander Nevsky Monastery in Leningrad; son of Mikhail Andreevich (a physician) and Maria Fedorovna (Nechaeva) Dostoevsky; married Maria Dmitrievna Konstant Isaeva (died April 15, 1864); married Anna Grigorievna Snitkina (a stenographer), February 15, 1867; children: (second marriage) Sofia, Lyubov, Fyodor, Aleksei.

Education: Military Engineering School, St. Petersburg, 1837- 43.

Career: Novelist, journalist, and short-story writer. Member of the Petrashevsky Circle (a radical group of socialist thinkers), 1847-1849; political prisoner at a prison labour camp in Tobolsk, Russia, 1850-54; *Vremya* (journal), Russia, co-owner and editor, 1861-63; *Epokha* (journal), Russia, co-owner and editor, 1864-65; *Grazhdanin* (journal; title means "The Citizen"), Russia, editor and columnist, 1871-74; *Dnevnik pisatelya* (monthly journal), Russia, owner, author, and publisher, 1876-77, 1881. Public Speaker.

Military Service: Russian Army, 1843-44, served in engineering; rank of lieutenant; and 1854-59, served in Semipalatinsk; became lieutenant.

Fyodor Dostoevsky (1821-1881) was a Russian novelist, journalist, short-story writer whose psychological penetration into the human soul had a profound influence on the 20th century novel. Fyodor Dostoevsky (1821-1881) was a Russian novelist, journalist, short-story writer whose psychological penetration into the human soul had a profound influence on the 20th century novel.

Dostoevsky was born in Moscow, as the second son of a former army doctor. He was educated at home and at a private school. Shortly after the death of his mother in 1837 he was sent to St. Petersburg, where he entered the Army Engineering College. In 1839 Dostoevsky's father died probably of apoplexy but there were strong rumors that he was murdered by his own serfs. Dostoevsky graduated as a military engineer, but resigned in 1844 to devote himself to writing. His first novel, *Poor Folk* appeared in 1846. It was followed by *The Double,* which depicted a man who was haunted by a look-alike who eventually usurps his position.

In 1846 he joined a group of utopian socialists. He was arrested in 1849 and sentenced to death. The sentence was commuted to imprisonment in Siberia. Dostoevsky spent four years in hard labour and four years as a soldier in Semipalatinsk.

Dostoevsky returned to St. Petersburg in 1854 as a writer with a religious mission and published three works that derive in different ways from his Siberia experiences: *The House of the Dead,* (1860) a fictional account of prison life, *The Insulted and Injured,* which reflects the author's refutation of naive Utopianism in the face of evil, and *Winter Notes on Summer Impressions,* his account of a trip to Western Europe.

In 1857 Dostoevsky married Maria Isaev, a 29-year old widow. He resigned from the army two years later. Between the years 1861 and 1863 he served as editor of the monthly periodical *Time,* which was later suppressed because of an article on the Polish uprising.

In 1864-65 his wife and brother died and he was burdened with debts, and his situation was made even worse by gambling. From the turmoil of the 1860s emerged *Notes from the Underground,* psychological study of an outsider, which marked a watershed in Dostoevsky's artistic development. The novel starts with the confessions of a mentally ill narrator and continues with the promise of spiritual rebirth. It was followed by *Crime and Punishment,* (1866) an account of an individual's fall and redemption, *The Idiot,* (1868) depicting a Christ-like figure, Prince Myshkin, and *The Possessed,* (1871) an exploration of philosophical nihilism.

In 1867 Dostoevsky married Anna Snitkin, his 22-year old stenographer, who seems to have understood her husband's manias and rages. They traveled abroad and returned in 1871. By the time of *The Brothers Karamazov,* which appeared in 1879-80, Dostoevsky was recognized in his own country as one of its great writers.

An epileptic all his life, Dostoevsky died in St. Petersburg on February 9, 1881. He was buried in the Aleksandr Nevsky monastery, St. Petersburg.

Chapter 2

Fyodor Dostoevsky: Biography

Russian novelist, journalist, short-story writer, whose psychological penetration into the human soul profoundly influenced the 20th century novel. Dostoevsky's novels have much autobiographical elements, but ultimately they deal with moral and philosophical questions. He presented interacting characters with contrasting views or ideas about freedom of choice, Socialism, atheisms, good and evil, happiness and so forth. Dostoevsky's central obsession was God, whom his characters constantly search through painful errors and humiliations.

"But you're a poet, and I'm a simple mortal, and therefore I will say one must look at things from the simplest, most practical point of view. I, for one, have long since freed myself from all shackles, and even obligations. I only recognize obligations when I see I have something to gain by them. You. of course, can't look at things like that, your legs are in fetters and your taste is morbid. You yearn for the ideal, for virtue. But, my dear friend, I am ready to recognize anything you tell me to, but what shall I do if I know for a fact that at the root of all human virtues lies the most intense egoism?" (Prince Valkovsky in *The Insulted and Humiliated,* 1861)

Fyodor Dostoevsky was born in Moscow, as the second son of a staff doctor at the Hospital for the Poor - later Dostoevsky's father acquired an estate and serfs. Dostoevsky was educated at home and at a private school. With his pious mother he made annual pilgrimages to the monastery of the

Trinity and Saint Sergei. Shortly after her death in 1837, he was sent to St. Petersburg, where he entered the Academy for Military Engineers. Dostoevsky was commissioned as a 2nd lieutenant in 1842 and next years he graduated as a War Ministry draftsman. He had no interest in military engineering but at the academy he could also study Russian and French literature.

Dostoevsky's father Mikhail Andreevich died in 1839, probably of apoplexy, but there was strong rumors that he was murdered by his own serfs in a quarrel. With the help of a small income from the estate, he resigned in 1844 his commission to devote himself to writing. His first novel, *Poor Folk* (1846), which he wrote in a little over nine months in his small room, gained a great success with the critics, who hailed Dostoevsky as the new Gogol. "We all came from Gogol's overcoat," Dostoevsky said. One critic remarked dryly, "You have Gogols growing like mushrooms." The leading literary critic Vissarion Belinsky called *Poor Folk* "the first attempt at a social novel we've had".

Poor Folk was followed by *The Double* (1846), subtitled "A Petersburg Poem", which irritated Dostoevsky's former admirer, Vissarion Belinsky. In the story a man is losing his mind - he is haunted by a look-alike who eventually usurps his position. Belinsky remarked that such atypical "psychopathic" characters belonged in madhouses rather than in works of art.

In 1846 Dostoevsky joined a group of utopian socialists, who gathered Mihail Petrashevsky's home. Petrashevsky was an eccentric and socialist, who once went to a church dressed as a woman. The secret police had placed an agent in the group, and on April 23 in 1849 Dostoevsky was arrested during a reading of Vissarion Belinsky's radical letter 'Selected Passages from Correspondence with Friends,' and sentenced to death. With mock execution, which thoroughly shocked the writer, the sentence was commuted to imprisonment in Siberia. Dostoevsky spent four years in hard labour in a stockade, wearing fetters. Many of the other convicts had committed murder. On his release in 1854 he was assigned as a common soldier in Semipalatinsk. Eventually he became an ensign. These experiences provided subject matter for the his future works. His heroes and heroines reflected moral values which were vitally important for the author. They also were men and women of action, whose thoughts influenced deeply the young in Russia. During the years in Siberia Dostoevsky became a monarchist and a devout follower of the Russian Orthodox Church.

Dostoevsky returned to St. Petersburg in 1859 as a writer with a religious mission. He published three works that derive in different ways from his Siberia experiences: *The House of the Dead* (1861-62), a fictional account of prison life, *The Insulted and Injured* (1861), which reflects the author's refutation of naive Utopianism in the face of evil, and *Winter Notes on Summer Impressions* (1863), his account of trip to Western Europe.

The Insulted and Injured was greeted by Dostoevsky's old and new readers with enthusiasm. It was completed after his penal service and exile, and published on his return to Petersburg. The narrator is Ivan Petrovich, a young aspiring writer. His literary debut, working methods, and social situation were taken from Dostoevsky's own life. The hero falls from the fame into poverty. When the book appeared it was coldly received by the critics. Dostoevsky defended the work in an open letter, writing that he knew for certain that even though the novel should be a failure, there would be poetry in it, and the two most important characters would be portrayed truthfully and even artistically.

In 1857 Dostoevsky married Maria Isaev, a 29-year old widow. He resigned from the army two years later. Between the years 1861 and 1863 he served as the editor of the monthly periodical *Time*. The paper was later suppressed because of an article on the Polish uprising. In 1862 Dostoevsky went to abroad for the first time, traveling in France and England. He traveled Europe again in 1863 and 1865. During this period his wife and brother died, he was obsessed with gambling, and plagued by debts and frequent epileptic seizures.

From the turmoil of the 1860s emerged *Notes from Underground* (1864), a psychological study of an outsider. The book marked a watershed in Dostoevsky artistic development. *Notes from Underground* starts with a confession by the narrator. "I am a sick man.... I am a spiteful man. I am a most unpleasant man. I think my liver is diseased." The story continues with the monologue of the Underground man, who reveals his inner self to his imaginary reader. He is humiliated by his former schoolmates in a party and he gets very drunk. In a dark shop, which functions as a brothel in the evenings, he makes impressive speeches to a humble prostitute, Liza. "What are you giving up here? What are you enslaving? Why, you're enslaving your soul; something you don't really own, together with your body! You're giving away your love to be defiled by any drunkard! Love! After all, that's all there is!" He humiliates her, gives money when she only shows her real caring, but eventually she demonstrates her moral superiority. *Notes from Underground* was followed by *Crime and Punishment* (1866), an account of an individual's fall and redemption, *The Idiot* (1868-69), depicting a Christ-like figure, Prince Myshkin, through whom the author revealed the spiritual bankruptcy of Russia, and *The Possessed* (1872), an exploration of philosophical nihilism.

Crime and Punishment was serialized in *Ruskii vestnik* (The Russian Messenger) from January through December 1866 and appeared in a book form next year. On one level the novel belongs to the genre of detective fiction, but Dostoevsky's interest lies on the criminal - the sinner. The story is set in St. Petersburg, which Dostoevsky called the "most fantastic city in the world". The city, with its mythology, also becomes the accomplice of the protagonist, Raskolnikov, a young resentful student. An assiduous readers of newspapers, Dostoevsky saw in the crime reports symbolic meanings, signs of the hidden ills of the whole society.

Raskolnikov kills a pawnbroker, a greedy old woman, and her half-witted stepsister as well. He attempts to justify the murder in terms of its advantageous social consequences. He argues that each age gives birth to a few superior beings who are not constrained by ordinary morality - and he is one of such beings. Under the influence of the meek, Christian prostitute Sonia, he confronts the hollowness of his thoughts, which eventually leads to confession and redemption. Raskolnikov's nemesis is Porfiry Petrovich, a police investigator, who knows his guilt. In the demonic Svidrigailov, who commits suicide, Raskolnikov sees his own picture. "You know," confesses Svidrigailov to Raskolnikov, "from the very beginning I always thought it was a pity that your sister had not chanced to be born in the second or third century of our era, as the daughter of a ruling prince somewhere, or some governor or proconsul in Asia minor. She would doubtless have been one of those who suffered martyrdom, and she would, of course, have smiled when they burned her breast with red-hot pinchers. She would have deliberately brought it on herself." In his agony Raskolnikov realises, that in murdering he has killed the essentially human in himself. Raskolnikov goes to Siberia for seven years. Sonia follows him to his imprisonment.

The novel has been filmed several times. Josef von Sternberg's version from 1935, starring Peter Lorre as Raskolnikov, was primarily a detective story. In the same year Pierre Chenal made his adaptation, *Crime et châtiment*. Denis Sanders moved the action to contemporary California in 1959. Lev Kulidjanov's version from 1969 was long - 3 hours and 20 minutes - and the most ambitious of all.

Dostoevsky married in 1867 Anna Grigoryevna Snitkina, his 22-years old stenographer, who seems to have understood her husband's manias and rages. To avoid his creditors Dostoevsky left Russia with her and spent time in Germany, Italy, and Switzerland, mostly in poverty. He was obsessed with gambling, but in Russia his literary fame only grew. When *The Possessed* turned out to be a success, he returned to Russia, and purchased a house in the provincial town of Staraya Russa. From 1873 to 1874 Dostoevsky was editor of the conservative weekly *Citizen*. Among his friends was Konstantin Pobedonostsev, a reactionary and the tutor to the czarevitch

Alexander. In 1876 he founded his own monthly, *The Writer's Diary*. From its writings he collected *The Diary of a Writer* (1876).

Dostoevsky's short story from this period 'The Gentle Maiden' (1876) inspired later Robert Bresson's film *Une Femme Douce* (1969). In the story, narrated in first-person, a husband searches the reason for his wife's suicide and goes through their life together. "How it has happened I cannot tell, I try, again and again, to explain it to myself. Ever since six o'clock I have been trying to explain it, yet cannot bring my thoughts to a focus. Perhaps it is through trying so much that I fail." Gradually his narration reveals him as pompous, cruel, and tyrannical man. "She could go nowhere without my leave," he says, and the reader realises that suicide offered her the only way to escape from her domineering husband.

By the time of *The Brothers of Karamazov* (1879-80), Dostoevsky was recognized in his own country as one of its great writers. He enjoyed his role as a prophet, an original public voice in the crisis period of his country. Dostoevsky final novel culminated his lifelong obsession with patricide - the assumed murder of his father had left deep marks on the author's psyche. The novel is constructed around a simple plot, dealing with the murder of the father of the Karamazov family. One of the sons, Dmitri, is arrested. The brothers represent three aspects of man's being: reason (Ivan), emotion (Dmitri) and faith (Alesha). This material is transcended into a moral and spiritual statement of contemporary society.

An epileptic all his life, Dostoevsky died in St. Petersburg on February 9 (New Style), 1881. He was buried in the Aleksandr Nevsky monastery, St. Petersburg. Anna Grigoryevna devoted the rest of her life to cherish the literary heritage of her husband. Dostoevsky's novels anticipated many of the ideas of Nietzsche and Freud. Dostoevsky himself was strongly influenced by such thinkers as Aleksandr Herzen and Vissarion Belinsky. He saw that great art must have liberty to develop on its own terms, but it always deals with central social concerns. He supported the Russian war against Turkey, and like much later Aleksandr Solzhenitsyn, he emphasized more the spiritual transformation of the individual than social revolution. In the notorious essay 'The Jewish Question' the author did not hide his anti-Semitism. Dostoevsky's novels have been read in many ways - according to some biographical interpretations, he raped a young girl, which he revealed in a fictionalized form in his writings. Dostoevsky nerver met his great contemporary writer Leo Tolstoy. The Westernizing Turgenev was in many ways his opposite.

Chapter 3

List of Works: Fyodor Dostoevsky

SELECTED WORKS

Dostoyevsky is considered one of the greatest writers in world literature. Best-known for his novels *Prestupleniye I nakazaniye* (1866; *Crime and Punishment*) and *Bratya Karamazovy* (1880; *The Brothers Karamazov*), he attained profound philosophical and psychological insights which anticipated important developments in twentieth-century thought, including psychoanalysis and existentialism. In addition, Dostoyevsky's powerful literary depictions of the human condition exerted a profound influence on modern writers, such as Franz Kafka, whose works further develop some of the Russian novelist's themes. The writer's own troubled life enabled him to portray with deep sympathy characters who are emotionally and spiritually downtrodden and who in many cases epitomize the traditional Christian conflict between the body and the spirit.

WRITINGS

- (Translator) Honore de Balzac, *Eugenie Grandet*, [Russia], 1844.
- *Bednye lyudi* (title means *Poor Folk*), [Russia], 1846.
- *Dvoinik* (translation published as *The DoubleDouble*), [Russia], 1846.
- Roman v devyati pis'makh (title means A Novel in Nine Letters Novel in Nine Letters), [Russia], 1847.

- Chuzhaya zhena i muzh pod krovat'yu (title means Another Man's Wife and a Husband under the Bed), [Russia], 1848.
- Elka i svad'ba (title means A Christmas Party and a WeddingChristmas Party and a Wedding), [Russia], 1848.
- *Netochka Nezvanova,* [Russia], 1849; translated as *Netochka Nezvanova* by Jane Kentish, Viking, 1986.
- *Dyadyushkin son* (novella; title means *Uncle's Dream*), [Russia], 1859.
- Selo Stepanchikovo (novella; title means The Friend of the FamilyFriend of the Family), [Russia], 1859.
- Zapiski iz mertvogo doma (title means The House of the DeadHouse of the Dead), [Russia], 1860-62.
- Unizhennye i oskorblennye (translations published as The Insulted and InjuredInsulted and Injured and Injury and Insult), [Russia], 1861.
- *Prestuplenie i nakazanie,* [Russia], 1866, translation by Jessie Coulson published as *Crime and Punishment,* edited by George Gibian, [New York], 1964.
- *Igrok* (novella; title means *The GamblerGambler*), [Russia], 1867.
- *Idiot,* [Russia], 1868.
- Vechnyi muzh (novella; title means The Eternal HusbandEternal Husband), [Russia], 1870.
- *Besy* (title means *The PossessedPossessed*), [Russia], 1872.
- *Dnevnik pisatelya* (title means *The Diary of a WriterDiary of a Writer*) (essays and short stories), [Russia], 1873-77; translated as *A Writer's Diary,Writer's Diary,* by Kenneth Lantz, Northwestern University Press, 1993.
- *Podrostok* (title means *A Raw YouthRaw Youth* or *The AdolescentAdolescent*), [Russia], 1875; translated as *An Accidental Family,Accidental Family,* by Richard

Freeborn, with introduction and notes, Oxford University Press, 1994.

- *Brat'ya Karamazovy,* [Russia], 1880, translation by Constance Garnett published as *The Brothers Karamazov,Brothers Karamazov,* edited by Ralph Matlaw, [New York], 1976.
- The Notebooks for "Crime and Punishment,"Notebooks for "Crime and Punishment," translated by Edward Wasiolek, [Chicago], 1967.
- The Notebooks for "The Idiot,"Notebooks for "The Idiot," translated by Katharine Strelsky, [Chicago], 1968.
- The Notebooks for "The Possessed,"Notebooks for "The Possessed," translated by Victor Terras, [Chicago], 1968.
- The Notebooks for "A Raw Youth,"Notebooks for "A Raw Youth," translated by Terras, [Chicago], 1969.
- The Notebooks for "The Brothers Karamazov," Notebooks for "The Brothers Karamazov," translated by Wasiolek, [Chicago], 1971.

Collections

- *Novels,* translated by Constance Garnett, [New York], 1912.
- Polnoe sobranie khudozhestvennykh proizvedenii; Dnevnik pisatelya; stat'i, edited by B. Tomashevskii and K. Khalabaev, 13 volumes, 1926-30.
- *Pis'ma,* edited by A. S. Dolinin, volumes 1-3, 1928-34, volume 4, 1959.
- The Short Novels of Dostoevsky,Short Novels of Dostoevsky, translated by Garnett, [New York], 1945.

- The Short Stories of Dostoevsky,Short Stories of Dostoevsky, translated by Garnett, [New York], 1946.
- *Dostoevsky's Occasional Writings,* translated and edited by David Magarshack, [New York], 1963.
- *Polnoe sobranie sochinenii v tridtsati tomakh,* edited by G. M. Fridlender and others, 1972—.
- The Unpublished Dostoevsky, Diaries and Notebooks, 1860-1881,Unpublished Dostoevsky, Diaries and Notebooks, 1860-1881, three volumes, [Ann Arbor, MI], 1973-76.

Other

- *Complete Letters,* 5 volumes, translated by David A. Lowe, Ardis, 1989-91.
- Also author of short stories, including "Mr. Prokharchin," 1846; Khozyaika (translation published as The Landlady), 1847; Belye nochi (title means White Nights), 1848; Polzunkov, 1848; Slaboe serdtse (title means A Faint Heart), 1848; Chestnyi vor (title means An Honest Thief), 1848; Skvernyi anekdot (title means A Vile Anecdote), 1861; Zapiski iz podpol'ya (translation published as Notes from Underground), 1864; Neobyknovennoe sobytie, ili passazh v passazhe (title means The Crocodile, or Mauled in the Mall), 1865; Bobok, 1873; Krotkaya (title means A Gentle Creature or The Meek One), 1876; and Son Smeshnogo cheloveka (title means The Dream of a Ridiculous Man), 1877.

PERIODICALS

- *American Imago,* April, 1947; Spring, 1959.
- Canadian Slavonic Papers, 10, Number 1, 1968.
- *Chimera,* Winter, 1943.
- *College English,* December, 1955.
- *Commentary,* February, 1987; June, 1992.
- Cross-Currents, Fall, 1952.

- *Economist*, July 9, 1988.
- *Explicator*, Fall, 1981; Spring, 1982; Fall, 1982.
- *Hudson Review*, Spring, 1948; Summer, 1960.
- Journal of Aesthetics and Art Criticism, Winter, 1968.
- Journal of American Folklore, July-September, 1956.
- Journal of Criminal Law and Criminology, November-December, 1937.
- Journal of Religions, April, 1956.
- Literature and Psychology, 22, Number 1, 1972.
- *London Mercury*, November, 1927.
- Michigan Quarterly Review, Fall, 1983.
- *Minnesota Review*, January-April, 1965.
- Modern Fiction Studies, Autumn, 1958.
- National Review, May 22, 1987.
- *New Republic*, June 15, 1915; April 27, 1987; December 5, 1988; March 6, 1989; October 12, 1992.
- *New York Review of Books*, January 17, 1991; June 13, 1991.
- *New York Times Book Review*, June 14, 1987; February 21, 1988; June 4, 1989; April 26, 1992; February 27, 1994.
- Psychoanalytic Review, April, 1930.
- Russian Literature Triquarterly, Fall, 1971.
- *Russian Review*, January, 1951; April, 1971.
- Slavic and East European Journal, Spring, 1966; Spring, 1973.
- Slavonic and East European Review, May, 1949.
- Soviet Literature, December, 1981.
- Studies in Short Fiction, Fall, 1973.
- Texas Studies in Literature and Language, Fall, 1972.
- *Yale Review*, December, 1977.

Chapter 4

Dostoevsky As a Writer

Dostoevsky grew up in a middle-class family in Moscow. His father, a doctor, was a tyrant toward his family, and his mother was a mild, pious woman who died before Dostoyevsky was sixteen. Partly to escape the oppressive atmosphere of his father's household, the boy acquired a love of reading, especially the works of Nikolai Gogol, E. T. A. Hoffmann, and Honore de Balzac. At his father's insistence, Dostoevsky trained as an engineer in St. Petersburg. While the youth was at school, his father was murdered by his own serfs at the family's small country estate. Dostoevsky rarely mentioned his father's murder, but Oedipal themes are recurrent in his work, and Sigmund Freud suggested that the novelist's epilepsy was a manifestation of guilt over his repressed wish for his father's death.

Dostoevsky graduated from engineering school but chose a literary career. His first published work, a translation of Balzac's novel *Eugenie Grandet,* appeared in a St. Petersburg journal in 1844. Two years later, he published his first novel, *Bednye lyudi* (1846;*Poor Folk*), a naturalistic tale with a clear social message as well as a delicate description of life's tragic aspects as manifested in everyday existence. The twenty-four-year-old author became an overnight celebrity when Vissarion Belinsky, the most influential critic of the day, praised Dostoyevsky for his social awareness and declared him the literary successor of Gogol. Dostoyevsky joined Belinsky's literary circle but later broke with it when the critic reacted coldly to his subsequent works. Belinsky judged the novel *Dvoynik* (1846;*The Double*) and the short stories Gospodin Prokharchin (1846;Mr. Prokharchin) and Khozyayka (1847; The Landlady) as devoid of a social message.

In 1848 Dostoevsky joined a group of young intellectuals, led by Mikhail Petrashevsky, which met to discuss literary and political issues. In the reactionary political climate of mid-nineteenth-century Russia, such groups were illegal, and in 1849 the members of the so-called Petrashevsky Circle were arrested and charged with subversion. Dostoyevsky and several of his associates were imprisoned and sentenced to death. As they were facing the firing squad, an imperial messenger arrived with the announcement that the Czar had commuted the death sentences to hard labour in Siberia. This scene was to haunt the novelist the rest of his life. Dostoyevsky described his life as a prisoner in *Zapiski iz myortvogo doma* (1862; *The House of the Dead*), a novel demonstrating both an insight into the criminal mind and an understanding of the Russian lower classes. While in prison the writer underwent a profound spiritual and philosophical transformation. His intense study of the *New Testament,* the only book the prisoners were allowed to read, contributed to his rejection of his earlier liberal political views and led him to the conviction that redemption is possible only through suffering and faith, a belief which informed his later work.

Dostoevsky was released from the prison camp in 1854; however, he was forced to serve as a soldier in a Siberian garrison for an additional five years. When Dostoyevsky was finally allowed to return to St. Petersburg in 1859, he eagerly resumed his literary career, founding two periodicals and writings articles and short fiction.

The articles expressed his new-found belief in a social and political order based on the spiritual values of the Russian people. These years were marked by further personal and professional misfortunes, including the forced closing of his journals by the authorities, the deaths of his wife and his brother, and a financially devastating addiction to gambling. It was in this atmosphere that Dostoyevsky wrote *Zapiski iz podpolya* (1864; *Notes from the Underground*) and *Crime and Punishment*. In *Notes from the Underground* Dostoyevsky satirizes contemporary social and political views by presenting a narrator whose notes reveal that his purportedly progressive beliefs lead only to sterility and inaction. Dostoyevsky's portrayal of this bitter and frustrated Underground Man is hailed as the introduction of an important new type of literary figure. *Crime and Punishment* brought him acclaim but scant financial compensation. Viewed by critics as one of his masterpieces, *Crime and Punishment* is the novel in which Dostoyevsky first develops the theme of redemption through suffering.

The protagonist Raskolnikovwhose name derives from the Russian word for schism or splitis presented as the embodiment of spiritual nihilism. The novel depicts the harrowing confrontation between his philosophical beliefs, which prompt him to commit a murder in an attempt to prove his supposed superiority, and his inherent morality, which condemns his actions.

In 1867, Dostoyevsky fled to Europe with his second wife to escape creditors. Although they were distressing due to financial and personal difficulties, Dostoyevsky's years abroad were fruitful, for he completed one important novel and began another. *Idiot* (1869; *The Idiot*), influenced by Hans Holbein's painting *Christ Taken from the Cross* and by Dostoyevsky's opposition to the growing atheistic sentiment of the times, depicts the Christ-like protagonist's loss of innocence and his experience of sin. Dostoyevsky's profound conservatism, which marked his political thinking following his Siberian experience, and especially his reaction against revolutionary socialism, provided the impetus for his great political novel *Besy* (1871-72; *The Possessed*). Based on a true event, in which a young revolutionary was murdered by his comrades, this novel provoked a storm of controversy for its harsh depiction of ruthless radicals. In his striking portrayal of Stavrogin, the novel's central character, Dostoyevsky described a man dominated by the life-denying forces of nihilism.

Dostoyevsky returned to Russia in 1871 and began his final decade of prodigious literary activity. In sympathy with the conservative political party, he accepted the editorship of a reactionary weekly, *Grazhdanin* (*The Citizen*). In his *Dnevnik pisatelya* (1873-1877; *The Diary of a Writer*), initially a column in the *Citizen* but later an independent periodical, Dostoyevsky published a variety of prose works, including some of his outstanding short stories. Dostoyevski's last work was *Bratya Karamazovy* (1880; *The Brothers Karamazov*), a family tragedy of epic proportions, which is viewed as one of the great novels of world literature. The novel recounts the murder of a father by one of his four sons. Initially, his son Dmitri is arrested for the crime, but as the story unfolds it is revealed that the illegitimate son Smerdyakov has killed the old man at what he believes to be the instigation of his half-brother Ivan. Ivan's philosophical essay, The Legend of the Grand Inquisitor, is a work now famous in its own right. Presented as a debate in which the Inquisitor condemns Christ for promoting the belief that mankind has the freedom of choice between good and evil, the piece explores the conflict between intellect and faith, and between the forces of evil and the redemptive power of Christianity. Dostoyevsky envisioned this novel as the first of a series of works depicting The Life of a Great Sinner, but early in 1881, a few months after completing *The Brothers Karamazov*, the writer died at his home in St. Petersburg.

To his contemporary readers, Dostoyevsky appeared as a writer primarily interested in the terrible aspects of human existence. However, later critics have recognized that the novelist sought to plumb the depths of the psyche, in order to reveal the full range of the human experience, from the basest desires to the most elevated spiritual yearnings. Above all, he illustrated the universal human struggle to understand God and self. Dostoyevsky was, Katherine Mansfield wrote, a being who loved, in spite of everything, adored life, even while he knew the dank, dark places.

Chapter 5

Crime and Punishment: Critical Analysis

When Dostoyevsky started work on Crime and Punishment in the summer of 1865 he was depressed and in serious financial straits. A recent gambling spree had depleted his savings, and he owed money for personal expenses as well as bills for Epokha, the journal he founded and had been forced to discontinue. Threatened with debtors' prison, he was approached by an unscrupulous publisher who offered a ridiculously exploitative contract under which Dostoyevsky signed over the copyrights to all his existing works and agreed to write a work of fiction by the end of the following year. For all this he was paid the sum of three thousand rubles, most of which was quickly swallowed up by promissory notes; what little remained was squandered at the gaming tables. Destitute once again, Dostoyevsky forced himself to concentrate on his writing, and by that fall had conceived of the idea for a novel-length work about a family ruined by alcohol.

The roots of Crime and Punishment can be found in various episodes in Dostoyevsky's life. His original idea, a murderer's first-person confession, came to him during his prison term in Siberia—an experience that profoundly changed his political views and instilled in him a life-long respect for order and authority. There is also evidence that he conceived of the Marmaledov family as the basis for a novel to be titled "The Drunkards," but which was never published. Finally, Dostoyevsky was reacting to the political climate in St.

Petersburg, where the impulses of the revolution could be found in the nihilist and radical movements, which Dostoyevsky abhorred. Regardless of its origins, Dostoyevsky meant the novel to be as close to perfect as possible. He took extensive—now famous—notes regarding its structure, toying with different points of view, character, structure, plot, and a variety of thematic strains.

The efforts paid off. Crime and Punishment is a superbly plotted, brilliant character study of a man who is at once an everyman and as remarkable as any character ever written. It poses a simple question, "Can evil means justify honourable ends?" and answers it convincingly without didacticism or naiveté. Dostoyevsky intimates himself so closely with Roskolnikov's consciousness, and describes his turmoil and angst so precisely and exhaustively, that it is easy to forget that the events take place over the course of a mere two weeks. He encourages us to identify with Roskolnikov: the painstaking descriptions of the student's cramped, dingy quarters; the overpowering sights and sounds of a stifling afternoon on the streets of St. Petersburg; the excruciating tension of Porfiry's interrogation—all serve to place the reader at the heart of the action: Roskolnikov's fevered, tormented mind.

The murder itself is almost incidental to the novel; Dostoyevsky devotes no more than a few pages to describing its execution, although he details the painful vacillations that precede the incident and, of course, exposes every aspect of its aftermath. Similarly, Roskolnikov's punishment, in the literal sense, is put off until the epilogue, with his sentence—reduced to seven years due to the accused's apparent temporary insanity—to a Siberian labour camp.

Thus Dostoyevsky brilliantly invites readers to put forth their own notions of Crime and Punishment, and engages us in an irresistible debate: Who is the real criminal? Marmeladov, for abandoning his family? Luzhin for exploiting Dunya? Svidrigailov for murdering his wife? Sonya for prostituting herself? The greedy pawnbroker whom Roskolnikov murdered? Or, to turn the question around: Who among us is not a criminal? Who among us has not attempted to impose his or her will on the natural order?

Furthermore, we are made to understand that Roskolnikov's true punishment is not the sentence imposed on him by the court of law, but that imposed on him by his own actions: the psychological and spiritual hell he has created for himself; the necessary sentence of isolation from his friends and family; the extreme wavering between wanting to confess his crime, and desperately hoping to get away with it. Compelled, ultimately, to confess his crime—and the confession scene is the only incident in which Roskolnikov actually admits to the crime—we feel that Roskolnikov has suffered sufficiently. Indeed, the epilogue with its abbreviated pace and narrative distance feels like a reprieve for the reader as well as for the criminal. Finally, in Siberia, Roskolnikov has found space.

The public reception of Crime and Punishment was enthusiastic—if a little stunned. There was much discussion about the novel's overwhelming power and rumors of people unable to finish it. Readers were shocked by Dostoyevsky's gruesome descriptions and enthralled by his use of dramatic tension. Perhaps the most virulent, and unexpected, criticism came from readers who felt that Dostoyevsky's portrait of the nihilist movement was an indictment of Russian youth and that its premise was inconceivable.

For more than a century, critics have argued about the book's message: Is it a political novel? A tale of morality? A psychological study? A religious epic? As Peter McDuff points out in his Introduction to the Penguin Classics edition, interpretations may be more revealing of the critic than of the text. Whatever Dostoyevsky's purpose—political, moral, psychological, or religious (and most likely he meant to touch on each of these themes)—one thing is certain. In Roskolnikov, Dostoyevsky has created a man who is singular yet universal. He is someone with whom we can sympathize, empathize, and pity, even if we cannot relate to his actions. He is a character we will remember forever, and whose story will echo throughout history.

The family was poor, but their descent from 17th-century nobility entitled them to own land and serfs. Dostoyevsky's mother, Maria, was loving and religious; his father, Mikhail, tended toward alcoholism and violence, and his cruel behaviour toward the peasants on their small estate resulted in his murder when Fyodor was eighteen years old.

Fyodor was the second of eight children. He was particularly close to his younger sister, Varvara, whose unfortunate marriage may have inspired Dostoyevsky's portraits of both Dunya and Sonya. His older brother, Mikhail, shared Dostoyevsky's literary and journalistic interests as well as his early social ideals. Together they attended secondary schools in Moscow, then the military academy in St. Petersburg, followed by service in the Russian army.

Dostoyevsky broadened his education by reading extensively in an attempt to sharpen his literary skills. As a youth he read and admired writers of all nationalities, including Dickens, Hugo, and Zola, and imitated some of Russia's literary geniuses, particularly Gogol. He also began a tortured acquaintance with Turgenev, which was to continue throughout his life.

His first novel, Poor Folk, was published in 1846. This tale of a young clerk who falls haplessly in love with a woman he cannot possess led the literary lion Victor Belinsky to proclaim Dostoyevsky as the next Gogol. Dostoyevsky's entrance into St. Petersburg literary society had begun—but his celebrity status was quickly overshadowed by his somewhat obnoxious behaviour. Eventually, Dostoyevsky found another group to join, this time a circle of intellectual socialists run by Mikhail Petrashevsky. Given the reactionary climate of the time, the Petrashevsky group's revolutionary ideas were both exciting and dangerous, and, although Dostoyevsky was far from being a revolutionary, his alignment with the faction brought him to the attention of the police. In 1849 he and the rest of the Petrashevsky group were arrested for subversion.

Dostoyevsky was imprisoned at the Peter and Paul Fortress where he and others were subject to a mock execution—an understandably traumatic experience which seems to have triggered an epileptic condition that would plague Dostoyevsky throughout his life. He spent the next five years at hard labour in Siberia, where his acquaintance with the criminal community would provide him with the themes, plots, and characters that distinguish many of his greatest works, including Crime and Punishment.

Dostoyevsky returned to St. Petersburg in 1859. The next decade was filled with emotional and physical turmoil. In 1864 the deaths of his wife, Maria, and his beloved brother, Mikhail, deepened his debt and drove him to gambling. He embarked on a doomed affair with Apollinaria Suslova, who vacillated between admiring and despising him. He also witnessed the dissolution of his literary journal and formed a disadvantageous relationship with an unscrupulous publisher. Yet the 1860s were also a period of great literary fervor, and in 1865, the publication of Crime and Punishment paved the way for a series of novels—including The Idiot, The Devils, and The Brothers Karamazov—that both reclaimed his position in Russia's pantheon of great living writers, and brought stability to his personal and financial affairs. He married his stenographer, Anna Grigorievna Snitkin, with whom he fathered four children, and established himself as a leading conservative who often spoke out against revolutionary activity.

In June of 1880, Dostoyevsky attended a celebration of the great novelist, Pushkin, during which he delivered a speech in praise of the writer. His words were met with great adulation, and the event marked what was perhaps the highest point of public approbation Dostoyevsky would ever attain. Little more than six months later, on January 28, 1881, Dostoyevsky died of a lung hemorrhage. His funeral, attended by nearly thirty thousand mourners, was a national event.

Chapter 6

Context of the Novel

Fyodor Dostoevsky (also spelled Dostoyevsky) is renowned as one of the world's greatest novelists and literary psychologists. His works grapple with deep political, social, and religious issues while delving into the often tortured psychology of characters whose lives are shaped by these issues. Born in Moscow in 1821, the son of a doctor, he was educated first at home and then at a boarding school. His father sent him to the St. Petersburg Academy of Military Engineering, from which he graduated in 1843. But, as he had long set his sights on literature, Dostoevsky immediately resigned his position as a sublieutenant in exchange for the much less stable life of a fiction writer. His first book, *Poor Folk,* was published to critical acclaim in 1846.

In 1847, Dostoevsky became active in socialist circles, largely because of his opposition to the institution of serfdom. On April 23, 1849, he was arrested for his participation in a group that illegally printed and distributed socialist propaganda. After spending eight months in prison, he was sentenced to death for membership in the group and led, with other members of the group, to be shot. But the execution turned out to be a mere show, meant to punish the prisoners psychologically. Dostoevsky then spent four years at a labour camp in Siberia, followed by four years of military service. Raskolnikov's time in a Siberian prison, described in the Epilogue of Crime and Punishment, is based on Dostoevsky's own experiences at a similar prison.

During his time in prison, Dostoevsky suffered the first of many epileptic seizures. He also underwent something of a political conversion, rejecting the radical socialist positions that had led to his arrest in favour of a conservative concern for traditional values. His dismissal of leftist political thought is evident in *Crime and Punishment*.

For instance, Raskolnikov's crime is motivated, in part, by his theories about society. Lebezyatnikov, whose name is derived from the Russian word for "fawning," is obsessed with the so-called new philosophies that raged through St. Petersburg during the time that Dostoevsky was writing the novel. Luzhin, a mid-level government official, is continually afraid of being "exposed" by "nihilists."

In 1857, Dostoevsky married Mariya Dmitriyevna Isayeva, who died of consumption seven years later. He spent much of the 1860s in Western Europe experiencing the culture that was slowly invading Russia and struggled with poverty, epilepsy, and an addiction to gambling. But with the 1866 publication of *Crime and Punishment*, a long, delirious trip through the psyche of a tormented murderer, his fortunes improved. The novel's popular and critical success allowed him to keep ahead, just barely, of daunting debts and the burden of supporting a number of children left in his care after the deaths of his brother and sister.

In 1867, he was married a second time, to Anna Grigoryevna Snitkina, who helped him cope with his epilepsy, depression, and gambling problems, and who had served as his stenographer for his novel *The Gambler*. After *Crime and Punishment*, Dostoevsky went on to write a number of other classics of world literature. These include *The Idiot*, published in 1868, and another masterwork, *The Brothers Karamazov*, published in 1880. He died in 1881.

Dostoevsky's novels and other writings were major influences on twentieth-century literature and philosophy. Some people saw the political themes of his novels as prescient depictions of life under the Soviet regime. The existentialist movement that took shape in the middle of the twentieth century looked to him for his descriptions of human beings confronting mortality, despair, and the anxiety of choice.

Writers such as Albert Camus and Jean-Paul Sartre valued Dostoevsky's writing for his profound insights into human dilemmas, which, along with his style, themes, and unforgettable characters, continue to influence writers more than a century after his death.

Chapter 7

Plot Overview

Rodion Romanovich Raskolnikov, a former student, lives in a tiny garret on the top floor of a run-down apartment building in St. Petersburg. He is sickly, dressed in rags, short on money, and talks to himself, but he is also handsome, proud, and intelligent. He is contemplating committing an awful crime, but the nature of the crime is not yet clear. He goes to the apartment of an old pawnbroker, Alyona Ivanovna, to get money for a watch and to plan the crime. Afterward, he stops for a drink at a tavern, where he meets a man named Marmeladov, who, in a fit of drunkenness, has abandoned his job and proceeded on a five-day drinking binge, afraid to return home to his family. Marmeladov tells Raskolnikov about his sickly wife, Katerina Ivanovna, and his daughter, Sonya, who has been forced into prostitution to support the family. Raskolnikov walks with Marmeladov to Marmeladov's apartment, where he meets Katerina and sees firsthand the squalid conditions in which they live.

The next day, Raskolnikov receives a letter from his mother, Pulcheria Alexandrovna, informing him that his sister, Dunya, is engaged to be married to a government official named Luzhin and that they are all moving to St. Petersburg. He goes to another tavern, where he overhears a student talking about how society would be better off if the old pawnbroker Alyona Ivanovna were dead. Later, in the streets, Raskolnikov hears that the pawnbroker will be alone in her apartment the next evening. He sleeps fitfully and wakes up the next day, finds an ax, and fashions a fake item to pawn to distract the pawnbroker. That night, he goes to her apartment and kills her. While he is rummaging through her bedroom, looking for money, her sister, Lizaveta, walks in, and Raskolnikov kills her as well. He barely escapes from the apartment without being seen, then returns to his apartment and collapses on the sofa.

Waking up the next day, Raskolnikov frantically searches his clothing for traces of blood. He receives a summons from the police, but it seems to be unrelated to the murders. At the police station, he learns that his landlady is trying to collect money that he owes her. During a conversation about the murders, Raskolnikov faints, and the police begin to suspect him. Raskolnikov returns to his room, collects the goods that he stole from the pawnbroker, and buries them under a rock in an out-of-the-way courtyard. He visits his friend Razumikhin and refuses his offer of work. Returning to his apartment, Raskolnikov falls into a fitful, nightmare-ridden sleep. After four days of fever and delirium, he wakes up to find out that his housekeeper, Nastasya, and Razumikhin have been taking care of him. He learns that Zossimov, a doctor, and Zamyotov, a young police detective, have also been visiting him. They have all noticed that Raskolnikov becomes extremely uncomfortable whenever the murders of the pawnbroker and her sister are mentioned. Luzhin, Dunya's fiancé, also makes a visit. After a confrontation with Luzhin, Raskolnikov goes to a café, where he almost confesses to Zamyotov that he is the murderer. Afterward, he impulsively goes to the apartment of the pawnbroker. On his way back home, he discovers that Marmeladov has been run over by a carriage. Raskolnikov helps to carry him back to his apartment, where Marmeladov dies. At the apartment, he meets Sonya and gives the family twenty rubles that he received from his mother. Returning with Razumikhin to his own apartment, Raskolnikov faints when he discovers that his sister and mother are there waiting for him.

Raskolnikov becomes annoyed with Pulcheria Alexandrovna and Dunya and orders them out of the room.

He also commands Dunya to break her engagement with Luzhin. Razumikhin, meanwhile, falls in love with Dunya. The next morning, Razumikhin tries to explain Raskolnikov's character to Dunya and Pulcheria Alexandrovna, and then the three return to Raskolnikov's apartment. There, Zossimov greets them and tells them that Raskolnikov's condition is much improved. Raskolnikov apologizes for his behaviour the night before and confesses to giving all his money to the Marmeladovs. But he soon grows angry and irritable again and demands that Dunya not marry Luzhin. Dunya tells him that she is meeting with Luzhin that evening, and that although Luzhin has requested specifically that Raskolnikov not be there, she would like him to come nevertheless. Raskolnikov agrees. At that moment, Sonya enters the room, greatly embarrassed to be in the presence of Raskolnikov's family. She invites Raskolnikov to her father's funeral, and he accepts. On her way back to her apartment, Sonya is followed by a strange man, who we later learn is Svidrigailov—Dunya's lecherous former employer who is obsessively attracted to her.

Under the pretense of trying to recover a watch he pawned, Raskolnikov visits the magistrate in charge of the murder investigation, Porfiry Petrovich, a relative of Razumikhin's. Zamyotov is at the detective's house when Raskolnikov arrives. Raskolnikov and Porfiry have a tense conversation about the murders. Raskolnikov starts to believe that Porfiry suspects him and is trying to lead him into a trap. Afterward, Raskolnikov and Razumikhin discuss the conversation, trying to figure out if Porfiry suspects him. When Raskolnikov returns to his apartment, he learns that a man had come there looking for him. When he catches up to the man in the street, the man calls him a murderer. That night Raskolnikov dreams about the pawnbroker's murder. When he wakes up, there is a stranger in the room.

The stranger is Svidrigailov. He explains that he would like Dunya to break her engagement with Luzhin, whom he esteems unworthy of her. He offers to give Dunya the enormous sum of ten thousand rubles. He also tells Raskolnikov that his late wife, Marfa Petrovna, left Dunya three thousand rubles in her will. Raskolnikov rejects Svidrigailov's offer of money and, after hearing him talk about seeing the ghost of Marfa, suspects that he is insane. After Svidrigailov leaves, Raskolnikov and Razumikhin walk to a restaurant to meet Dunya, Pulcheria Alexandrovna, and Luzhin. Razumikhin tells Raskolnikov that he is certain that the police suspect Raskolnikov. Luzhin is insulted to find that Raskolnikov, contrary to his wishes, is in attendance at the meal.

They discuss Svidrigailov's arrival in the city and the money that has been offered to Dunya. Luzhin and Raskolnikov get into an argument, during the course of which Luzhin offends everyone in the room, including his fiancée and prospective mother-in-law. Dunya breaks the engagement and forces him to leave. Everyone is overjoyed at his departure. Razumikhin starts to talk about plans to go into the publishing business as a family, but Raskolnikov ruins the mood by telling them that he does not want to see them anymore. When Raskolnikov leaves the room, Razumikhin chases him down the stairs. They stop, face-to-face, and Razumikhin realises, without a word being spoken, that Raskolnikov is guilty of the murders. He rushes back to Dunya and Pulcheria Alexandrovna to reassure them that he will help them through whatever difficulties they encounter.

Raskolnikov goes to the apartment of Sonya Marmeladov. During their conversation, he learns that Sonya was a friend of one of his victims, Lizaveta. He forces Sonya to read to him the biblical story of Lazarus, who was resurrected by Jesus. Meanwhile, Svidrigailov eavesdrops from the apartment next door.

The following morning, Raskolnikov visits Porfiry Petrovich at the police department, supposedly in order to turn in a formal request for his pawned watch. As they converse, Raskolnikov starts to feel again that Porfiry is trying to lead him into a trap. Eventually, he breaks under the pressure and accuses Porfiry of playing psychological games with him. At the height of tension between them, Nikolai, a workman who is being held under suspicion for the murders, bursts into the room and confesses to the murders. On the way to Katerina Ivanovna's memorial dinner for Marmeladov, Raskolnikov meets the mysterious man who called him a murderer and learns that the man actually knows very little about the case.

The scene shifts to the apartment of Luzhin and his roommate, Lebezyatnikov, where Luzhin is nursing his hatred for Raskolnikov, whom he blames for the breaking of his engagement to Dunya. Although Luzhin has been invited to Marmeladov's memorial dinner, he refuses to go. He invites Sonya to his room and gives her a ten-ruble bill. Katerina's memorial dinner goes poorly. The widow is extremely fussy and proud, but few guests have shown up, and, except for Raskolnikov, those that have are drunk and crude. Luzhin then enters the room and accuses Sonya of stealing a one-hundred-ruble bill. Sonya denies his claim, but the bill is discovered in one of her pockets. Just as everyone is about to label Sonya a thief, however, Lebezyatnikov enters and tells the room that he saw Luzhin slip the bill into Sonya's pocket as she was leaving his room. Raskolnikov explains that Luzhin was probably trying to embarrass him by discrediting Sonya. Luzhin leaves, and a fight breaks out between Katerina and her landlady.

After the dinner, Raskolnikov goes to Sonya's room and confesses the murders to her. They have a long conversation about his confused motives. Sonya tries to convince him to confess to the authorities. Lebezyatnikov then enters and informs them that Katerina Ivanovna seems to have gone mad—she is parading the children in the streets, begging for money. Sonya rushes out to find them while Raskolnikov goes back to his room and talks to Dunya. He soon returns to the street and sees Katerina dancing and singing wildly. She collapses after a confrontation with a policeman and, soon after being brought back to her room, dies. Svidrigailov appears and offers to pay for the funeral and the care of the children. He reveals to Raskolnikov that he knows Raskolnikov is the murderer.

Raskolnikov wanders around in a haze after his confession to Sonya and the death of Katerina. Razumikhin confronts him in his room, asking him whether he has gone mad and telling him of the pain that he has caused his mother and sister. After their conversation, Porfiry Petrovich appears and apologizes for his treatment of Raskolnikov in the police station. Nonetheless, he does not believe Nikolai's confession. He accuses Raskolnikov of the murders but admits that he does not have enough evidence to arrest him.

Finally, he urges him to confess, telling him that he will receive a lighter sentence if he does so. Raskolnikov goes looking for Svidrigailov, eventually finding him in a café. Svidrigailov tells him that though he is still attracted to Dunya, he has gotten engaged to a sixteen-year-old girl. Svidrigailov parts from Raskolnikov and manages to bring Dunya to his room, where he threatens to rape her after she refuses to marry him. She fires several shots at him with a revolver and misses, but when he sees how strongly she dislikes him, he allows her to leave. He takes her revolver and wanders aimlessly around St. Petersburg. He gives three thousand rubles to Dunya, fifteen thousand rubles to the family of his fiancée, and then books a room in a hotel. He sleeps fitfully and dreams of a flood and a seductive five-year-old girl. In the morning, he kills himself.

Raskolnikov, who is visiting his mother, tells her that he will always love her and then returns to his room, where he tells Dunya that he is planning to confess. After she leaves, he goes to visit Sonya, who gives him a cross to wear. On the way to the police station, he stops in a marketplace and kisses the ground. He almost pulls back from confessing when he reaches the police station and learns of Svidrigailov's suicide. The sight of Sonya, however, convinces him to go through with it, and he confesses to one of the police officials, Ilya Petrovich.

A year and a half later, Raskolnikov is in prison in Siberia, where he has been for nine months. Sonya has moved to the town outside the prison, and she visits Raskolnikov regularly and tries to ease his burden. Because of his confession, his mental confusion surrounding the murders, and testimony about his past good deeds, he has received, instead of a death sentence, a reduced sentence of eight years of hard labour in Siberia. After Raskolnikov's arrest, his mother became delirious and died. Razumikhin and Dunya were married. For a short while, Raskolnikov remains as proud and alienated from humanity as he was before his confession, but he eventually realises that he truly loves Sonya and expresses remorse for his crime.

Chapter 8

Character Sketch

CHARACTER LIST

Rodion Romanovich Raskolnikov ("Rodya," "Rodka")

The protagonist of the novel. A former student, Raskolnikov is now destitute, living in a cramped garret at the top of an apartment building. The main drama of the novel centres on his interior conflict, first over whether to kill the pawnbroker and later over whether to confess and rejoin humanity. Raskolnikov is ill throughout the novel, overwhelmed by his feelings of alienation and self-loathing.

Sofya Semyonovna Marmeladov ("Sonya," "Sonechka")

Raskolnikov's love and Marmeladov's daughter. Sonya is forced to prostitute herself to support herself and the rest of her family. She is meek and easily embarrassed, but she maintains a strong religious faith. She is the only person with whom Raskolnikov shares a meaningful relationship.

Avdotya Romanovna Raskolnikov ("Dunya," "Dunechka")

Raskolnikov's sister. Dunya is as intelligent, proud, and good-looking as her brother, but she is also moral and compassionate. She is decisive and brave, ending her engagement with Luzhin when he insults her family and fending off Svidrigailov with gunfire.

Arkady Ivanovich Svidrigailov

Dunya's depraved former employer. Svidrigailov appears to believe, almost until the end of the novel, that he can make Dunya love him. The death of his wife, Marfa Petrovna, has made him generous, but he is generally a threatening presence to both Dunya and Raskolnikov.

Dmitri Prokofych Razumikhin -

Raskolnikov's friend. A poor ex-student, he responds to his poverty not by taking from others but by working even harder. Razumikhin is Raskolnikov's foil, illustrating through his kindness and amicability the extent to which Raskolnikov has alienated himself from society. To some extent, he even serves as Raskolnikov's replacement, stepping in to advise and protect Pulcheria Alexandrovna and Dunya. His name comes from the Russian word *razum*, which means "reason" or "intelligence."

Katerina Ivanovna Marmeladov

The consumptive wife of Marmeladov. Katerina Ivanovna's serious illness gives her flushed cheeks and a persistent, bloody cough. She is very proud and repeatedly declares her aristocratic heritage.

Porfiry Petrovich

The magistrate in charge of investigating the murders. Porfiry Petrovich has a shrewd understanding of criminal psychology and is exquisitely aware of Raskolnikov's mental state at every step along the way from the crime to the confession. He is Raskolnikov's primary antagonist, and, though he appears only occasionally in the novel, his presence is constantly felt.

Semyon Zakharovich Marmeladov

An alcoholic public official whom Raskolnikov meets at a tavern. Marmeladov is fully aware that his drinking is ruining himself and his family, but he is unable to stop. It is unclear whether his death by falling under the wheels of a carriage was a drunken accident or intentional.

Pulcheria Alexandrovna Raskolnikov

Raskolnikov's mother. Pulcheria Alexandrovna is deeply devoted to her son and willing to sacrifice everything, even her own and her daughter's happiness, so that he might be successful. Even after Raskolnikov has confessed, she is unwilling to admit to herself that her son is a murderer.

Pyotr Petrovich Luzhin

Dunya's fiancé. Luzhin is stingy, narrow-minded, and self-absorbed. His deepest wish is to marry a beautiful, intelligent, but desperately poor girl like Dunya so that she will be indebted to him.

Andrei Semyonovich Lebezyatnikov

Luzhin's grudging roommate. Lebezyatnikov is a young man who is convinced of the rightness of the "new philosophies" such as nihilism that are currently raging through St. Petersburg. Although he is self-centred, confused, and immature, he nonetheless seems to possess basic scruples.

Alyona Ivanovna

An old, withered pawnbroker whom Raskolnikov kills. Raskolnikov calls Alyona Ivanovna a "louse" and despises her for cheating the poor out of their money and enslaving her own sister, Lizaveta.

Lizaveta Ivanovna

Alyona Ivanovna's sister. Lizaveta is simple, almost "idiotic," and a virtual servant to her sister. Sonya later reveals to Raskolnikov that she and Lizaveta were friends.

Zossimov

Raskolnikov's doctor and a friend of Razumikhin. Zossimov is a young, self-congratulating man who has little insight into his patient's condition. He suspects that Raskolnikov is mentally ill.

Nastasya Petrovna ("Nastenka," "Nastasyushka")

A servant in the house where Raskolnikov rents his "closet." Nastasya brings him tea and food when he requests it and helps care for him in his illness after the murders.

Ilya Petrovich ("Gunpowder")

The police official whom Raskolnikov encounters after committing the murder and to whom he confesses at the end of the novel. Unlike Porfiry Petrovich, Ilya Petrovich is rather oblivious and prone to sudden bouts of temper (thus the nickname "Gunpowder").

Alexander Grigorievich Zamyotov

A junior official in the police station who suspects that Raskolnikov is the killer of Alyona Ivanovna and Lizaveta.

Nikolai Dementiev ("Mikolka")

A painter working in an empty apartment next to Alyona Ivanovna's on the day of the murders. Suspected of the murders and held in prison, Nikolai eventually makes a false confession.

Polina Mikhailovna Marmeladov ("Polya," "Polenka," "Polechka")

The oldest daughter of Katerina Ivanovna from her former marriage.

ANALYSIS OF MAJOR CHARACTERS

Raskolnikov

Raskolnikov is the protagonist of the novel, and the story is told almost exclusively from his point of view. His name derives from the Russian word *raskolnik,* meaning "schismatic" or "divided," which is appropriate since his most fundamental character trait is his alienation from human society. His pride and intellectualism lead him to disdain the rest of humanity as fit merely to perpetuate the species. In contrast, he believes that he is part of an elite "superman" echelon and can consequently transgress accepted moral standards for higher purposes such as utilitarian good. However, that guilt that torments him after he murders Alyona Ivanovna and Lizaveta and his recurring faintness at the mention of the murders serve as proof to him that he is not made of the same stuff as a true "superman" such as Napoleon. Though he grapples with the decision to confess for most of the novel and though he seems gradually to accept the reality of his mediocrity, he remains convinced that the murder of the pawnbroker was justified. His ultimate realization that he loves Sonya is the only force strong enough to transcend his ingrained contempt of humanity. Raskolnikov's relationships with the other characters in the novel do much to illuminate his personality and understanding of himself. Although he cares about Razumikhin, Pulcheria Alexandrovna, and Dunya, Raskolnikov is so caught up in his skeptical outlook that he is often unappreciative of their attempts to help him. He turns to Sonya as a fellow transgressor of social norms, but he fails to recognize that her sin is much different from his: while she truly sacrifices herself for the sake of others, he essentially commits his crime for his sake alone. Finally, his relationship with Svidrigailov is enigmatic. Though he despises the man for his depravity, he also seems to need something from him—perhaps validation of his own crime from a hardened malcontent.

Sonya

Sonya is quiet, timid, and easily embarrassed, but she is also extremely devout and devoted to her family. Her sacrifice of prostituting herself for the sake of her family is made even more poignant by the fact that it would not be necessary were her father able to control his drinking habit. Initially scared of the half-delirious Raskolnikov, Sonya, in her infinite capacity for understanding, begins to care deeply about him. She is not horrified by his crimes, but rather, concerned for his soul and mental well-being, urges him to confess. Raskolnikov thinks of her, at first, as a fellow transgressor, someone who has stepped over the line between morality and immorality, just as he has. But there is a crucial difference between their transgressions that Raskolnikov is unwilling to acknowledge: she sins for the sake of others, whereas he sins for no one but himself. Sonya illustrates important social and political issues that were of concern to Dostoevsky, such as the treatment of women, the effects of poverty, the importance of religious faith, and the importance of devotion to family.

Dunya

Dunya is Raskolnikov's sister and shares many of his traits. She is intelligent, proud, beautiful, and strong-willed. But in most other ways, she is Raskolnikov's exact opposite. Whereas he is self-centred, cruel, and prone to intellectualizing, she is self-sacrificing, kind, and exhibits endless compassion. The relationship between Dunya and Raskolnikov is always based on mutual love and respect, but it swings from one extreme of emotion to the other as Raskolnikov slowly approaches the moment of confession. In many ways, Dunya is more mature than her brother: while he grows angry and dizzy confronting Luzhin, she remains confident and in control, even when she becomes just as angry. She is the strongest female character in the novel, neither as crushed by poverty nor as timid as Sonya. If there are any heroes in *Crime and Punishment*, she, along with Razumikhin, is certainly one of them, which makes their marriage at the end of the novel particularly appropriate.

Svidrigailov

Svidrigailov is one of the most enigmatic characters in *Crime and Punishment*. Dostoevsky leaves little doubt as to Svidrigailov's status as a villain. But all of Svidrigailov's crimes, except for his attempted rape of Dunya, are behind him. We witness Svidrigailov perform goods deeds, such as giving money to the family of his fiancée, to Katerina Ivanovna and her children, and to Dunya. Although he is a violent and sneaky individual, Svidrigailov possesses the ability to accept that he cannot force reality to conform to his deepest desires. In this regard, he functions as a foil to Raskolnikov, who can accept only partially the breakdown of his presumed "superman" identity. Further, whereas Raskolnikov believes unflinchingly in the utilitarian rationale for Alyona Ivanovna's murder, Svidrigailov doesn't try to contest the death of his romantic vision when Dunya rejects him. Although the painful realization that he will never have the love of someone as honest, kind, intelligent, and beautiful as she is compels him to commit suicide, he is one of the few characters in the novel to die with dignity.

Chapter 9

Major Themes of the Novel

THEMES

Alienation from Society

Alienation is the primary theme of *Crime and Punishment*. At first, Raskolnikov's pride separates him from society. He sees himself as superior to all other people and so cannot relate to anyone. Within his personal philosophy, he sees other people as tools and uses them for his own ends. After committing the murders, his isolation grows because of his intense guilt and the half-delirium into which his guilt throws him. Over and over again, Raskolnikov pushes away the people who are trying to help him, including Sonya, Dunya, Pulcheria Alexandrovna, Razumikhin, and even Porfiry Petrovich, and then suffers the consequences. In the end, he finds the total alienation that he has brought upon himself intolerable. Only in the Epilogue, when he finally realises that he loves Sonya, does Raskolnikov break through the wall of pride and self-centredness that has separated him from society.

The Psychology of Crime and Punishment

The manner in which the novel addresses crime and punishment is not exactly what one would expect. The crime is committed in Part I and the punishment comes hundreds of pages later, in the Epilogue. The real focus of the novel is not on those two endpoints but on what lies between them—

an in-depth exploration of the psychology of a criminal. The inner world of Raskolnikov, with all of its doubts, deliria, second-guessing, fear, and despair, is the heart of the story. Dostoevsky concerns himself not with the actual repercussions of the murder but with the way the murder forces Raskolnikov to deal with tormenting guilt. Indeed, by focusing so little on Raskolnikov's imprisonment, Dostoevsky seems to suggest that actual punishment is much less terrible than the stress and anxiety of trying to avoid punishment. Porfiry Petrovich emphasizes the psychological angle of the novel, as he shrewdly realises that Raskolnikov is the killer and makes several speeches in which he details the workings of Raskolnikov's mind after the killing. Because he understands that a guilt-ridden criminal must necessarily experience mental torture, he is certain that Raskolnikov will eventually confess or go mad. The expert mind games that he plays with Raskolnikov strengthen the sense that the novel's outcome is inevitable because of the nature of the human psyche.

The Idea of the Superman

At the beginning of the novel, Raskolnikov sees himself as a "superman," a person who is extraordinary and thus above the moral rules that govern the rest of humanity. His vaunted estimation of himself compels him to separate himself from society. His murder of the pawnbroker is, in part, a consequence of his belief that he is above the law and an attempt to establish the truth of his superiority. Raskolnikov's inability to quell his subsequent feelings of guilt, however, proves to him that he is not a "superman." Although he realises his failure to live up to what he has envisioned for himself, he is nevertheless unwilling to accept the total deconstruction of this identity.

He continues to resist the idea that he is as mediocre as the rest of humanity by maintaining to himself that the murder was justified. It is only in his final surrender to his love for Sonya, and his realization of the joys in such surrender, that he can finally escape his conception of himself as a superman and the terrible isolation such a belief brought upon him.

Nihilism

Nihilism was a philosophical position developed in Russia in the 1850s and 1860s, known for "negating more," in the words of Lebezyatnikov. It rejected family and societal bonds and emotional and aesthetic concerns in favour of a strict materialism, or the idea that there is no "mind" or "soul" outside of the physical world. Linked to nihilism is utilitarianism, or the idea that moral decisions should be based on the rule of the greatest happiness for the largest number of people. Raskolnikov originally justifies the murder of Alyona on utilitarian grounds, claiming that a "louse" has been removed from society. Whether or not the murder is actually a utilitarian act, Raskolnikov is certainly a nihilist; completely unsentimental for most of the novel, he cares nothing about the emotions of others. Similarly, he utterly disregards social conventions that run counter to the austere interactions that he desires with the world. However, at the end of the novel, as Raskolnikov discovers love, he throws off his nihilism. Through this action, the novel condemns nihilism as empty.

MOTIFS

Poverty

Poverty is ubiquitous in the St. Petersburg of Dostoevsky's novel. Almost every character in the novel—except Luzhin, Svidrigailov, and the police officials—is desperately poor, including the Marmeladovs, the Raskolnikovs, Razumikhin, and various lesser characters. While poverty inherently forces families to bond together, Raskolnikov often attempts to distance himself from Pulcheria Alexandrovna and Dunya. He scolds his sister when he thinks that she is marrying to help him out financially; he also rejects Razumikhin's offer of a job. Dostoevsky's descriptions of poverty allow him to address important social issues and to create rich, problematic situations in which the only way to survive is through self-sacrifice. As a result, poverty enables characters such as Sonya and Dunya to demonstrate their strength and compassion.

SYMBOLS

The City

The city of St. Petersburg as represented in Dostoevsky's novel is dirty and crowded. Drunks are sprawled on the street in broad daylight, consumptive women beat their children and beg for money, and everyone is crowded into tiny, noisy apartments. The clutter and chaos of St. Petersburg is a twofold symbol. It represents the state of society, with all of its inequalities, prejudices, and deficits. But it also represents Raskolnikov's delirious, agitated state as he spirals through the novel toward the point of his confession and redemption. He can escape neither the city nor his warped mind. From the very beginning, the narrator describes the heat and "the odor" coming off the city, the crowds, and the disorder, and says they "all contributed to irritate the young man's already excited nerves." Indeed, it is only when Raskolnikov is forcefully removed from the city to a prison in a small town in Siberia that he is able to regain compassion and balance.

The Cross

The cross that Sonya gives to Raskolnikov before he goes to the police station to confess is an important symbol of redemption for him. Throughout Christendom, of course, the cross symbolizes Jesus' self-sacrifice for the sins of humanity. Raskolnikov denies any feeling of sin or devoutness even after he receives the cross; the cross symbolizes not that he has achieved redemption or even understood what Sonya believes religion can offer him, but that he has begun on the path toward recognition of the sins that he has committed. That Sonya is the one who gives him the cross has special significance: she gives of herself to bring him back to humanity, and her love and concern for him, like that of Jesus, according to Christianity, will ultimately save and renew him.

Chapter 10

Chapter Wise Summary

PART I: CHAPTER I

Summary: Chapter I

A young man leaves his boardinghouse room on an uncomfortably hot summer's day in St. Petersburg. As he descends the steps, he is overcome with a dread of meeting his landlady, who lives on the floor below. He owes her several months' rent and recoils at the thought of having to make excuses to her. The narrator states that this young man "had fallen into a state of nervous depression akin to hypochondria" and so avoids contact with other people. As he leaves the boardinghouse, the young man turns his thoughts to an extreme, though unspecified, act that he is thinking about committing. He considers himself incapable of the act—if he lacks the stomach even to face his landlady, it seems impossible that he would ever go through with the deed that he now mulls. The narrator identifies the young man as the protagonist ("our hero") and describes him as tall and handsome, with "dark auburn hair and fine dark eyes."

The young man wears ridiculously tattered clothes, but he is so contemptuous of the people who live in his wretched neighbourhood—which is filthy and populated with drunks, prostitutes, and tradesmen—that he feels no embarrassment about his shoddy appearance. He walks along in a trancelike state, thinking over his awful plan, again considering the idea and then dismissing it. The narrator informs us that, over the last month, the young man has grown increasingly serious about taking action, even though the idea of doing so has disturbed and troubled him. At this particular moment, he is in the middle of a "rehearsal" of the act. He arrives at the apartment house of Alyona Ivanovna, a pawnbroker. As he walks up the stairs to her apartment, he carefully observes the building and its inhabitants in connection with his plan. He introduces himself to the pawnbroker, whom he had first met a month earlier, as a student, and we learn that the young man's name is Raskolnikov. The pawnbroker is an unattractive, shabbily dressed old woman who is suspicious, crude, and has "eyes sparkling with malice."

Though the apartment's furnishings are old and ugly, Raskolnikov notices that they are immaculately clean, thanks to the hard work of the old woman's younger sister, Lizaveta. The pawnbroker treats the young man rudely, reminding him of the money that he already owes her and offering him a small, inadequate sum for a watch that he now offers her. Raskolnikov grudgingly accepts the money, remembering that his purpose is twofold, as he is both pawning the watch for much-needed money and rehearsing the crime that he may commit. He observes that the old woman keeps her money and "pledges," or pawned items, in a chest in a back room and her keys on a ring in her right pocket. Before leaving, he tells her that he will return in a few days with another pledge and asks whether Lizaveta is usually at home at that time. Once outside, Raskolnikov is physically overcome with disgust at his plan and renounces it. Filled with a sudden thirst for alcohol, he descends into a tavern for the first time in his life and sits in a dark corner. After drinking a beer, he feels much better and again scoffs at his plan.

Analysis: Chapter I

The opening chapter of *Crime and Punishment* illuminates aspects of Raskolnikov's character that prove central to the novel. He is extremely proud, contemptuous, emotionally detached from the rest of humanity, and is in a complex, semidelirious mental state. Why he has developed this troubling mix of qualities remains an important question throughout the novel. A few clues are given at the outset: Raskolnikov is tall and handsome, which may foster his pride, while his squalid surroundings—the neighbourhood in which Raskolnikov and the pawnbroker live is described in vivid terms that convey the chaos and filthiness of poor, urban neighbourhoods—may have helped bring about his deteriorated mental condition. The narrator describes the heat and "the odor" coming off of the city, as well as the crowds and disorder, saying that all of these factors "contributed to irritate the young man's already excited nerves." Most important, though, each quality seems to reinforce the others, and Raskolnikov seems caught in an ever-deepening spiral: his pride leads him to perceive others as inferior, his lack of human contact leads him to increasingly abstract and inhuman ideas, and his crazed ideas cause him to separate himself from society.

Chapter I also explores the character of the pawnbroker. In some respects, Alyona Ivanovna is a foil to Raskolnikov—that is, her character contrasts with his and serves to emphasize his distinct characteristics. She is old and unattractive, while he is young and handsome; she is alert and concerned with practical business matters, while he is semidelirious and deeply in debt. The only apparent similarity between the two is that they both wear worn and tattered clothes. But even this similarity, examined more closely, reveals the difference in wealth between the two, since Raskolnikov dresses in rags because of poverty whereas the pawnbroker does so out of miserliness.

The conflict in this chapter is primarily internal, as it is throughout the novel. Here, the struggle is mostly between Raskolnikov's desire to commit the crime and his revulsion at the thought of doing so. Significantly, this inner conflict is not between his hatred of the pawnbroker and a moral objection to killing but rather between his desire to kill her and his disgust at the idea of the actual, physical performance of the deed. Morality seems to play little role in his decision and does not become a strong force in his life until the very end of the novel.

Whatever degree of innocence or harmlessness is still intact in Raskolnikov's character disappears upon his symbolic entrance into the tavern. This descent into a tavern's dingy darkness—the first of his life—parallels his descent into the seamy realm of discontent and malice. Though he already seems somewhat disturbed and though the beer seems to calm him, Raskolnikov has now crossed a figurative threshold into the muddled, violent mindset that alcohol induces.

In this opening chapter and throughout the novel, Dostoevsky withholds information to create suspense. He even delays informing us of the protagonist's name until several pages into the work, when it comes up naturally in the course of the plot. Dostoevsky informs us on the first page that the young man is contemplating some sort of "desperate deed," but he doesn't tell us what this deed is. Instead, we are given clues as the chapter progresses—for instance, that it will involve the pawnbroker and take place in her apartment. This slow revelation of detail helps to pique the reader's interest, creating suspense that adds momentum to the plot and increases the emotional impact of each event or revelation as it occurs.

PART I: CHAPTERS II–IV

Summary: Chapter II

Inside the tavern, Raskolnikov meets a drunk man who looks like a retired government official. The man's physical appearance has obviously suffered as a result of his habitual drinking. Although his clothes are tattered, he manages to convey an air of dignity and education. Despite the jeers of the tavern's patrons and staff, the man proceeds to tell his life story to Raskolnikov. He is a self-professed drunkard married to a proud woman of noble background, Katerina Ivanovna. She married him out of desperation after a bad first marriage that resulted in three children and her disinheritance. The man, whose name is Marmeladov, has a daughter of his own, named Sonya, who has been forced to prostitute herself to support her family. Recently, Marmeladov managed to regain a job in the civil service, raising the hopes of his wife, but he lost the job in a fit of drunkenness and has not dared return home for five days. Throughout his story, Marmeladov alternates between self-reproach and justification of his behaviour. He leaves the tavern for his home, taking Raskolnikov with him. The nearby Marmeladov household is a scene of misery. Though no older than thirty, Katerina is sickly and agitated. Upon seeing Marmeladov, she grabs him by the hair and loudly criticizes him. Other tenants arrive to mock the family squabble, and the landlady orders Katerina to move out. As Raskolnikov departs, he leaves the family a small amount of money, something he promptly regrets doing. He holds the Marmeladovs in disdain, especially for forcing Sonya to sacrifice herself for their sake.

Summary: Chapter III

The next morning, Raskolnikov, in his room, is awakened by the maid, Nastasya, who brings him tea and soup and a letter from his mother, Pulcheria Alexandrovna. Nastasya tells him that the landlady wants to evict him for not paying rent. In the letter, his mother relates the experience of his sister, Dunya, as a maid. Dunya was trying to earn money to help support Raskolnikov but her employer, Svidrigailov, made improper advances toward her and her reputation in the town was nearly ruined. She has now accepted a proposal of marriage from a man named Pyotr Petrovich Luzhin, who wants to marry her because she is poor and thus will regard him as her savior. Pulcheria Alexandrovna adds that she and Dunya were not sure about the marriage at first but that Dunya agreed to it after much consideration. Both hope that Dunya's new husband will eventually be able to help Raskolnikov with his career. Mother, daughter, and fiancé will be arriving in St. Petersburg shortly. Crying, Raskolnikov finishes reading the letter and goes for a walk, talking to himself like a drunk.

Summary: Chapter IV

On his walk, Raskolnikov decides that he will not allow the marriage to take place, as Dunya is plainly sacrificing herself to help him. Luzhin sounds stingy and disrespectful, and Raskolnikov develops a passionate hatred of him. The sight of an older man pursuing a drunk young woman interrupts his thoughts. Disgusted, he confronts the older man. A policeman shows up, and Raskolnikov explains the situation, giving the policeman some money for a cab to take the girl home. The girl goes, followed by the stranger and the policeman. Raskolnikov grows annoyed at this waste of money. The policeman, he thinks, will let the man have the girl as soon as Raskolnikov is out of sight. He suddenly realises that he has been walking toward the home of his best friend from university, Razumikhin, whom he has not seen in four months. Razumikhin is described as warm and outgoing.

Analysis: Chapters II–IV

Chapter II vividly illustrates the characters of Marmeladov and his wife, Katerina Ivanovna. Each is pathetic, he in his way and she in hers, but, at the same time, each possesses an inherent sense of pride. Marmeladov is an interestingly paradoxical figure, largely because he refuses to accept responsibility for his actions even though he acknowledges that his behaviour is at the root of his family's problems. Unable to escape a cycle of failure and unemployment, he goes on his drinking binge in part as a reaction to the respect and esteem that his wife gives him upon hearing of his new job. It is almost as if success of any kind is too much for him; as soon as he can, he ruins his prospects of making money and bringing the family out of its abject poverty. Nonetheless, he clings to a shred of dignity in public, and Raskolnikov can discern that he is an educated man despite his degenerate appearance. Katerina is an even more tragic figure than her husband; unlike him, she bears almost no responsibility for her condition. Her illness and bad luck in her choice of husbands has doomed her to a life of weakness and squalor. But, despite these overwhelming obstacles, her pride and dignity still remain strong.

The Marmeladovs' suffering constitutes a major subplot of the novel. Their trials and troubles are interesting in their own right, as Katerina, Marmeladov, and Sonya struggle to make ends meet and overcome daunting circumstances. Their poverty also allows Dostoevsky to include striking examples of the damaging effects of urban deprivation on quality of life. The Marmeladov subplot also intersects with the main plot at various points and illustrates aspects of Raskolnikov's character. One such point occurs at the end of Chapter II: Raskolnikov's gift of money to the Marmeladovs seems to reflect the awakening of his compassionate side. But his pride extinguishes this sentiment almost as soon as it is kindled, as he congratulates himself that "they would be in great straits tomorrow without that money of mine!" Instead of feeling pity for the family, he judges them coldly as cowards who profit willingly from Sonya's degradation and then curses himself for having given them money, which he is certain that they will waste. This pattern of acting compassionately and then pushing away the objects of his compassion repeats itself throughout the novel as Raskolnikov struggles to reconcile his haughty disdain for others with his desire to rejoin society.

Raskolnikov's pride is explored further in Chapters III and IV. The devotion of his mother and sister, who are willing to make enormous sacrifices for him, can be seen as another source of Raskolnikov's haughtiness. His reaction to Dunya's engagement further reveals his self-absorption, as he assumes that she is marrying solely for his sake and ignores the possibility that she might be marrying Luzhin to provide a better life for herself and her mother. He determines not to let her sacrifice herself for his sake, self-importantly declaring, "No, mother, it shall never be, not whilst I live. I will not have it." Whether or not Dunya herself wishes it never enters his mind.

The character of Raskolnikov's mother, Pulcheria Alexandrovna, comes through clearly in her letter. She is devoted to her son, even ready to condone her daughter's self-sacrifice for his benefit. Her letter to him serves the important role of introducing the subplot of Dunya's engagement. The letter also discusses and introduces Dunya's former employer, Svidrigailov, who becomes important to the development of the plot, and his recently deceased wife, Marfa Petrovna. Dostoevsky skillfully uses Pulcheria's letter as a device to provide these bits of context and background, so that when Raskolnikov first talks to his mother, sister, and Luzhin, we have a deeper sense of the meaning of the interaction than we would have if the characters had not already been described.

PART I: CHAPTERS V–VII

Summary: Chapter V

Raskolnikov resolves not to meet with his old friend Razumikhin until after he has committed his awful act, if he ever does commit it. After drinking some brandy, he falls asleep in a grassy area. He dreams of an incident from his childhood in which he witnessed a group of peasants sadistically beating an old mare to death and delighting in their cruelty. In his dream, a young boy cries out against the act and nestles the dead mare's head in his arms before his father carries him away. Raskolnikov wakes stricken with horror at the act that he is contemplating and again renounces it. On a whim, he walks home through a public market, the Haymarket, where he happens to overhear Lizaveta, the pawnbroker's sister, say that she will be out of the house the next day at seven. Raskolnikov realises that such a chance will not present itself again. He walks home terror-stricken, feeling that "all liberty of action and free-will were gone."

Summary: Chapter VI

The narrator recounts how Raskolnikov first developed the idea to kill Alyona Ivanovna (the first explicit identification of the awful deed that he is contemplating committing). Raskolnikov developed a strong hatred of her the first time he saw her. Soon after, in a bar, he overheard a conversation between a student and an officer in which the student denounced the old woman as a hateful parasite and argued that humanity would be better off if she were killed and her wealth distributed among the poor. These ideas echoed Raskolnikov's own thoughts, and he was struck by the coincidence of hearing them spoken by someone else. He became sure that it was his destiny to kill the pawnbroker.

The narrative then shifts back to the present. Raskolnikov falls into a deep sleep and doesn't wake until the following evening. Realizing it is already six o'clock, he hastily makes preparations for the crime, preparing a fake "pledge" to give to Alyona and a loop in his overcoat in which he plans to carry the ax that he will use to commit the murder. Still unsure at first, his resolve increases when he conveniently finds an ax in the caretaker's shed. He goes to Alyona's apartment, his intent to commit the crime stronger than ever. At seven-thirty, he is at Alyona's door, ringing the bell in a deliberately nonchalant manner. Someone inside unlocks the door.

Summary: Chapter VII

The old woman lets the feverish-looking Raskolnikov in. He presents her with a fake cigarette case wrapped with a difficult knot in order to distract her. As she turns away to undo the knot, he reaches for the ax. After several blows, Alyona lies dead on the floor in a bloody heap. Raskolnikov takes her keys and goes to the back room, overcoming an urge to give up and leave. He takes a purse that had hung on her neck but is unable to find more than a few trinkets in the back room. Just then, Lizaveta enters the apartment and is paralyzed with horror at the sight of her dead sister. Raskolnikov kills her with a single blow but then realises that the door to the apartment has been open the whole time. Terrified and desperate, he washes the blood from his hands and the ax and locks the door. Two strange men come to the door, determined to enter. When they leave for a minute, Raskolnikov manages to escape by hiding in a vacant apartment in which two painters have been working until it is safe to leave the building through the front door. Feverish, Raskolnikov takes a circuitous route home and puts the ax back where he found it before returning to his room.

Analysis: Chapters V–VII

In these chapters, Dostoevsky makes effective use of the literary techniques of suspense, foreshadowing, and coincidence. To build suspense, the author delays the actual commission of the crime with a dream sequence, one more renunciation of the crime, a flashback, and a description of Raskolnikov's thoughts and preparations for the crime. These postponements also reveal different aspects of Raskolnikov's character and reasoning, giving the reader a sense of his mental process as he builds up the crime. Nevertheless, much about him remains ambiguous. We still do not understand his real motives for the crime, the reasons for his poverty and isolation from society, and his surprising carelessness before and during the actual execution of the murder. Despite the elements of suspense, there is never much doubt that Raskolnikov *will* commit the crime, but the nagging question of *why* haunts the novel until, and even long after, the actual murders.

Chapter V provides a glimpse of Raskolnikov's buried capacity for compassion. His disgust at the thought of killing Alyona after he dreams of an incident from his childhood signifies his deep ambivalence about committing murder. One part of him, rational and abstract, thinks that he has every right to do it, while another part, emotional and compassionate, is repulsed by the idea. The gruesome description of the killing of the old mare in his dream also serves to foreshadow the killing of Alyona in the next chapter. The barbaric beating of the mare is described in vivid terms, heightening the emotional tone of the novel and preparing the reader for the horror of the murder. Finally, the compassionate reaction of the young Raskolnikov to the brutal act might be seen as a foreshadowing of Raskolnikov's ultimate repentance of his crime.

Coincidences abound in *Crime and Punishment*. At this point in the novel, they serve as the plot device by means of which Raskolnikov's resolve to commit the crime is made firm. His determination results from a chance discovery of a prime opportunity to commit the crime. Though Raskolnikov takes the mention of Lizaveta's impending absence as a sign that he is meant to commit the murder, it is perhaps more telling as a sign of Raskolnikov's own personality. Nothing in the world forces him to commit the crime. Instead, he searches the environment around him for excuses and opportunities that allow him to justify the horrible action that he is about to take. It is almost as though, by investing chance events with personal importance, Raskolnikov is trying to avoid his own responsibility for the crime. As coincidences that make the crime increasingly plausible accumulate, he starts to feel that he is losing control over himself and that the forces of fate are taking over. This belief in coincidences as signs of fate is tied to Raskolnikov's pride: since he believes that he is superior to other human beings, it is only natural for him to feel that circumstances should conspire to make his crime more easily accomplished. Raskolnikov is convinced, or, at least, is trying hard to *be* convinced, that he is an instrument of fate and that his actions are thus justified.

The fallacy of Raskolnikov's supposedly rational reasoning behind the crime is that his unplanned murder of Lizaveta destroys all of his justifications. Although Raskolnikov assures himself that he is committing a principled act in doing away with Alyona, the murder of her harmless sister has none of the utilitarian consequences that Raskolnikov believes the death of Alyona will have. Rather, killing Lizaveta is a selfish act that serves only to protect Raskolnikov from arrest. Committed to a path of crime from the moment he first raises the ax against Alyona, Raskolnikov unhesitatingly murders them both.

PART II: CHAPTERS I–IV

Summary: Chapter I

It was no longer possible for him to address these people... in any way at all.

After a night of restless sleep, Raskolnikov frantically searches his clothes for traces of blood. In a pocket he discovers the pawned items that he stole and tries to hide them. He imagines that his judgment is escaping him. "Can this be the punishment already beginning? Indeed it is," he exclaims to himself. Around noon, Nastasya and the porter enter the room and hand Raskolnikov a summons to the police station. Although he is worried, Raskolnikov figures that the summons cannot be related to the murders. He proceeds to the police station, where he finds that his landlady has reported him as a debtor. He is semidelirious and argumentative. After overhearing a detective discuss the killing of the pawnbroker and her sister, Raskolnikov passes out. When he comes to, the detective, Ilya Petrovich, asks him what he was doing the previous day. Raskolnikov leaves the station deeply shaken and worried that the police suspect him of the murders.

Summary: Chapter II

Raskolnikov returns to his room, gathers the stolen goods from the hole in the wall where he hid them, and goes for a walk. He considers dumping the items in the river but ends up burying them under a large stone in a courtyard. He walks around in an angry mood, wondering about his motives for the crime. On a whim, he visits his friend Razumikhin. The friendly Razumikhin worries about Raskolnikov's health and offers him work doing translations. Raskolnikov refuses and leaves in a huff. He wanders the streets listlessly and returns home at eight in the evening. He falls into a deep sleep, during which he dreams that the police detective is beating his landlady. He is sure it is reality and not a dream. Nastasya wakes him and brings him food the next day. She tells him that he has imagined the scene between the landlady and the detective.

Summary: Chapter III

Raskolnikov starts to experience hallucinations and becomes extremely weak. He wakes one morning surrounded by Nastasya, his landlady, Razumikhin, and a stranger. The stranger brings Raskolnikov thirty-five rubles from Pulcheria Alexandrovna. Raskolnikov learns that he hasn't been fully conscious in four days, and that Razumikhin, Nastasya, and the landlady have been taking care of him. Zossimov, a doctor, and Zamyotov, a detective, have also been to visit during this time. Razumikhin has managed to keep Raskolnikov's creditors—his landlady, in particular—at bay. Razumikhin is very concerned about his friend and has brought him some new clothes, which only annoys Raskolnikov. Zossimov then enters.

Summary: Chapter IV

Zossimov, a punctilious, well-dressed man, accepts Razumikhin's invitation to a housewarming party that evening at which Zamyotov and others will be present. Zossimov, Razumikhin, and Nastasya discuss the murder of the pawnbroker and her sister. Razumikhin has been working to clear the name of a painter who was working in the vacant apartment next to the pawnbroker's and who has been charged with the murders. Apparently, the painter was found to be in possession of some earrings that had been pawned to the old woman. Razumikhin argues that the earrings could have been dropped by the real murderer on his way out of the building and then found by the painter. As Razumikhin finishes this explanation, a strange face appears in the doorway.

Analysis: Chapters I–IV

Whereas Part I of *Crime and Punishment* was devoted to the crime, the remaining six parts of the novel are concerned with the punishment. At the beginning of Part II, less than a day after the crime is committed, Raskolnikov's punishment begins to unfold. As he himself notes, his punishment is to suffer emotionally and, though he would hesitate to use the word, spiritually. He becomes paranoid, worried that his senses will betray him and that he will forget some crucial detail in disposing of the stolen goods or overlook a spot of blood on his clothes. At this point, his main concern is with being caught, and he has not yet begun to worry about atoning for the crime. It is already clear that the feelings of superiority and accomplishment that he hoped would accompany the completion of the crime are nowhere to be found. Instead, he is weak, anxious, and delirious.

The main drama of the novel, the struggle between Raskolnikov's desire to confess and his desire to remain free, commences in Part II. Raskolnikov's fainting spell in the police station evidences the pressure that he feels to navigate these conflicting desires and his inability to do so. This tension and the feelings of alienation from society that Raskolnikov experiences are key elements of one of the main themes of the novel—that the individual who commits such a crime begins to feel estranged from the rest of humanity and that this suffering constitutes his true punishment.

Raskolnikov's attempt to get rid of the stolen goods, evidence of his guilt, parallels his attempt to suppress the feelings of guilt in his own mind. He opts not to dispose of the goods in the river for fear they will float to the surface, visible to all; similarly, he must stamp out any acknowledgment of guilt lest he unwittingly exhibit signs of this guilt. His burying of the goods under a heavy stone represents the smothering of his conscience.

These chapters develop the character of Razumikhin. He is a kind, caring person, willing to go out of his way to help even a surly and ungrateful friend. He is a foil to Raskolnikov—his cheerful, friendly, and relaxed manner accentuates Raskolnikov's disgruntled, antisocial, and agitated state of mind. While Raskolnikov is proudly aloof and suffers the torment brought on by his pride, Razumikhin is outgoing and seems to enjoy life. Razumikhin's accommodating qualities help to show that by engaging with humanity, one can avoid the pains of alienation from society. These qualities also help to confirm that circumstances alone do not cause Raskolnikov to commit his crime: Razumikhin, like his friend, is a poor student, but he manages to support himself without even contemplating, let alone putting into action, Raskolnikov's extreme measures.

PART II: CHAPTERS V–VII

Summary: Chapter V

The strange man who appears in Raskolnikov's doorway introduces himself as Luzhin, Dunya's fiancé. He is pompous and affected and immediately seems to resent Razumikhin friendly familiarity. He makes a show of interest in progressive ideas and reforms in an unsuccessful attempt to impress the younger men. Both Raskolnikov and Razumikhin treat him coldly. As Luzhin gets up to leave, Razumikhin and Zossimov return to discussing the murders. Razumikhin argues that an amateur must have committed the crime, since only a few trinkets but not the fifteen hundred rubles in the apartment were stolen. Luzhin breaks in with another attempt to make a display of his intelligence, and Razumikhin uses the opportunity to criticize his ideas. The feverish Raskolnikov then enters the conversation, denouncing Luzhin for wanting to be a benefactor to his impoverished sister. Luzhin takes great offense and storms out. Razumikhin and Zossimov are shocked at Raskolnikov's behaviour. Raskolnikov angrily throws them and Nastasya out of the room. On the way out, Zossimov remarks to Razumikhin that the mere mention of the murders seems to cause Raskolnikov great irritation.

Summary: Chapter VI

Raskolnikov, feeling suddenly clearheaded and resolute, throws on the clothes that Razumikhin bought for him and goes out. Wandering the streets, he wildly interrogates passing strangers. He enters a café, the Crystal Palace, and orders tea and a newspaper. There he meets the police inspector Zamyotov. The visibly ill Raskolnikov begins to tease the inspector about the murders and crime in general, claiming to know a great deal about both. He starts a crazed conversation in which he nearly confesses to the crime and seems to arouse Zamyotov's suspicions, but he finishes on a note that leaves Zamyotov convinced that he is merely a bit eccentric. Raskolnikov leaves hastily, bumping into Razumikhin on the stairs on his way out. They have a heated exchange, in which Razumikhin chastises his friend for going out by himself and then invites him to his party. Raskolnikov declines and walks on alone. Crossing a bridge, he is disgusted by the sight of a suicide attempt. He continues to wander and soon finds himself outside Alyona Ivanovna's home. He impulsively enters her apartment and sees two workmen redecorating it. In a daze, he asks them why the blood has been removed. He then fails to respond to their questions and is thrown out by the porter. Walking along, he notices a crowd gathered in the middle of the street.

Summary: Chapter VII

Raskolnikov sees the drunken Marmeladov lying injured in the street, having been trampled by a horse-drawn carriage. He takes the dying man to his home nearby. There, Katerina Ivanovna tearfully tries to care for him. A doctor declares that Marmeladov is dying. Marmeladov calls for a priest, who tells Katerina to forgive, but she rejects the priest's shallow ideas, tending to her husband even as she curses him as worthless. Marmeladov dies in Sonya's arms. Raskolnikov leaves twenty rubles for the family and promises his future support. Another of Katerina's daughters, Polenka, runs after him as he leaves and asks his name on behalf of Sonya and her mother. She hugs him and he asks her to pray for him.

Full of self-satisfaction, Raskolnikov considers himself partially redeemed. He goes to visit Razumikhin, who is rather tipsy from his party. Razumikhin confides that Zossimov believes Raskolnikov to be mad, a belief reinforced by the knowledge of Raskolnikov's conversation with Zamyotov. Raskolnikov is quite faint and can barely stand up straight. Together, he and Razumikhin return to Raskolnikov's room, where they are surprised to find Pulcheria Alexandrovna and Dunya awaiting him. The two are grief-stricken, having heard of Raskolnikov's condition from Nastasya. Once inside his room, Raskolnikov collapses and Razumikhin takes charge of caring for him.

Analysis: Chapters V–VII

Luzhin is convincingly depicted as a pompous boor. This opinion is strengthened by the fact that the good-natured and tolerant Razumikhin, with whose sentiments the reader feels comfortable aligning him- or herself, shares it. Indeed, Dostoevsky purposely gives Luzhin an unwelcome introduction, making him appear ominously at the end of the preceding chapter. Neither his identity nor his intentions are clear. His attempts to show off his knowledge further estrange him from Raskolnikov and Razumikhin. Raskolnikov's uncontrollable pride manifests itself when he deliberately offends Luzhin; although he has good reason to dislike the man, it hardly seems appropriate for him to insult his sister's fiancé.

In Chapter VI, Raskolnikov displays an apparent desire to be found out that rivals the intensity of his desire to escape suspicion. This internal conflict becomes visible in the scene in the Crystal Palace, in which, under the influence of a wild impulse, he nearly confesses to Zamyotov. He again nearly confesses during his visit to the scene of the crime. In later chapters, Porfiry Petrovich reveals that both incidents aroused suspicion among the police. In very definite ways, Raskolnikov's impulsive and dangerous actions make him an instrument of his own downfall and his own worst enemy.

In the following chapter, Raskolnikov is shown to be capable of compassion, or at least desirous to atone for his crime, when he offers his support to the Marmeladov family. Unlike Razumikhin, who helps Raskolnikov out of nothing but kindness and a genuine sense of humanity, Raskolnikov clearly acts out of an unavoidable sense of guilt. After donating money to the Marmeladovs, he experiences "a feeling akin to that of a dead man upon suddenly receiving his pardon." Dostoevsky himself had exactly this experience, having been subjected to a mock execution after his conviction for being a member of an illegal socialist group, and he refers to it frequently in his fiction. But Raskolnikov's rebirth or resurrection does not last. He is "simply catching at a straw," according to the narrator, and it takes a much deeper repentance for him to experience peace. Nonetheless, he appears to have taken the first, minuscule step on the road to reconciliation.

Dostoevsky continues to employ the narrative device of coincidence to propel the plot forward. Here, coincidence brings Raskolnikov back into contact with the Marmeladov family, thereby uniting the main plot and a subplot, as Raskolnikov implausibly happens upon the scene just after Marmeladov is injured. This type of coincidence gives the novel a quick, almost frantic pace, as Dostoevsky forces his characters to act within the confines of the world that he has established for them.

PART III: CHAPTERS I–III

Summary: Chapter I

Pulcheria Alexandrovna and Dunya are grief-stricken at Raskolnikov's condition, but he becomes annoyed with them and orders them out. He upsets them both by commanding Dunya to break off her engagement. Razumikhin promises to abandon his party and stay the night with Raskolnikov. Speaking to them on the stairs, the half-drunk Razumikhin tries to convince Dunya and Pulcheria Alexandrovna to leave Raskolnikov alone, offering to bring Zossimov to look after him. At first, Razumikhin frightens them with his intensity, but they soon both trust him. He, in turn, appears to be strongly attracted to Dunya. He makes drunken declarations of loyalty to her and says that Luzhin is unworthy of her. The mother and daughter return to their lodgings. The narrator describes Razumikhin's attraction to Dunya, explaining that she is beautiful, self-confident, strong, and tender, and, as if that weren't enough, Razumikhin is also somewhat drunk.

After checking up on Raskolnikov, Razumikhin visits the two women, first by -himself, then accompanied by Zossimov, who is thrilled to calm their fears. He remarks, however, that he believes Raskolnikov to be suffering from some sort of obsession. Outside, Razumikhin becomes violently jealous when the doctor idly compliments Dunya, and he tries to fix the doctor up with Raskolnikov's -landlady instead.

Summary: Chapter II

At times, however, he's... just inhumanly cold and callous, as if there really were two opposite characters in him.

The next morning, Razumikhin rises from bed overcome with regret at the bold things that he said the previous night. He renounces his desire for Dunya as absurd. Still, he washes and dresses himself with extra care in preparation for his next visit with Dunya and Pulcheria Alexandrovna. He finds them quite glad to see him. He relates how Raskolnikov is doing, emphasizing his self-involvement and even cruelty. He remains calm for most of the conversation but cannot help letting his feelings for Dunya slip out again. They show him a worrisome letter from Luzhin in which Luzhin asks not to see Raskolnikov again. Luzhin also tells them that Raskolnikov donated a large portion of the money that they sent him to Marmeladov's family. Razumikhin advises Pulcheria Alexandrovna to follow her daughter's wishes in the matter. Dunya thinks Raskolnikov should meet with her fiancé despite Luzhin's request. Pulcheria Alexandrovna declares her trust in Razumikhin, to his delight. The three then go to Raskolnikov's room.

Summary: Chapter III

Zossimov greets mother, daughter, and friend and informs them that Raskolnikov's condition has greatly improved. Raskolnikov pretends to be in a better mood and apologizes profusely to Zossimov and Razumikhin for his ingratitude. He apologizes to Pulcheria Alexandrovna for his thoughtlessness and warmly extends his hand to Dunya, a gesture that touches everyone in the room. Raskolnikov confesses to having given the money that he received from Pulcheria Alexandrovna to the Marmeladovs, and she forgives him. But the tranquillity of the scene is soon ruined when Raskolnikov becomes anxious and annoyed again. He commands Dunya not to marry Luzhin, saying that the engagement is dirty and "sordid." She retorts that she is doing nothing wrong, stating, for emphasis, that she is "guilty of no one's death." At this remark, Raskolnikov faints but recovers quickly. His sister explains to him her plan for testing her fiancé, showing him Luzhin's letter, and adding that she plans to defy his request that Raskolnikov not meet with them that evening. Luzhin's response to the situation, she declares, will reveal his true feelings for her. Raskolnikov agrees to meet with them that night.

Analysis: Chapters I–III

Razumikhin's falling in love with Dunya complicates the subplot of her engagement to Luzhin. His attachment comes about with almost incredible suddenness, as he becomes infatuated with her almost as soon as he meets her. This development can be explained plausibly by Razumikhin's honesty and straightforwardness, Dunya's undeniable charms, and Razumikhin's state of drunkenness when he first meets her. Besides illustrating Razumikhin's character and advancing the plot, his mad declarations of loyalty and burning affection provide a break in the heavy tone of the novel, which has been dominated so far by descriptions of Raskolnikov's delirious downward spiral and the suffering of the Marmeladovs. In fact, the subplot of Dunya's engagement constitutes one of the few bright spots in an otherwise overwhelmingly gloomy narrative.

With the character of Zossimov, the novel takes another short break from its seriousness to inject a bit of dry humour. Zossimov, while certainly not a boor like Luzhin, has a high opinion of himself and is not afraid to show it: "the doctor retired delighted with his call, and still more with himself." But Zossimov is a minor character in the novel, and the fact that he is a doctor has little effect beyond impressing Pulcheria Alexandrovna and Dunya. Perhaps his most important contribution is his suspicion that Raskolnikov is mentally ill. That others perceive Raskolnikov's guilty conscience as mental illness may be a comment on the connection between a criminal mindset and madness, or on the inability of the medical profession to tell the difference between the two.

Dostoevsky develops Dunya thoroughly in these chapters. He shows her to be intelligent, thoughtful, and practical. Her plan for testing her fiancé and her willingness to leave herself stranded in St. Petersburg if he doesn't measure up show that she is much stronger and more resourceful than Raskolnikov believes her to be. Dunya, in fact, faces the same problems that Raskolnikov does, but she confronts them with dignity and pride. It is interesting to note that, in Raskolnikov's behaviour toward Dunya, Dostoevsky reverses the conventional gender roles in nineteenth-century fiction: Dunya, a woman, proves the model of collected rationality and practicality, while Raskolnikov, a man, is lost in abstractions and prone to fainting.

Raskolnikov continues to demonstrate his complete self-absorption as the anxiety that his guilt produces gnaws at his ability to maintain his composure. His thoughtless treatment of his mother and sister, whom he has not seen in three years and whom he knows dote on him, reflects his insensitivity. Razumikhin's frank evaluation of his friend's personality reinforces this impression of Raskolnikov's misanthropy. Additionally, Raskolnikov's inner turmoil comes closer to the surface in these chapters. Zossimov's recognition of Raskolnikov's recent obsessiveness demonstrates that Raskolnikov's agitation is becoming increasingly visible, even to strangers such as the doctor. Raskolnikov's fainting spell when his sister makes a remark about not having killed anyone is another sign that he lacks the self-control needed to avoid giving himself away. In the aftermath of a crime committed according to the dictates of his intellect, his emotions are finally starting to take control.

PART III: CHAPTERS IV–VI

Summary: Chapter IV

Sonya timidly enters Raskolnikov's room, interrupting the conversation among Raskolnikov, Pulcheria Alexandrovna, Dunya, and Razumikhin. She bashfully invites Raskolnikov to Marmeladov's funeral and the memorial dinner that Katerina has planned to follow it. She is astonished at Raskolnikov's apparent poverty. Dunya and Pulcheria Alexandrovna politely leave. Raskolnikov tells Razumikhin that he had pawned a valuable watch to Alyona Ivanovna and would like it back. He asks Razumikhin if he should speak to Porfiry Petrovich, the magistrate in charge of the case and a relative of Razumikhin's, about the missing items. Razumikhin replies that he should. Raskolnikov agrees to go visit the Marmeladovs the next day, and all three leave. As Sonya walks back to her room, a strange, middle-aged man (Svidrigailov) follows her; it turns out that he lives in the room next to hers. Meanwhile, Razumikhin and Raskolnikov go to Porfiry Petrovich's house. Along the way, Raskolnikov teases Razumikhin about his attraction to Dunya, laughing loudly and trying to appear at ease. He secretly wonders whether Porfiry has heard of his visit the previous day to the scene of the crime and contemplates confessing.

Summary: Chapter V

Razumikhin is somewhat embarrassed by Raskolnikov, who bursts out laughing at him as they enter Porfiry's house. Raskolnikov tries to appear calm and confident before Porfiry, but the forced laughter comes off strangely. He becomes even more uneasy when he notices Zamyotov's presence. Razumikhin then makes things even worse by mentioning Raskolnikov's obvious distress at the mere mention of the murder case. Raskolnikov imagines that Porfiry is suspicious of him and nearly loses his cool when Porfiry mentions that Raskolnikov was the only one of the pawnbroker's clients not to come for his things immediately after the murder. Raskolnikov becomes very excited discussing his delirious wanderings of the night before. He starts to feel as though Porfiry is playing games with him. The men enter a discussion on crime, and Porfiry mentions an article that Raskolnikov had written, "On Crime," which, unbeknownst to Raskolnikov, had been published two months earlier. In the article, he argued that certain men were above the general run of humanity, and, as such, they have a right to commit murder. Porfiry coaxes Raskolnikov into elaborating on this thesis. Razumikhin finds it difficult to believe that his friend holds such a view. Just before Raskolnikov leaves, Porfiry asks him if he saw any painters at work in the building on his last visit to Alyona's, two days before the crime. Raskolnikov recognizes the trap, recalling that there were painters there on the day of the murder but not two days before, and says no.

Summary: Chapter VI

The old woman was a mistake perhaps, but... it wasn't a human being I killed, it was a principle!

Razumikhin argues with Raskolnikov about whether or not the police suspect him of the murders. Raskolnikov believes that they do; Razumikhin counters that if they did suspect him, they would never have engaged him so openly in a discussion of crime. But Razumikhin eventually admits that he, too, got the impression that the police suspected Raskolnikov. The two try to analyse Porfiry Petrovich's methods, arguing over whether his final question was a trap. Raskolnikov declares that it was and that he escaped it with his answer. The two reach Raskolnikov's house, where the porter tells them that a man has just been inquiring after Raskolnikov. Raskolnikov overtakes the man in the street. "Murderer," the man calls to him, giving him a cold look but no further explanation. Raskolnikov returns to his room and feverishly wonders about the stranger's accusation and Porfiry's suspicions. He tries to convince himself that Alyona's life was worthless. Yet he also questions his own motives for the crime and whether he actually is the sort of extraordinary "superman" that he had written about in his article. That night, he has a nightmare in which he tries to murder the pawnbroker; instead of dying, however, she laughs. He wakes to find a stranger in his room.

Analysis: Chapters IV–VI

In these chapters, Raskolnikov's interior conflict intensifies. He is faced with the dual task of avoiding the suspicion of Porfiry Petrovich and dealing with his own emotional turmoil. His difficulty in controlling himself at Porfiry's home and his strange dream at the end of Part III demonstrate that he is just barely avoiding a complete breakdown. The ongoing struggle between his desire to avoid suspicion and his compulsion to confess leads him to act erratically, sometimes trying to appear healthy and innocent and other times boldly risking discovery.

Raskolnikov's article "On Crime" clues the reader in to some of the rationale for committing the murder. Introducing the theme of Raskolnikov's idea of a "superman," the article argues that certain extraordinary people are above the masses of humanity and so have the right to violate moral codes, for instance, by committing murder. Razumikhin's strongly moral character reveals itself in his immediate rejection of this notion. Porfiry Petrovich, however, takes great interest in the idea—not because he agrees with it, but because he sees it as a piece of psychological evidence pointing to Raskolnikov's guilt. The discussion takes place on an intellectual plane, but the fact that Raskolnikov has actually followed through with his idea and that Porfiry suspects him of it lends the otherwise abstract discussion a tense immediacy. The conversation serves to illustrate the enormous gap between talking about violating moral boundaries and actually doing so. Interestingly, Raskolnikov's inner turmoil belies the superiority and righteousness with which his ideal "superman" is supposed to commit crimes.

The ideas that Raskolnikov expresses in his article have strong ties to nihilism, a philosophical position developed in Russia in the 1850s and 1860s. Nihilism rejected the traditional bonds of family and society as well as emotional and aesthetic concerns in favour of a strict materialism promoting the idea that there is no mind or soul outside of the physical world. A central tenet of nihilism was utilitarianism—the idea that actions are moral insofar as they work toward the greatest possible happiness for the largest number of people. As is made clear in this section, Raskolnikov's justifications for murdering Alyona are strongly utilitarian and nihilist.

Raskolnikov's nightmare reflects not so much his feelings of guilt as his fear that he doesn't actually measure up to his theoretical "superman"—and that his actions, therefore, have no justification. Even before Raskolnikov has his nightmare, the stranger's simple, direct labeling of him as "[m]urderer" makes the grandiose identity that he had created for himself begin to crumble. The defence that he mounts against this deconstruction of his assumed identity constitutes a counterattack on the debased identity that the stranger has imposed on him. In devaluing Alyona's life, Raskolnikov seeks to mitigate the criminality of the murder by emphasizing his own worth and her worthlessness. In his nightmare, however, he cannot pretend that he acted as a "superman" in killing Alyona. Indeed, the nightmare forces him to confront his mediocrity; that Alyona laughs at him when he tries to kill her reveals to him his impotency and inadequacy.

The suspense mounts in these chapters, especially with the introduction of the strange man who follows Sonya in Chapter IV and then appears in Raskolnikov's doorway at the end of Chapter VI. The more strangers that enter Raskolnikov's life, the more complicated his situation gets. Each time he pushes them away, he is, in part, trying to keep himself separate from the humanity that he disdains and maintain the abstract, lonely position from which he originally formulates his plan of killing Alyona. The entrance into the drama of the stranger, who we later find out is Svidrigailov, threatens Raskolnikov's sense of his role and thrusts him one step closer toward reengagement with society, whether he likes it or not.

PART IV: CHAPTERS I–III

Summary: Chapter I

Svidrigailov explains that he has come to ask Raskolnikov's help in his pursuit of Dunya. Raskolnikov immediately refuses. Svidrigailov contends that he has only the purest feelings for Dunya and that, contrary to rumor, he had nothing to do with the recent death of his wife, Marfa Petrovna. He argues that he is not a monster, only a slave to passion. He then tells a story about how he came to marry his wife, saying that she took advantage of a predicament that he was in to control and dominate him. He claims to have been visited by the ghost of his dead wife several times. Raskolnikov wonders whether his visitor is insane. Svidrigailov says that he has heard of Dunya's engagement to Luzhin, who is a relative of his, and offers to help break off this inappropriate match. Svidrigailov claims that, though he once obsessed over Dunya, he is no longer in love with her but cannot bear her taking such an unsuitable husband. He wants to give her ten thousand rubles as an apology before he either marries or goes on a journey. Raskolnikov assures him that his sister will refuse the gift. Svidrigailov also tells him that his wife has left Dunya three thousand rubles in her will. He leaves, passing Razumikhin on his way out.

Summary: Chapter II

Razumikhin and Raskolnikov walk to a restaurant. Razumikhin says that he has spoken with Porfiry Petrovich and Zamyotov and discovered that they suspect Raskolnikov of the murders, which Razumikhin finds absurd. Raskolnikov privately wonders what his friend will think when he finds out that Raskolnikov is indeed guilty. They meet with Luzhin, Dunya, and Pulcheria Alexandrovna and seat themselves around a table. Luzhin's pride is wounded by the presence of the two young men, whose absence he had specifically requested, and he resolves to punish the women. He upsets them by breaking the news of Svidrigailov's arrival in St. Petersburg. He goes on to describe the crimes and depravities that he has heard attributed to Svidrigailov, but Dunya rejects his stories as baseless gossip. Raskolnikov abruptly informs the party of his meeting with Svidrigailov and the money that was willed to Dunya by Marfa Petrovna. He refuses to say what Svidrigailov wants with Dunya. Dunya then confronts Luzhin about his annoyance at her brother's presence, and Luzhin manages to offend everyone in the room with his response. There is an angry confrontation between mother, daughter, and son on one side and fiancé on the other. Dunya orders Luzhin to leave.

He does so only after insulting them. As he leaves, he blames his loss of Dunya on Raskolnikov, for whom he now harbors a deep hatred. He convinces himself that he may still have a chance with Dunya.

Summary: Chapter III

After Luzhin departs, the group is overjoyed. Razumikhin is the happiest of all. Raskolnikov, however, quickly becomes anxious again. He tells them about Svidrigailov offering to give Dunya ten thousand rubles, which both women refuse. Razumikhin offers to guard Dunya from the man, and Dunya consents. He suggests that Dunya and her mother stay on in St. Petersburg and proposes that they all go into the publishing business together. Dunya is thrilled with this idea and Raskolnikov assents as well. But then Raskolnikov abruptly gets up to leave. He states that he has resolved to separate himself from them for a long time and that they must not pursue him. The rest of the group is dismayed. Razumikhin chases after him, but Raskolnikov sends him back, telling his friend to stay with Pulcheria Alexandrovna and Dunya. The two stare at each other, and Razumikhin realises that Raskolnikov is the murderer. He returns to the table.

Analysis: Chapters I–III

Svidrigailov is depicted as a morally weak man who doesn't seem to understand when he is unwelcome or perhaps simply doesn't care. But, unlike most of the other characters, such as the kind and compassionate Razumikhin or the miserly Alyona Ivanovna, Svidrigailov is not drawn quickly and decisively. His mental state, motives, and true nature remain enigmatic throughout the novel. Svidrigailov's entrance into the plot is almost identical to that of Luzhin: like Luzhin in Part II, Chapter IV, Svidrigailov appears unexpectedly in Raskolnikov's room, his entrance made ominous by the fact that he, a stranger, hovers over Raskolnikov at the close of the preceding chapter. Additionally, both discuss their interest in Dunya with Raskolnikov. One subtle difference between these two encounters is that Razumikhin is not present when Svidrigailov shows up; rather, Raskolnikov is alone in his room. Svidrigailov is an unreal shadow of Raskolnikov, a figment of his imagination, delusional like he is and equally dysfunctional in society.

Luzhin returns to cause mischief later in the narrative, but it is clear that his engagement with Dunya is permanently broken. In her decision to reject Luzhin, Dunya is revealed as an intelligent, confident, and decisive woman who, though willing to make sacrifices for the sake of her family, is unwilling to disgrace herself by marrying a man as crude as Luzhin. Her pride is as strong as Raskolnikov's, but, unlike his, it is laced with dignity and motivates her to maintain her integrity in the face of such ill-conceived possibilities as her engagement to Luzhin.

The breaking of the engagement is a major event not only for Dunya but also for Raskolnikov. Raskolnikov's sudden irritation after Luzhin's departure seems, at first, abrupt, but a close look at the timing of his decision to leave reveals its significance. Only after he realises that Razumikhin will take care of Dunya and Pulcheria Alexandrovna does Raskolnikov announce his need to separate from them. Tainted by his crime, he wishes to distance himself from them, but he is unwilling to do so until he knows that they will be cared for. This consideration marks the beginning of a change in his character. For the first time, he seems to care for others and not just for himself. While Raskolnikov's decision to leave is of a different order than Sonya's prostitution and Dunya's decision to become engaged to Luzhin, it nevertheless reflects his understanding of the importance of family. The contrast between Raskolnikov's lonely, alienated thoughts and the generous affection of Pulcheria Alexandrovna and Dunya only heightens Raskolnikov's inner turmoil and his compulsion to detach himself from his family. His departure from them makes it clear that he either intends to confess voluntarily or believes that he will soon be found out—or, perhaps, that he simply cannot face the people who love him with the secret of the murders hanging over him.

PART IV: CHAPTERS IV–VI

Summary: Chapter IV

Raskolnikov goes to Sonya's room. She is surprised and frightened by his visit. They discuss Katerina Ivanovna, whom Sonya defends as kind, childlike, and fiercely proud, though she concedes that misfortune has more or less deranged Katerina. Sonya clearly cares immensely for her stepmother and is deeply troubled to think that she might soon die, leaving her children defenceless. Yet she clings to the belief that God will provide for the family and take care of them. Sonya reveals that she was a friend of the murdered Lizaveta. In fact, Lizaveta gave Sonya a cross and a copy of the Gospels. Raskolnikov commands Sonya to read him the story of Lazarus. Sonya manages to overcome her terror of the crazed Raskolnikov and reads, shaking as she does so. It is clear that the passage has special significance for her. Raskolnikov shares with her his resolution to separate from his family and asks her to go away with him. He thinks of her as a kindred spirit, someone who has, as a prostitute, also transgressed moral law and "destroyed a life—her very own." He tells her that she will soon know who killed Lizaveta. Meanwhile, in a vacant room next door, Svidrigailov eavesdrops on the conversation.

Summary: Chapter V

Freedom will no longer be dear to him, he'll fall to thinking, get entangled... he'll worry himself to death!

The following morning, Raskolnikov pays a visit to Porfiry Petrovich at the police station. While he waits in the lobby, he mulls over his hatred for the magistrate. Once inside Porfiry's office, Raskolnikov presents him with a written request for his pawned possessions. The two embark on a long conversation in which Raskolnikov quickly starts to feel as though he has fallen into a trap. Frustrated by the games that he thinks Porfiry is playing, he asks the magistrate to submit him to the questioning discussed the previous day. Porfiry tries to put Raskolnikov at ease and become friendly with him. He chatters away, speaking mostly nonsense, though occasionally adding an enigmatic remark. He discusses the psychological methods by which he hopes to catch the murderer. He includes observations about the "youth" and "intelligence" of his suspect that are pointed directly at Raskolnikov. Throughout Porfiry's rambling monologue, Raskolnikov, though agitated, stays quiet. But after a while, he bursts out wildly, accusing the official of suspecting him and challenging Porfiry either to accuse him outright or to let him be. Porfiry tries to calm him down. But even as he does so, he reveals that he knows of Raskolnikov's recent visit to the scene of the crime. He tries to trick Raskolnikov into admitting that he sent Razumikhin to ask Porfiry about his suspicions. Raskolnikov becomes violently upset, but then a "singular incident" occurs.

Summary: Chapter VI

Suddenly, Nikolai, the prisoner who is under suspicion for the murders, rushes into the office and confesses to the crime. Although Porfiry does not believe the man, he takes the confession seriously. He shows Raskolnikov out. As Raskolnikov is on the stairs, Porfiry detains him to say that he will need to see him again soon for more questions. Raskolnikov goes home, where he realises that, if Nikolai hadn't burst into Porfiry's office, he might have confessed to the murders. He decides to go to the memorial dinner for Marmeladov. Just then, the stranger who had called him a murderer the previous day appears in the doorway. The man, who identifies himself as a tenant of the pawnbroker's building, says that he witnessed Raskolnikov's visit to the crime scene and heard him question the workers about the blood. He reveals that he knows nothing more and, having overheard his conversation with Porfiry at the police station, is now sympathetic to Raskolnikov's plight. Raskolnikov is greatly relieved and feels renewed hope that he will not be caught after all.

Analysis: Chapters IV–VI

Dostoevsky's inclusion of the Lazarus story provides both Raskolnikov and Sonya with a model of hope for their lives. In the Christian tradition, the raising of Lazarus from death is the most profound miracle that Jesus performed while on earth. Sonya may adapt the story to her life as a promise that a similar miracle will rectify her situation, a kind of death induced by her poverty and self-sacrifice. The story also carries deep significance for the skeptical Raskolnikov. Although he claims not to believe in the story, he is moved by it, since it no doubt resonates with his sense of total alienation from society. His death has been a death of the soul. Separated from those who love him by his own pride and his terrible secret, Raskolnikov longs for some kind of chance to start anew, to be, like Lazarus, resurrected. He is still proud, but his veneer of superiority is beginning to crack.

The Lazarus story also serves as allegorical foreshadowing, predicting Raskolnikov's return to humanity at the end of the novel. Despite his conviction that killing Alyona Ivanovna was justified, Raskolnikov already feels his guilt and alienation on a deep, almost physical level. He is eventually driven to confess, if for no other reason than to put an end to the doubt and emotional turmoil that now hound him. His ultimate confession and subsequent imprisonment lead him to some form of redemption.

Sonya's humility is much more profound than her embarrassment about being a prostitute. She is a pious Christian, believing that her fate is firmly in God's hands and trusting that he is just, as Raskolnikov observes, against all proof to the contrary. It is Sonya's faith that allows her to continue surviving and helping her family to survive. The contrast between Sonya and Raskolnikov is striking, illuminating the depth of Sonya's devotion and self-sacrifice and the shallowness of Raskolnikov's pride. Raskolnikov's attempt to compare himself to Sonya as a fellow sinner falls flat, since she has turned to prostitution only out of the need to help her family, and laments her sin, while Raskolnikov has not yet repented for the murders, the first of which is shakily predicated on utilitarian grounds and the second of which is purely self-serving. Raskolnikov's blindness to these differences shows that he is still a long way from recognizing his guilt.

The psychological conflict between Raskolnikov and Porfiry Petrovich comes to a head in Chapter V. Though Raskolnikov is rightly confident that Petrovich has no evidence of his guilt, Porfiry makes full use of Raskolnikov's unease. Raskolnikov seems almost ready to confess at the end of Chapter IV, but he steps back from the edge, and, by the end of Part IV, seems to have renewed his resolve to evade punishment. His sarcastic, prideful side returns in full force, and he pulls himself away from the people around him, criticizing himself for his "weakness." The internal conflict between his pride and his desire to confess intensifies, weaving back and forth and prolonging the suspense over the eventual outcome of the struggle.

Dostoevsky continues to employ all of his characters to masterful effect, setting up an infinite number of possible coincidences and obstacles for Raskolnikov. The revelation of Svidrigailov's eavesdropping is intended purely for the reader and clearly foreshadows that Svidrigailov will use the information that he has garnered for some sinister purpose. Additionally, Dostoevsky inserts Nikolai's dramatic confession, an unexpected but perfectly timed event for Raskolnikov's benefit that allows Dostoevsky to shift the direction of the plot. As when Raskolnikov heard someone talking about a desire to kill the pawnbroker, echoing his thoughts, Raskolnikov believes that Nikolai's confession is evidence of some master plan for him.

PART V: CHAPTERS I–IV

Summary: Chapter I

Luzhin is in his room with Lebezyatnikov, a younger man who is his roommate. Luzhin now realises that his engagement with Dunya is irrecoverably broken. He nurses a deep hatred for Raskolnikov, and shivers to think of the money that he lost on deposits for their newlywed home and furnishings. He fantasizes that if he had given his fiancée and her mother more presents, they would not have broken the engagement. Meanwhile, he and Lebezyatnikov have been invited to the memorial dinner that Katerina Ivanovna, who lives in the same building, is holding for Marmeladov. Lebezyatnikov is a pompous fool, though Luzhin initially thought of him as a thoughtful young man who could help him navigate the new political waves of liberalism, radicalism, and nihilism washing over Russia. Luzhin invites Sonya to his room and gives the embarrassed girl a ten-ruble note.

Summary: Chapter II

The narrator considers Katerina Ivanovna's reasons for spending more than half of the money given to them by Raskolnikov on the memorial banquet and concludes that it is probably because of her pride. Only Raskolnikov and the lowliest of the tenants, who behave rudely, attend the affair. Katerina, who claims repeatedly to be of a "noble, if not aristocratic," family, hurls insults at her low-class guests. Meanwhile, she appears increasingly unwell, coughing up blood during the meal. She ends up fighting with her landlady while her guests egg her on. In the middle of the fight, Luzhin appears in the doorway and Katerina rushes to him.

Summary: Chapter III

Luzhin insultingly brushes Katerina aside as she implores his protection from the landlady. Turning to Sonya, he accuses her of stealing a one-hundred-ruble note. Sonya denies the theft. Katerina becomes incensed at the insult to her stepdaughter and starts raving against Luzhin and the landlady. To prove Sonya's innocence, she defiantly turns the girl's pockets out and is shocked when a one-hundred-ruble note falls out. Luzhin magnanimously agrees not to press charges. To Luzhin's horror, however, Lebezyatnikov appears and declares that he saw Luzhin place the note in Sonya's pocket earlier. Raskolnikov then explains that Luzhin was probably trying to embarrass him about his association with Sonya. Luzhin, faced with the complete ruin of his plan, tries to extricate himself by maintaining his innocence and insulting Lebezyatnikov and Raskolnikov. After Luzhin leaves, the fight between Katerina and the landlady continues. In the end, the Marmeladovs are evicted.

Summary: Chapter IV

Raskolnikov visits Sonya in her room. He tells her that her family has been turned out of their building but urges her not to go to help them. He confesses the murders to her. Sonya responds with immense pity and promises to support Raskolnikov and not abandon him. She is astonished when he tells her that his poverty was not the motive. Rather, he says, "I was ambitious to become another Napoleon; that was why I committed a murder." He also confesses that he feels detached from other people and believed, and perhaps still believes, in his superiority over most other people. Sonya tells him that he has been punished for turning away from God. He reiterates that self-absorption fueled his actions, that he wished to prove that he was somehow extraordinary and able to transgress the moral codes that bind ordinary people. Sonya tells him that he must confess his sins publicly for God to give him peace. At first he resists, but he soon consents. Sonya promises to come to see him in prison and support him. She gives him a pendant cross to wear, similar to the one that she wears, saying that they will both bear their crosses. Just then, Lebezyatnikov knocks at the door.

Analysis: Chapters I–IV

Luzhin's profoundly materialistic and self-serving nature is brought to the fore in this section. Obsessed with money and material objects, he blames Dunya's rejection of him on entirely material motives, thinking that once she had the inheritance from Marfa Petrovna, she and her mother no longer needed him. His plan to frame Sonya solidifies his status as one of the novel's villains. His ploy is clumsy and mean-spirited, and, although he tries to maintain his pride, it is clear that he will never regain Dunya's favour. After this scene, Luzhin disappears from the narrative, never to return again, since he has played his last cards and been beaten. Dunya is now completely free to turn her attention to Razumikhin, the man whose rightness for her has been clear from the start.

Lebezyatnikov functions as a humourous and sarcastic caricature of the pompous but stupid intellectual, a proverbial emperor with no clothes. Even as he rushes to Sonya's defence, Lebezyatnikov feels the need to make little speeches about the ethics of private charity. In depicting Lebezyatnikov as obsessed with intellectual fads and unrealistic utopias, Dostoevsky criticizes the actual intellectual currents that were sweeping Russia in the 1860s, such as nihilism, and emphasizes how much more profound, albeit equally misguided, Raskolnikov's theories are.

Katerina Ivanovna appears as a tragic figure, portrayed in vivid images of coughed-up blood and inflamed cheeks. Her pride, unlike Raskolnikov's, is deeply pathetic and intertwined with her poverty. She rails against a world that she believes has unjustly punished her. Her pride motivates her to spend too much money on Marmeladov's memorial dinner, even though, with his death, the family is certain to starve. She sees the dinner as one last chance to pretend that she truly is "noble, even aristocratic." Instead, the event proves to be only one more illustration of the impossibility of escaping the poverty that surrounds her. The subplot of the Marmeladovs' unrelenting misfortune provides the reader a broader context for Raskolnikov's struggle against a society filled with injustice, poverty, anonymity, and hopelessness.

Raskolnikov's confession to Sonya and his promise to confess to the police are major developments. At the end of this section, Raskolnikov seems finally to have started on the path to resolving the torment that he has felt since the murders. His pride has given way to the realization that he is not the "superman" that he once fantasized himself to be. Still, it is important to note that his return to humanity is not happy; he still thinks of the people around him as despicable creatures and, understanding himself as part of humanity, views himself as necessarily despicable. This realization that he is only human constitutes the first big step toward confession and redemption. Though true remorse stands a long way off, the simple act of confessing to Sonya and receiving her sympathy—his first meaningful connection with another person—helps him break through his alienation from all of humanity.

These developments occur in tandem with a shift for Raskolnikov from a theoretical to a realistic understanding of matters. Whereas he initially justifies the murder of Alyona Ivanovna on the nihilist grounds of ridding humanity of a parasite, he now admits that his actions were based less in philosophy than in emotional insecurity: "All I wanted was to do some daring thing, Sonya; that was my sole motive!" By committing an exceptional act, by stepping over the normal bounds of human behaviour, he had hoped to prove that he himself was exceptional. The self-serving nature of his actions, however, contradicts and undermines the utilitarian and nihilist motives that he originally professes.

PART V: CHAPTER V

In some editions, the fifth chapter of Part V is set as a chapter-long Part VI. In such editions, Crime and Punishment is divided into seven parts plus an epilogue, rather than the six parts plus an epilogue into which this SparkNote divides the text.

Summary: Chapter V

Lebezyatnikov informs Sonya that Katerina Ivanovna has apparently gone mad. Katerina has visited the homes of well-to-do people, demanding their assistance, and has been violently thrown out. She has now resolved to become an organ-grinder, is tearing up her children's clothes, and has sent her children to dance in the street and beg for charity. She hopes to perform in front of one of the houses from which she was turned out to shame its inhabitants and the public. Lebezyatnikov reports that she cries, "People shall see the children of a noble family beg in the public streets!"

Sonya rushes out to find Katerina. Raskolnikov goes to his room, where Dunya soon comes to see him. She says that she has heard from Razumikhin of her brother's "persecution" by the police and pledges her support. Raskolnikov tells her that he thinks highly of Razumikhin. After she leaves, Raskolnikov goes out into the street, where Lebezyatnikov catches up with him and tells him that Katerina has truly gone mad and may soon be taken by the police. Lebezyatnikov leads Raskolnikov to Katerina and the children, around whom a crowd has formed. Katerina looks ghastly. She is obviously in the throes of her disease; she is animated by a mad energy, singing, dancing, and beating her children. She tries to appeal to the sympathies of well-dressed passersby, explaining that her children are of "noble, nay, even aristocratic family." She and the children are all crying. Katerina refuses Sonya's pleas that she return home. She has a confrontation with a policeman and coughs up a great deal of blood. She is taken back to their home, where she is laid on a couch. The policeman, Lebezyatnikov, Raskolnikov, Sonya, the children, the landlord, the landlady, and some strangers crowd around her as she dies. She refuses the services of a priest, saying she has no need for them. She starts having hallucinations. She calls for Sonya and, in a fit of convulsions, dies. Sonya, sobbing, throws herself onto the corpse.

Svidrigailov appears and tells Raskolnikov that he will use a portion of the money that he had promised Dunya to pay for a funeral and to provide for the children, who will be sent to an orphanage. He then reveals that he overheard Raskolnikov confessing the murders to Sonya.

Analysis: Chapter V

This chapter centres on the climax of the Marmeladov subplot, with the frenzied death of Katerina Ivanovna. The combination of Luzhin's accusation of Sonya with the family's eviction by their landlady pushes Katerina over the edge, and she explodes in a frenzy of activity that culminates in her death. She desperately turns to illusions of her nobility and fantasies of the rich offering her support. When the rich treat her as badly as everyone else, however, it is more than her defences can take, and she breaks down. In contrast to Raskolnikov, who accepts the deconstruction of the "superman" identity that he has envisioned for himself, Katerina defiantly plows through the reality that her proclaimed nobility is meaningless.

Although Katerina is delusional about the world around her, her sense of dignity is very real and quite strong. When her dignity bears the brunt of an intolerable attack, she responds by singing, dancing, and screaming her outrage against the world. Even her death, marked by sighs and convulsions, comes in a burst of activity. The juxtaposition of her grotesque behaviour and repeated claims to nobility accentuates her obstinate refusal to alter her perception of herself in response to circumstances. Her pathetic claim to nobility becomes an increasingly angry assertion. On her deathbed, Katerina irritably refuses the services of a priest, declaring, "A priest? I am not in need of one. My conscience is free from sin! And, even were it not, God must forgive me. He knows how I have suffered!" Believing that her unending and highly visible tribulations have rendered her a martyr, Katerina believes that not even God can legitimately find fault with her.

This final portrait of Katerina Ivanovna completes the picture of the ruined Marmeladovs, a family that includes a drunk husband trampled to death in the streets, a proud but consumptive mother reduced to beating her children and begging, and an older daughter forced into prostitution. Sonya's suffering and devotion to her family stands out remarkably against this backdrop of utter despair. She has long understood and accepted her identity and role, despite the cruel and crushing reality of her life.

Svidrigailov's appearance at Katerina's deathbed moves the plot in two important directions. First, by offering to pay for the funeral and provide for Katerina's children, he frees Sonya from the overwhelming burden of caring for them, just as Razumikhin's willingness to care for Pulcheria Alexandrovna and Dunya enables Raskolnikov to separate himself from them without feeling that he is abandoning them. Second, Svidrigailov draws Raskolnikov into his web by revealing that he has overheard Raskolnikov's confession of the murders. He, Sonya, and Raskolnikov himself are now the only three people who know without a doubt that Raskolnikov is the murderer. While Sonya uses this knowledge for good—to try to persuade Raskolnikov to confess—it is unclear what Svidrigailov intends to do with it, but it is certain to be something much less honourable. Raskolnikov is losing control of his secret, and his control over events is about to unravel rapidly as well.

PART VI: CHAPTERS I–V

Summary: Chapter I

A delirious haze settles over Raskolnikov in the days following Katerina Ivanovna's death and his confession to Sonya. He wanders the streets, hanging around in bars and outside the building in which Sonya lives. One day, Razumikhin comes to visit him in his room. He says that he has come to find out once and for all whether or not Raskolnikov has gone mad. Razumikhin decides that he has not. He tells Raskolnikov that Pulcheria Alexandrovna is heartbroken and feels abandoned. The always compassionate Razumikhin finally seems to have lost patience with Raskolnikov's selfishness, now that he has seen the pain that it causes his family. He informs Raskolnikov of a mysterious and upsetting letter that Dunya has received. He also mentions that Porfiry Petrovich apparently believes that the painter, Nikolai, is guilty of the murders. When Raskolnikov tells him of Dunya's earlier visit, Razumikhin becomes suspicious of a "conspiracy" between the two. After Razumikhin leaves, Porfiry appears.

Summary: Chapter II

Porfiry tells Raskolnikov that he wants to apologize for his treatment of him, admitting that he was trying to extract a confession from him. He attributes his suspicions to Raskolnikov's article, his fainting on his first visit to the police station, and his remarks to Zamyotov at the Crystal Palace. But the official soon admits that he still does not believe Nikolai's confession, since the painter seems too childlike and is ignorant of most of the details of the crime. Raskolnikov, Porfiry claims, is the true murderer. Raskolnikov denies the accusation, but Petrovich repeats the charge with confidence. He has not arrested Raskolnikov, he says, because he has not gathered enough evidence. He is sympathetic to Raskolnikov, he says, and urges him to confess. He claims that he has proof of Raskolnikov's guilt and that Raskolnikov would look better in the eyes of the judge if he confessed before the evidence was produced. If he confesses, Porfiry promises to put in a good word with the judge. He is confident that Raskolnikov's guilt will eventually cause him to confess. Before leaving, he asks Raskolnikov to leave a note disclosing the location of the stolen loot should he decide to commit suicide. Raskolnikov leaves his room soon after.

Summary: Chapter III

Raskolnikov goes looking for Svidrigailov. He finds him in a café, being entertained in one of the back rooms by a singer. After a series of elusive exchanges with Svidrigailov,

Raskolnikov, unsettled, threatens to kill him if he uses "some recent discovery" about Raskolnikov to force his will upon Dunya. Svidrigailov tells Raskolnikov that he enjoys observing him, and then begins to talk about his life. Thinking Svidrigailov a worthless and depraved man, Raskolnikov gets up to leave. Svidrigailov, however, persuades him to stay by mentioning Dunya.

Summary: Chapter IV

Svidrigailov proceeds to tell Raskolnikov at length about his relationship with Marfa Petrovna, who allowed him to be unfaithful to her, and his attraction to Dunya. Raskolnikov notices that Svidrigailov is becoming drunk and announces that he is convinced that Svidrigailov still has designs on Dunya. Svidrigailov tries to deflect Raskolnikov's concerns by telling him that he has found himself a young, vulnerable fifteen-year-old girl and has recently become engaged to her. According to Svidrigailov, this girl possesses a mixture of childlike qualities and mature intelligence that he finds alluring. Raskolnikov is disgusted at the engagement and the depraved pleasure that the older man clearly takes in it, but Svidrigailov is unfazed. He leaves, amused by Raskolnikov's disapproval. Raskolnikov follows Svidrigailov into the street, worried that he might still be a threat to Dunya despite his engagement.

Summary: Chapter V

Svidrigailov notices Raskolnikov pursuing him and again tells him goodbye. Raskolnikov decides not to follow Svidrigailov after Svidrigailov boards a carriage for a distant part of the city. He fails to notice that Svidrigailov rides the carriage for only a hundred paces before getting off. Svidrigailov lures Dunya to his room by reminding her that he knows about her brother's secret, referring to the information that he promised to reveal in the mysterious letter mentioned by Razumikhin. Dunya is incredulous when Svidrigailov reveals that he overheard Raskolnikov confessing to the murders of Alyona Ivanovna and Lizaveta. While Dunya becomes faint with anger and confusion, Svidrigailov offers to help Raskolnikov avoid punishment if she will marry him. In horror, she runs to the door, only to discover that Svidrigailov has locked it. He threatens to rape her, warning that he can report her brother if she reports him. She pulls out a revolver, threatens him with it, and accuses him of poisoning his late wife. He dares her to fire, and she does, twice, but manages only to graze his temple. Svidrigailov moves to embrace her but, realizing that she will never love him, lets her go. Putting the revolver in his pocket, he goes out shortly thereafter.

Analysis: Chapters I–V

The mind game between Raskolnikov and Porfiry Petrovich reaches its climax in Part VI, Chapter II. Porfiry's shrewd expertise in psychology leads him to the bold move of declaring his suspicions to Raskolnikov. He guesses correctly that his suspect is tormented by his guilt. By placing the possibility of confession before Raskolnikov, he provides him with a method of resolving his unhappiness and thus appeals to his human side.

Svidrigailov embodies the qualities of immorality and self-absorption. Although he is human in a way that Luzhin and Raskolnikov are not, he greatly exceeds both in his capacity to be sneaky and calculating. While Luzhin is plainly nothing more than a cold, self-centred materialist, Svidrigailov is a complex character. His actions are ambiguous and his generosities can all be interpreted in ways that cast doubt on his good intentions. One can argue that his donation in support of the Marmeladov children is not, as it first seems, the kind gesture of a sinful but repentant man, but merely an attempt to get closer to Raskolnikov and, through him, Dunya. Conflicting stories about Svidrigailov's past, including whether he caused the death of one of his servants and whether he contributed to his wife's death, leave his motivations for his behaviour in doubt.

Nonetheless, Svidrigailov's attempted rape of Dunya removes any lingering doubts about his character. But even-here, the incident turns on more than just the pursuit of a goal. Although Dunya's gunshots cause no physical harm, they prove to Svidrigailov that she will never care for him. His subsequent urgency in asking her to leave evidences an intense inner struggle. He has managed to rein in, if only for a moment, the appetites that have driven him to sin in the past. Dostoevsky reveals that Svidrigailov, so often glib and cynical, suffers deeply when he sees his fantasy fractured. Svidrigailov's character adds depth and complexity to the novel's depiction of evil; in the extremity of his emotions, he is similar to the self-conscious, tormented Raskolnikov.

Dunya's use of the revolver in Chapter V presents a striking contrast to an earlier act of violence—the murders of Alyona and Lizaveta. Even with the justification of self-defence against an immediate physical threat, Dunya is unable to go through with the act, firing only twice before laying the gun down. Her unwillingness or inability to kill Svidrigailov renders irrelevant the philosophical rationalizations of murder that prompt Raskolnikov's actions. Dostoevsky seems to suggest that what matters is not whether the murder leads to the greatest good for the greatest number of people, but simply whether the individual with the gun can find it within him- or herself to kill another human being. Dunya clearly cannot, which distinguishes her from Raskolnikov.

PART VI: CHAPTERS VI–VIII

Summary: Chapter VI

Svidrigailov wanders aimlessly around St. Petersburg, soaking himself in the rain. In the evening, he visits Sonya. He assures her that her siblings will be provided for and offers her a three-thousand-ruble bond. He tells her that she is to use the money to accompany Raskolnikov to Siberia. He himself is going off to America. After leaving Sonya, Svidrigailov visits his fiancée's family, informs them that he will be going away for some time, and presents them with fifteen thousand rubles. He then proceeds to a hotel, where he has feverish dreams, imagining that he has found a five-year-old girl in a corner of the hotel, whimpering from the cold. He lovingly puts her in her bed and wraps a blanket around her, but she turns to him with a depraved, seductive look on her face. He also dreams that rain is flooding St. Petersburg. He wakes just before dawn in a daze and goes out, taking Dunya's revolver with him. He finds a soldier keeping watch, puts the revolver to his head, and, before killing himself, tells the soldier to tell anyone who asks that he has gone to America.

Summary: Chapter VII

Raskolnikov goes to see Pulcheria Alexandrovna. She says that she has read his article and was impressed by it, though she could not understand it all. Raskolnikov looks at the article with disgust. His mother has apparently convinced herself that her son is a genius destined for great things and that his eccentricities are all attributable to this fact. She is tearfully overjoyed to see him. Raskolnikov shocks her by asking if she will always love him no matter what. He tells her that he will always love her but that he must leave her. She tearfully tries to make him stay with her, but he leaves and returns to his apartment, where he finds Dunya waiting for him. He confesses to her that he contemplated suicide but could not go through with it. He tells her that he will confess, and she urges him to do so, arguing that it will help atone for his crime. But Raskolnikov becomes indignant. He argues that he only killed a "louse," and that if he had succeeded in profiting from his crime and doing some good by it, he would have nothing of which to be ashamed. Dunya is shocked at his response. Looking into her distraught face, he realises how much pain he has brought to his family. The two go out, stopping to take one last look at each other as they walk in opposite directions.

Summary: Chapter VIII

Raskolnikov goes to Sonya's lodging. The narrator tells us that Sonya and Dunya had become good friends during their visit the previous day, when Dunya discovered that Raskolnikov was guilty of the murders. Raskolnikov tells Sonya that he has come to pick up his cross. Sonya has him say a prayer before he leaves.

Raskolnikov starts walking toward the police station, dreading the public humiliation of a confession. He takes a detour to the Haymarket, remembering Sonya's suggestion that he declare his guilt at the crossroads. Along the way, he carefully observes every detail of the city around him, aware that he is taking his last look as a free man. At the Haymarket, he kisses the ground, but his action meets with jeers from the onlookers and he loses his nerve and decides not to confess publicly. But he then notices Sonya following him at a distance and feels renewed conviction. At the police station, he has a friendly chat with Ilya Petrovich, who apologizes for harboring suspicions about him. Ilya mentions Svidrigailov's suicide in passing, and Raskolnikov is so stunned that he leaves without confessing. But when he gets outside, he sees Sonya waiting for him, and he turns back into the police station and offers his confession to the shocked Ilya.

Analysis: Chapters VI–VIII

Svidrigailov's suicide sheds light on Raskolnikov's apparent inability to kill himself. Raskolnikov's disdain for humanity makes him think that suicide is a vulgar act reserved for common people (he earlier observes a suicide attempt with disgust). But though he is convinced, at times, that such an act is beneath him, it becomes clear that he lacks the moral strength to end his insidious life. Svidrigailov, on the other hand, is a realist; seeing his dreams fractured, he ends his life in a spree of utilitarian action—giving away money and removing a source of pain (himself) from Dunya's life. Raskolnikov hangs on to his idealism, unable to understand that killing himself would have been much more utilitarian than killing Alyona Ivanovna.

The climax of the Svidrigailov subplot occurs in Chapter VI, and the suspense surrounding Svidrigailov's true intentions builds in urgency until the last sentence of the chapter. Before he kills himself, Svidrigailov manages to tie up an important loose end in the plot, resolving the question of how Sonya can possibly act as Raskolnikov's companion when she has to support her younger siblings. Svidrigailov thus plays a critical practical role in the narrative. But even in the last minutes of his life, he is of great interest in his own right—a clearly cynical and depraved but also generous and enigmatic figure.

Raskolnikov's mother's desperate faith in her son's greatness adds poignancy to his decision to confess. Her pathetic attachment manifests itself in her being proud of her son's dreadful article ("On Crime"), a pride made all the more ridiculous by her admission that she didn't understand the article. The pain that she feels when he tells her that she cannot accompany him highlights their opposing views concerning the value of family relationships: while Pulcheria Alexandrovna, like Dunya and Sonya, places great weight on supportive relationships within the family, Raskolnikov shows concern for his family only in urgent circumstances, such as when he fears that Svidrigailov is planning to pursue Dunya aggressively. His ability to dismiss his mother somewhat callously, thinking first of his own needs, reveals the depth of his isolation from society.

Although Raskolnikov wonders why he visits Sonya before going to confess, it is clear to the reader that he needs to gather strength from her in order to go through with his confession. After he first leaves the police station, having failed to confess, it is the sight of Sonya, not the suspicions of the police or his own emotional turmoil that pushes him to finally make his confession. Sonya is thus a pivotal character in the plot of the novel. Her crucial role in encouraging Raskolnikov to confess foreshadows her indispensability to Raskolnikov's eventual start toward redemption.

Raskolnikov's confession at the end of the main body of the novel constitutes the climax of *Crime and Punishment*, drawing the suspense surrounding the consequences of Raskolnikov's crime to a close. Even at the very end, Dostoevsky heightens the anticipation with the long, irrelevant conversation between Raskolnikov and Ilya Petrovich, and the outcome is temporarily cast into doubt when Raskolnikov turns and leaves the police station. The long-awaited confession does not come until nearly the last sentence of the last chapter. Subsequently, the uncertainty about Raskolnikov's fate drives the reader on to the Epilogue.

EPILOGUE

Summary: Chapter I

Raskolnikov is in prison in Siberia. He has been there for nine months, and a year and a half has passed since the murders. At his trial, Raskolnikov confessed to the crime, establishing his guilt by explaining why Lizaveta was murdered and identifying the location of the stolen goods. The examining magistrates and judges had trouble believing that Raskolnikov would not know how much money was in the stolen purse, which was hidden under the rock along with the pawned items, but the psychologists at the trial explained this ignorance as a symptom of his temporary insanity and "monomania." The testimony of his friends corroborated his deteriorated condition. Raskolnikov himself refused to offer or accept any defence of his actions, although he told the court that he sincerely repented his crime. He received a relatively light punishment, largely because Porfiry Petrovich kept silent about his knowledge of Raskolnikov's guilt, which enabled Raskolnikov to confess without being forced. He thereby saved Nikolai from wrongful punishment. Razumikhin also testified to Raskolnikov's acts of charity while at the university, and his landlady testified about his heroism during a fire. Five months after first confessing, Raskolnikov was sentenced to eight years of hard labour in Siberia. Sonya went with him, while Razumikhin, Dunya, and Pulcheria Alexandrovna stayed in St. Petersburg. Before leaving St. Petersburg, Raskolnikov realised that his mother was on the verge of death.

Two months later, Razumikhin and Dunya married. They attempted to keep the truth about Raskolnikov's crime and imprisonment from his mother, but she eventually became delirious and died, revealing her knowledge of her son's fate before her death. Sonya serves as a link between the family in St. Petersburg and Raskolnikov in prison. She also lightens

Raskolnikov's burden in the prison by winning favour with the authorities. Eventually, Raskolnikov falls dangerously ill and spends some time in the hospital.

Summary: Chapter II

Infinite happiness lit up in her eyes... he loved her, loved her infinitely, and... at last the moment had come...

The narrator tells us that Raskolnikov does not mind the conditions of prison life but that his pride has been deeply wounded. He still believes that there was nothing wrong with his character and that what he did was not a sin but simply "an error." He considers his choice of confession over suicide the result of weakness rather than "a presentiment of future resurrection and a new life." The other prisoners don't like him much, though they adore Sonya. While Raskolnikov is ill, he has a dream that a virus is sweeping the country. The virus causes its victims to suffer a madness that causes each to think him- or herself the sole possessor of truth. People cannot get along and so tear each other apart.

Throughout Raskolnikov's imprisonment, Sonya comes to visit, sitting outside where Raskolnikov can see her from his window. One day, she manages to meet him outside. They sit next to each other for a moment, holding hands. Previously, when they had such opportunities and held hands, Raskolnikov felt a sense of revulsion. But this time is different. He collapses in tears and embraces her. They both realise that he truly loves her. They resolve to wait out the remaining seven years of his prison term. That evening, Raskolnikov thinks about Sonya and experiences the ecstasy of love. From underneath his pillow he takes a copy of the New Testament that Sonya had given him. He feels at one with her. The narrator closes the novel by stating that this man's renewal is the matter of another story.

Analysis: Chapters I–II

Some critics have argued that the Epilogue is an unnecessary and heavy-handed end to a novel that stands quite well without it. They criticize the dream of the virus spreading through Europe, the blossoming of Raskolnikov's love for Sonya, and the death of Raskolnikov's mother as blunt attempts to tie up the story and simplistic treatments of issues that the body of the novel deals with in much more complex and open-ended ways.

This analysis notwithstanding, the Epilogue serves to develop several of the important themes of the novel, particularly those of alienation and religious redemption. At the end of Part VI, we are left in doubt as to the ultimate consequences of Raskolnikov's confession. The suspense that this doubt creates drives the reader into the Epilogue in search of answers. The descriptions of Raskolnikov's life in prison confirm that Raskolnikov, despite having confessed, is not yet truly repentant of his crime. Convinced that his crime was an "error," not a sin, he remains isolated from his fellow inmates, even as Sonya befriends them.

The recounting of the trial, a locus of objective analytical attitudes about Raskolnikov, demonstrates the disparity between Raskolnikov's perception of himself and others' perceptions of him. His friends testified to the degeneration of his mind, and the court officials assumed that he must be mentally deranged since he didn't even make use of the money and goods that he stole from Alyona.

The testimonies of Razumikhin and the landlady about Raskolnikov's acts of goodness emphasize further how Raskolnikov's mental health was in serious decline by the time that he committed the murders. The narrator describes Raskolnikov's claims of repentance as exaggerated and coarse; Raskolnikov continues to cling to a belief in the morality, even nobility, of the murder of Alyona Ivanovna. Unwilling to let go of this belief, he is again forced to confront his mediocrity in the realm of the subconscious. His dream about the virus is aimed at stripping him of feelings of superiority, as the insanity and belief in the self as the sole possessor of truth infects everyone, thus dragging Raskolnikov back into the quagmire of banal humanity.

The scene in which Raskolnikov finally realises that he loves Sonya, collapsing at her feet and weeping, is the first time that he is portrayed as being truly happy. Though the change in his character seems abrupt, it is the culmination of months of suffering and thought. Sonya's willingness to care for Raskolnikov, despite his frequent rudeness and apparent lack of love for her, demonstrates her enormously generous and self-sacrificing nature. Even as Raskolnikov keeps trying to reject human relationships, she serves as a link between him and Razumikhin and Dunya in St. Petersburg, and works to ease Raskolnikov's burden in the prison camp.

The theme of religious redemption is closely paired with that of reintegration into society. The cross that Sonya gives Raskolnikov in Part V, Chapter IV and the Bible that he begins to read in the Epilogue are both symbols of his awakening religious faith. Interestingly, faith is represented not as necessarily good in and of itself but rather as a way for Raskolnikov to reconnect with the people around him. Faith in God becomes a channel for him to bond with Sonya, just as the story of Lazarus resonates for both of them even when Raskolnikov explicitly rejects religious beliefs. Raskolnikov's reach for the New Testament as he revels in his newfound love suggests that this love will effect his Lazarus-like resurrection.

Chapter 11

Quotes to be Quoted

Quotation

What was taking place in him was totally unfamiliar, new, sudden, never before experienced. Not that he understood it, but he sensed clearly, with all the power of sensation, that it was no longer possible for him to address these people in the police station, not only with heartfelt effusions, as he had just done, but in any way at all, and had they been his own brothers and sisters, and not police lieutenants, there would still have been no point in this addressing them, in whatever circumstances of life.

Explanation

This quote, from Part II, Chapter I, illustrates Raskolnikov's sudden realization that by murdering Alyona and Lizaveta, he has completely isolated himself from society. His separation, which began before the murders, is now complete, as he has truly crossed over the bounds that formerly kept him tied to the rest of humanity. Indeed, one can argue that only because of his increasing alienation and lack of empathy for other people is Raskolnikov able to actually commit the murders. Additionally, the act of having physically accomplished the crime makes it necessary for Raskolnikov to cement his understanding of himself as a "superman" so that he can evade the bothersome, banal consequences of his actions.

Much of the novel is concerned with Raskolnikov's gradual breakdown and deconstruction of this identity in the face of his alienation from others. Only when he confesses his guilt to Sonya, someone whom he sees as a fellow transgressor of morality, does he start on the path of rejoining society.

Quotation

I've known Rodion for a year and a half: sullen, gloomy, arrogant, proud; recently (and maybe much earlier) insecure and hypochondriac. Magnanimous and kind. Doesn't like voicing his feelings, and would rather do something cruel than speak his heart out in words. At times, however, he's not hypochondriac at all, but just inhumanly cold and callous, as if there really were two opposite characters in him, changing places with each other. At times he's terribly taciturn! He's always in a hurry, always too busy, yet he lies there doing nothing. Not given to mockery, and not because he lacks sharpness but as if he had no time for such trifles. Never hears people out to the end. Is never interested in what interests everyone else at a given moment. Sets a terribly high value on himself and, it seems, not without a certain justification.

Explanation

Razumikhin offers this description of Raskolnikov in Part III, Chapter II, to Sonya and Pulcheria Alexandrovna. His comments emphasize Raskolnikov's key character traits of self-centredness, intelligence, and simultaneous cruelty and kindness. However, the informal, ungrammatical, and free-flowing tone of Razumikhin's remarks contributes to the seeming inconsistency of his words ("magnanimous and kind... inhumanly cold and callous"). The specific mention of "two opposite characters in him" seems to point to the unrelenting tension that Raskolnikov experiences as a result of his conflicting desire to confess and to evade capture. As a whole, this impressionistic depiction captures Raskolnikov's essential schismatic nature: he has detached himself from humanity and thus only engages in social behaviour when it fits his needs.

Additionally, this passage sets up Razumikhin as Raskolnikov's foil, emphasizing the contrast between Razumikhin's friendliness and good nature and Raskolnikov's sullenness and antisocial nature. This difference constitutes strong counterevidence to the argument that Raskolnikov is compelled to commit the murders because of difficult circumstances in life. Razumikhin, like his friend, is a desperately poor ex-student, but he never even considers, much less commits, such a crime. To the contrary, he seems genuinely happy and takes a great deal of pleasure in life.

Quotation

> *The old woman was a mistake perhaps, but she's not the point! The old woman was merely a sickness... I was in a hurry to step over... it wasn't a human being I killed, it was a principle! So I killed the principle, but I didn't step over, I stayed on this side... All I managed to do was kill. And I didn't even manage that, as it turns out...*

Explanation

This ranting comes from Part III, Chapter VI, when Raskolnikov is lying in bed thinking to himself. The language, with its abrupt phrases and frequent use of ellipses, reflects Raskolnikov's fractured state of mind. It also shows that Raskolnikov is still trapped in a Napoleonic mindset—he believes that the only thing that matters is success in one's endeavors. Raskolnikov feels anxious not because he is a murderer but because he is an unsuccessful murderer, unable to use the crime to his advantage and dismiss the guilt from his mind. His need to assure himself of the intellectualized motivations for Alyona Ivanovna's murder ("it wasn't a human being I killed, it was a principle!") and his frantic, repetitive justification of his crime ("I stayed on this side") reveal his insecurity about the whole matter and accentuate how unlike his "superman" ideal he is. This quote also foreshadows Raskolnikov's stubborn protest to Dunya in Part

VI, Chapter VII, that the murder itself was not wrong, only his failure to profit from it.

Quotation

> *What is it, to run away! A mere formality; that's not the main thing; no, he won't run away on me by a law of nature, even if he has somewhere to run to. Have you ever seen a moth near a candle? Well, so he'll keep circling around me, circling around me, as around a candle; freedom will no longer be dear to him, he'll fall to thinking, get entangled, he'll tangle himself all up as in a net, he'll worry himself to death! ... he'll keep on making circles around me, narrowing the radius more and more, and—whop! He'll fly right into my mouth, and I'll swallow him, sir, and that will be most agreeable, heh, heh, heh!*

Explanation

Porfiry Petrovich speaks these words in Part IV, Chapter V, when Raskolnikov goes to Porfiry's office with the ostensible purpose of reclaiming his pawned possessions. This quotation gives the reader a sense of Porfiry's style of speech, energetic to the point of being frantic. It also demonstrates his method of focusing on the psychological aspects of the case, a method that seems to have been Dostoevsky's as well. Porfiry's confidence that Raskolnikov "won't run away on me by a law of nature"—that because he is human, Raskolnikov ultimately will not be able to evade his guilt—provides a sense of inevitability that Raskolnikov will either confess or go mad. Additionally, in Dostoevsky's writing, every character serves a specific function in the plot; we know that Porfiry's certainty of Raskolnikov's guilt will not rest idle for long. This subtle tension contributes to the novel's suspense throughout.

Finally, Porfiry functions as a mirror for Raskolnikov. His diatribe here seems tinged with the same obsessive, almost mad, tone as Raskolnikov's monologues. He is the only character whose intelligence is a match for Raskolnikov's. As such, the magistrate seems at times less like a real person and more like an imaginary conscience, pointing out the moves of Raskolnikov's mind to Raskolnikov and constantly reminding him that he will be found out eventually.

Quotation

How it happened he himself did not know, but suddenly it was as if something lifted him and flung him down at her feet. He wept and embraced her knees. For the first moment she was terribly frightened, and her whole face went numb. She jumped up and looked at him, trembling. But all at once, in that same moment, she understood everything. Infinite happiness lit up in her eyes; she understood, and for her there was no longer any doubt that he loved her, loved her infinitely, and that at last the moment had come....

Explanation

This quotation comes from the Epilogue, at the climactic moment in which Sonya finally realises that Raskolnikov truly loves her. The significance is both personal and public, since by showing that he loves a particular person, Raskolnikov demonstrates that he is willing to take his place as a member of society once again. The tears that Raskolnikov sheds represent his remorse over his sins and, perhaps, his joy in realizing that Sonya, the lone individual with whom he has enjoyed a meaningful relationship, loves him. It is only when he realises that he truly cares for another person that Raskolnikov is finally able to break his alienation from humanity and begin to sincerely repent for his crimes. This newfound love injects his life with fresh meaning and, one can argue, releases him from the bond of his destructive nihilism.

Chapter 12

Study Questions and Essay Topics

Q1. Why does Raskolnikov kill the pawnbroker?

Raskolnikov gives a number of different reasons for murdering Alyona, many of which involve pride. The clearest, most powerful reason seems to be a desire to prove his superiority to the rest of humanity. But he also claims, at times, that he committed the crime for utilitarian reasons—that the death of such a despicable "louse" would increase society's overall happiness—or that he did it solely out of a need for money. The narrator suggests in Part I that Raskolnikov's physical hunger, the squalid environment in which he lives, and his poor health may be responsible for weakening any impulses that might have prevented him from committing the murder.

Raskolnikov's deeper motivations for the murder are abstract, intellectual, and oddly rational. The discussion of Raskolnikov's article "On Crime" introduces the philosophical justifications for such a murder. In the article, Raskolnikov posits a class of "superm[e]n," who are superior, he argues, to the vast majority of humanity and thus have the right to violate moral codes. These ideas are strongly connected to nihilism, a philosophy rampant in late-nineteenth-century Russia that scorned traditional familial and societal bonds as well as emotional motivations. Central to nihilism was utilitarianism, the concept that moral decisions should be based on the rule of the greatest happiness for the largest number of people.

Although the inner turmoil that Raskolnikov experiences from the moment that he commits the crime is a far cry from the superiority and righteousness with which the abstract "superman" is supposed to commit his crimes, Raskolnikov's justifications for the pawnbroker's murder are strongly utilitarian and nihilist.

Q2. Discuss the development of the poverty motif over the course of the novel.

Almost everyone in the novel is struggling for money and the pressing need of it serves as a constant reminder of unhappiness. Most striking are the poverty of Raskolnikov and that of Marmeladov and his family. Raskolnikov's poverty becomes part of his motivation for killing the pawnbroker, since he perceives of her death as a chance to get enough money to resume his education and make progress toward a better life. His poverty also, at least in his own mind, becomes a motivation for Dunya to marry Luzhin, though, of course, Dunya is motivated by her own poverty as well. The Marmeladovs' situation is obviously more severe. Marmeladov's drunkenness, Katerina Ivanovna's illness, and Sonya's turning to prostitution all vividly demonstrate the vicious cycle in which the economically and socially downtrodden are caught. Over the course of the novel, the causes and consequences of this kind of poverty are made increasingly clear, as various characters make sacrifices and important decisions based on their desperate need for money.

At the end of the novel, Svidrigailov's generosity changes the tone. Suddenly, and almost miraculously, everyone has enough money to do what he or she needs to do. One can interpret this sudden change either as an unrealistic deus ex machina—an obvious contrivance on the part of the author to salvage a seemingly hopeless situation for his or her characters—or as hopeful evidence of the power of faith, or at least good luck, to make the most important things in life possible.

Q3. Discuss Dostoevsky's use of coincidence as a plot device in the novel. Does it affect the plausibility of the narrative? How does it affect the pacing?

Crime and Punishment abounds with coincidences. Two examples are Raskolnikov's overhearing of a discussion about killing the pawnbroker, which solidifies his resolve to commit the murder, and his discovery of the injured Marmeladov in the street. The first example is crucial to Raskolnikov's psychology. Although he is extremely reluctant to kill Alyona before he overhears the conversation, one can argue that he truly desires to kill her and is simply waiting for a sign that he is fated to do so. Support for this claim can be found in the fact that when he overhears that Alyona will be alone at home the next evening, he senses that circumstances support his decision to commit the murder. Raskolnikov's pride is tied up with what he interprets as coincidences and, even before the murder, he is somewhat paranoid and ready to read deep meanings into ostensibly trivial incidents.

The coincidence of Raskolnikov coming across the just-injured Marmeladov, on the other hand, makes no statement on his character. Rather, it serves primarily to advance the plot and give the narrative an almost frantic feeling. In fact, seemingly at every turn, Raskolnikov runs into some unexpected person or thing that drives the plot onward. Nearly every event or encounter contributes to the forward momentum of the plot, and the virtual lack of actionless time periods in the novel gives it a rushed, delirious pacing that serves to reflect Raskolnikov's own state of mind.

Q4. Discuss the subject of "Crime and Punishment".

by Emile Melchior, Vicomte de Vogüé

The subject is very simple. A man conceives the idea of committing a crime; he matures it, commits the deed, defends himself for some time from being arrested, and finally gives himself up to the expiation of it. For once, this Russian artist has adopted the European idea of unity of action; the drama, purely psychological, is made up of the combat between the man and his own project. The accessory characters and facts are of no consequence, except in regard to this influence upon the criminal's plans. The first part, in which are described the birth and growth of the criminal idea, is written with consummate skill and a truth and subtlety of analysis beyond all praise. The student Raskolnikov, a nihilist in the true sense of the word, intelligent, unprincipled, unscrupulous, reduced to extreme poverty, dreams of a happier condition. On returning home from going to pawn a jewel at an old pawnbroker's shop, this vague thought crosses his brain without his attaching much importance to it:

"An intelligent man who had that old woman's money could accomplish anything he liked; it is only necessary to get rid of the useless, hateful old hag."

This was but one of those fleeting thoughts which cross the brain like a nightmare, and which only assume a distinct from through the assent of the will. This idea becomes fixed in the man's brain, growing and increasing on every page, until he is perfectly possessed by it. Every hard experience of

his outward life appears to him to bear some relation to his project; and by a mysterious power of reasoning, to work into his plan and urge him on to the crime.

The influence exercised upon this man is brought out into such distinct relief that it seems to us itself like a living actor in the drama, guiding the criminal's hand to the murderous weapon. The horrible deed is accomplished; and the unfortunate man wrestles with the recollection of it as he did with the original design. The relations of the world to the murderer are all changed, through the irreparable fact of his having suppressed a human life. Everything takes on a new physiognomy, and a new meaning to him, excluding from him the possibility of feeling and reasoning like other people, or of finding his own place in life. His whole soul is metamorphosed and in constant discord with the life around him. This is not remorse in the true sense of the word.

Dostoevsky exerts himself to distinguish and explain the difference. His hero will feel no remorse until the day of expiation; but it is a complex and perverse feeling which possesses him; the vexation at having derived no satisfaction from an act so successfully carried out; the revolting against the unexpected moral consequences of that act; the shame of finding himself so weak and helpless; for the foundation of Raskolnikov's character is pride.

Only one single interest in life is left to him: to deceive and elude the police. He seeks their company, their friendship, by an attraction analogous to that which draws us to the extreme edge of a dizzy precipice; the murderer keeps up interminable interviews with his friends at the police office, and even leads on the conversation to that point, when a single word would betray him; every moment we fear he will utter the word; but he escapes and continues the terrible game as if it were a pleasure.

The magistrate Porphyre has guessed the student's secret; he plays with him like a tiger with its prey, sure of his game. Then Raskolnikov knows he is discovered; and through several chapters a long fantastic dialogue is kept up between the two adversaries; a double dialogue, that of the lips, which smile and wilfully ignore; and that of the eyes which know and betray all. At last when the author has tortured us sufficiently in this way, he introduces the salutary influence which is to break down the culprit's pride and reconcile him to the expiation of his crime. Raskolnikov loves a poor street-walker. The author's clairvoyance divines that even the sentiment of love was destined in him to be modified like every other, to be changed into a dull despair.

Sonia is a humble creature, who has sold herself to escape starvation, and is almost unconscious of her dishonour, enduring it as a malady she cannot prevent. She wears her ignominy as a cross, with pious resignation. She is attached to the only man who has not treated her with contempt; she sees that he is tortured by some secret, and tries to draw it from him. After a long struggle the avowal is made, but not in words. In a mute interview which is tragic in the extreme, Sonia reads the terrible truth in her friend's eyes. The poor girl is stunned for a moment, but recovers herself quickly. She knows the remedy; her stricken heart cries out:

"We must suffer, and suffer together; ... we must pray and atone; ... let us go to prison!..."

Thus are we led back to Dostoevsky's favourite idea, to the Russian's fundamental conception of Christianity: the efficacy of atonement, of suffering, and its being the only solution of all difficulties.

To express the singular relations between these twobeings, that solemn pathetic bond, so foreign to every preconceived idea of love, we should make use of the word *compassion* in the sense in which Bossuet used it: the suffering with and through another being. When Raskolnikov falls at the feet of the girl who supports her parents by her shame, she, the despised of all, is terrified at his self-abasement, and begs him to rise. He then utters a phrase which expresses the combination of all the books we are studying: "It is not only before thee that I prostrate myself, but before all suffering humanity." Let us here observe that our author has never yet once succeeded in representing love in any form apart from these subtleties, or the simple natural attraction of two hearts toward each other. He portrays only extreme cases; either that mystic state of sympathy and self-sacrifice for a distressed fellow-creature, of utter devotion, apart from any selfish desire; or the mad, bestial cruelty of a perverted nature. The lovers he represents are not made of flesh and blood, but of nerves and tears. Yet this realist evokes only harrowing *thoughts,* never disagreeable *images.* I defy any one to quote a single line suggestive of anything sensual, or a single instance where the woman is represented in the light of a temptress. His love scenes are absolutely chaste, and yet he seems to be incapable of portraying any creation between an angel and a beast.—From "Dostoevsky" in "The Russian Novelists," translated by J. L. Edmands (1887).

ANOTHER ABSTRACT ABOUT SUBJECT OF "CRIME AND PUNISHMENT"

by Kazimierz Waliszewski

Raskolnikov, the student who claims the right to murder and steal by virtue of his ill-applied scientific theories, is not a figure the invention of which can be claimed by the Russian novelist. It is probable that before or after reading the works of Victor Hugo, Dostoevsky had perused those of Bulwer Lytton. Eugene Aram, the English novelist's hero, is a criminal of a very different order, and of a superior species.

When he commits his crime, he not only thinks, like Raskolnikov, of a rapid means of attaining fortune, but also, and more nobly, of a great and solemn sacrifice to science, of which he feels himself to be the high priest. Like Raskolnikov, he draws no benefit from his booty. Like him, too, he hides it, and like him, he is pursued, not by remorse, but by regret—haunted by the painful thought that men now have the advantage over him, and that he no longer stands above their curiosity and their spite—tortured by his consciousness of the total change in his relations with the world. In both cases, the subject and the story, save for the voluntary expiation at the close, appear identical in their essential lines. This features stands apart. Yet, properly speaking, it does not belong to Dostoevsky.

In Turgenev's "The Tavern" (Postoïalyï Dvor), the peasant Akime, whom his wife has driven into crime, punishes himself by going out to beg, in all gentleness and humble submission Some students, indeed, have chosen to transform both subject and character, and have looked on Raskolnikov as a political criminal, disguised after the same fashion as Dostoevsky himself may have been, in his "Memories of the House of the Dead." But this version appears to me to arise out of another error. A few days before the book appeared, a crime almost identical with that related in it, and committed under the apparent influence of Nihilist teaching, though without any mixture of the political element, took place at St. Petersburg.

These doctrines, as personified by Turgenev in Bazarov, are, in fact, general in their scope. They contain the germs of every order of criminal attempt, whether public or private; and Dostoevsky's great merit lies in the fact that he has demonstrated the likelihood that the development of this germ in one solitary intelligence may foster a social malady. In the domain of social psychology and pathology, the great novelist owes nothing to anybody; and his powers in this direction suffice to compensate for such imperfections as I shall have to indicate in his work.

The "first cause" in this book, psychologically speaking, is that individualism which the Slavophil School has chosen to erect into a principle of the national life—an unbounded selfishness, in other words, which, when crossed by circumstances, takes refuge in violent and monstrous reaction. And indeed, Raskolnikov, like Bazarov, is so full of contradictions, some of them grossly improbable, that one is almost driven to inquire whether the author has not intended to depict a condition of madness. We see this selfish being spending his last coins to bury Marmeladov, a drunkard picked up in the street, whom he had seen for the first time in his life only a few hours previously. From this point of view Eugene Aram has more psychological consistency, and a great deal more moral dignity.

Raskolnikov is nothing but a poor half-crazed creature, soft in temperament, confused in intellect, who carries about a big ideas in a head that is too small to hold it. He becomes aware of this after he has committed his crime, when he is haunted by hallucinations and wild terrors, which convince him that his pretension to rank as a man of power was nothing but a dream. Then the ruling idea which has lured him to murder and to theft gives place to another—that of confessing his crime. And even here his courage and frankness fail him; he cannot run a straight course, and, after wandering round and round the police station, he carries his confession to Sonia.

This figure of Sonia is a very ordinary Russian type, and strangely chosen for the purpose of teaching Raskolnikov the virtue of expiation. She is a woman of the town, chaste in mind though not in deed, and is redeemed by one really original feature, her absolute humility. It may be inquired whether this element of moral redemption, in so far as it differs from those which so constantly occur to the imagination of the author of "Manon Lescaut," and to that of all Dostoevsky's literary forerunners, is more truthful than the rest, and whether it must not be admitted that certain moral, like certain physical conditions, necessarily result in an organic and quite incurable deformation of character. Sonia is like an angel who rolls in the gutter every night and whitens her wings each morning by perusing the Holy Gospels. We may just as well fancy that a coal-heaver could straighten the back bowed by the weight of countless sacks of charcoal by practising Swedish gymnastic!

The author's power of evocation, and his gift for analysing feeling, and the impressions which produce it, are very great, and the effects of terror and compassion he obtains cannot be denied. Yet, whether from the artistic or from the scientific point of view (since some of his admirers insist on this last), his method is open to numerous objections. It consists in reproducing, or very nearly, the conditions of ordinary life whereby we gain acquaintance with a particular character.

Therefore, without taking the trouble of telling us who Raskolnikov is, and in what his qualities consist, the story relates a thousand little incidents out of which the personal individuality of the hero is gradually evolved. And as these incidents do not necessarily present themselves, in real life, in any logical sequence, beginning with the most instructive of the series, the novelist does not attempt to follow any such course. As early as on the second page of the book, we learn that Raskolnikov is making up his mind to murder an old woman who lends out money, and it is only at the close of the volume that we become aware of the additional fact that he has published a review article, in which he has endeavoured to set forth a theory justifying this hideous design.

From "A History of Russian Literature" (1900).

CLASSICS OF RUSSIAN LITERATURE

Russian literature famously probes the depths of the human soul. These 36 half-hour lectures delve into this extraordinary body of work under the guidance of Professor Irwin Weil of Northwestern University, an award-winning teacher at Northwestern University and a legend among educators in the United States and Russia.

Professor Weil introduces you to such masterpieces as Tolstoy's *War and Peace*, Dostoevsky's *Crime and Punishment*, Pushkin's *Eugene Onegin*, Gogol's *Dead Souls*, Chekhov's *The Seagull*, Pasternak's *Doctor Zhivago*, and many other great novels, stories, plays, and poems by Russian authors.

You will study more than 40 works by a dozen writers, from Aleksandr Pushkin in the 19th century to Aleksandr Solzhenitsyn in the 20th. You will also investigate the origin of Russian literature itself, which traces to powerful epic poetry and beautiful renderings of the Bible into Slavic during the Middle Ages.

All of these works are treated in translation, but Professor Weil does something very unusual for a literature-in-translation course. For almost every passage that he quotes in English, he reads an extract in the original Russian, with a fluent accent and an actor's sense of drama.

You may not understand Russian, but there is no mistaking the expressive intonation, rhythm, and feeling with which Professor Weil performs these passages. At one point, reciting verses from Russia's most famous poet, he advises: "Listen to it once as a piece of music, and you will sense the linguistic genius of Pushkin."

Classics of Russian Literature explores Russian masterpieces at all levels—characters, plots, scenes, and sometimes even single sentences, including:

- Tolstoy's *Anna Karenina*, which has one of the most famous first sentences in all of literature, setting the stage for a novel that probes the tragic dimension of a subject—adultery—that had traditionally been treated as satire.

- Gogol's *Dead Souls*, with a concluding passage beloved to all Russians, in which the hero flees the scene of his fiendishly clever swindle in a *troika*—a fast carriage drawn by three horses—to the author's invocation, "Oh Rus' [Russia], whither art thou hurtling?"
- Dostoevsky's *The Brothers Karamazov*, whose long chapter "The Grand Inquisitor" is a gripping, haunting, mystifying parable that is often studied on its own, but that is all the more powerful in this great novel, which addresses faith, doubt, redemption, and other timeless themes.

The Golden Age and After

The central core of the course covers the great golden age of Russian literature, a period in the 19th century when Russia's writers equaled or surpassed the achievements of the much older literary cultures of Western Europe. The age commenced with Pushkin, developed with the fantastic and grotesque tales of Gogol', and grew to full flower with Dostoevsky and Tolstoy—who at the time were considered in Europe to be lesser writers than their talented contemporary Turgenev. As the 20th century approached, Chekhov's exquisitely understated plays and stories symbolized the sunset of the golden age.

Gorky straddled the next transformation, linking the turmoil preceding the Russian Revolution with the political oppression that affected all artists in the newly established Soviet Union from the 1920s on. You examine the brilliant revolutionary poet Maiakovsky; the novelist Sholokhov, who portrayed the revolution as a tragedy for the Cossack people; the satirist Zoshchenko, who used Soviet society as food for parody; and Pasternak, who produced beautiful poems and a single extraordinary novel. Your survey ends with Solzhenitsyn, who became the most influential literary voice speaking out against the tyranny of the Soviet system.

Inside, Outside, and Behind the Scenes

Professor Weil uses intriguing details to bring these authors and their works to life. For example, readers of English translations are probably unaware of the symbolic names that Russian writers routinely give their characters, names that are especially evocative in Russian:

- Roskol'nikov, the protagonist of *Crime and Punishment,* is named after the term for "schism," signifying a person who is separating himself from society. Dostoevsky gives other characters names that mean "mud puddle" and "intelligence," again, representing the person's inner nature.
- Iurii Zhivago, the hero of *Doctor Zhivago,* has a family name that is an older Russian form of the word "alive." Pasternak uses a grammatical case that emphasizes the animate nature of the noun, signifying life as it should be experienced.

In addition to such internal details that enrich your understanding of the text, Professor Weil also points you to outside resources, from films and operas to recommended attractions that you may wish to see if you travel to Russia:

- In order to get a sense of the powerful rhythms of Pushkin's masterpiece *Eugene Onegin,* readers who don't know Russian can turn to Tchaikovsky's famous operatic adaptation, which magnificently catches the meter and texture of the poem.
- A trip to Moscow should include a visit to Tolstoy's house, now preserved as a museum. There you will get a vivid sense of the contradictions in this man's life—in the marked contrast between the comfortable Victorian furnishings preferred by his wife and family and the Spartan austerity in which he closeted himself to write, a style that came increasingly to define his life.

Professor Weil also recounts behind-the-scenes stories, many of which relate to his own experiences in Russia. These anecdotes add a new dimension to your appreciation of the works covered in this course:

- *One Day in the Life of Ivan Denisovich,* Solzhenitsyn's moving novella about life in a Soviet forced labour camp, might never have appeared in print had not the mercurial Soviet premier Khrushchev found the story spellbinding. After reading the manuscript, Khrushchev admitted that it was one of the few literary works that he had managed to finish without sticking himself with pins to stay awake. The resulting publication stunned the Soviet reading public and the world.
- "The History of an Illness," a short story by Zoshchenko, gently lampoons the Soviet health care system, with which Professor Weil has personal experience from his visits to the country. He describes some of the maddening features of Soviet medicine, including a propensity to treat every illness with vodka.

RUSSIAN LANGUAGE AND LITERATURE

Russian Language

Russian is a Slav language belonging to the Indo-European family. The dispersion of the Slav tribes in prehistoric times resulted in the formation of various Slav dialects, of which Shafarik counted twelve, although other writers recognize only six or seven. The Slav dialects are divided into the South-Eastern dialects and the Western dialects. To the former, which culminate in the Bulgarian, belongs the Russian, or rather the three Russian dialects of Great Russia, Little Russia, and White Russia. Russian has many affinities with the Bulgarian and Servian languages, because Russia received her primitive literature from the Bulgarians and Servians.

The absence of documents, however, makes it impossible to define with precision the character of the primitive language of Russia, or rather the relations between that language and the Russian of literature. According to Sreznevski and Lavroff, the similarity between the two languages was almost complete, and consisted in turns of expression rather than in grammatical forms. Before the thirteenth century, the literary, ecclesiastical, and administrative language was one. But in the fourteenth century the ecclesiastical language began to differ from the literary language and this difference grew considerably in the fifteenth and sixteenth centuries.

The Palæoslavic or ecclesiastical language, however, varied little in either case from the language of the people. In time Russian underwent local changes of form that gave rise to the dialects of Kieff, Novgorod, Vladimir, and Moscow. The Vareghi, the Greeks, the Tatars, the Lithuanians, and the Poles left traces of their political domination on the language of Russia, and in the time of Peter the Great many words were added from German, French, and English. The question of the primitive language of Russia is connected with the ethnological question, and in the nineteenth century gave rise to lengthy and spirited polemics which, however, led to no definite results. A leading work for the study of this controversy is Buslaeff's "Historical Grammar of the Russian Language" (1858). Political and nationalist questions also enter into the philological researches concerning the primitive language of Russia. The Ruthenians, or Little Russians, claim that their language was the original Russian, and therefore that primitive Russian literature should rather be called Ruthenian. On the other hand Sobolevski and the nationalists of Great Russia declare that the present Ruthenian is not the primitive language of Kieff. This philological controversy between the nationalists of Little Russia and those of Great Russia has not yet terminated.

Ancient Popular Literature

Q5. Russian literature depicts its own culture. Discuss.

From its earliest history Russia has possessed a literature that was handed down by tradition from generation to generation. It was not before the seventeenth century that this literature took a written form. The collection of Russian proverbs was begun: in the eighteenth century Daniloff published the first collection of Russian *byline:* at the end of the same century and at the beginning of the nineteenth, Tchulkoff, Popoff, and Macaroff published the first collections of popular songs. Upon this literature, which conveys so much information on the religious, civil, and social life of primitive Russia, great light was thrown by the studies of Kalaidovitch, Snegireff, Sakharoff, Kirieevski, Bielinski, Athanasieff, Kostomoroff, Maikoff, Buslaeff, Bezsonoff, and Vselovski. The popular Russian songs are divided into several classes. There are the mystic or ritual songs (*obriadnyia piesni*), which were sung in the sacred games, and on other solemn occasions; they contain many memories of the ancient pagan feasts, celebrating the glories of Dazh-Bog (the sun-god), of Koliada (traced by Russian writers to the Latin *Calendœ*), and of Ovsen. Others, illustrating the promiscuity of pagan tradition, celebrate the birth of Jesus Christ (*sviatotchnyja piesni*); others relate to the spring feasts (*vesnianki*), or accompany the dance (*khorovodnyja*).

To this same class belong the nuptial songs (*svadebnyja*), the *kupal'skija* (literally, songs of the baths), the *rusal'nyja,* in honour of the *Rusalke,* a term that probably served to designate the souls of the departed. The *byline* are the most beautiful treasures of this popular literature, of which they form the heroic cycle. The term *byline* is derived from the verb *byl* (it was), and etymologically signifies the recital of that which happened in times gone by. They tell of the deeds of the legendary heroes of primitive Russia. History, legend, and mythology together furnish the matter of these epic songs. In them the Russian heroes are called *bogatyr*, a name that some believe to be derived from *Bog* (God), as if they were demigods; others believe that the term is derived from Tatar or Mongolian; and yet others from the Sanskrit (*bhaga,* force, happiness).

The heroes who are immortalized in the *byline* belong to the epoch of Vladimir the Great, or to more ancient times, and partake of a mythological character. These heroes, who act together with those of the time of Vladimir the Great, but nevertheless are endowed with a mythological character, are Sviatogor, Mikula Selianinovitch, Volga Sviatoslavitch, Sukhman Odikhmantévitch, and Don Ivanovitch; the historians of Russian literature designate them by the epithet of *starshie* ("ancient heroes"). The "young heroes" (*mladshie*) belong historically to the epoch of Vladimir; their names are Elia Muromec, Dobrynja Nikititch, Alesha Popovitch, Solovei Budimirovitch, etc. Kieff is so to speak, their geographical centre, and Vladimir their star. In the Russian chronicles they are mentioned between the eleventh and thirteenth centuries. Elia of Murom lived at the end of the twelfth century, and his remains rest in the grotto of the sanctuary of Petcherskaia at Kieff. They combat the monsters that assail Russia from within or from without, that is, paganism and thieves among the first, and the Petchenegi, the Polovcy, and the Chozari among the second. The historical, philological, and poetical importance of these ancient monuments of literature is very great. Other *byline* of later date, more commonly called historical songs, refer to the Tatar invasions, to the period of Ivan the Terrible, and also to that of Peter the Great. The songs and legends of Little Russia are called *dumy* (elegies, ballads), and celebrate the struggles of the Cossacks and Little Russians against the Turks or Tatars and the Poles, and the union of Little Russia with Great Russia.

The songs that refer to domestic life are called *bytovyja piesni*. They sing the popular feasts and games, and the sad as well as happy events of domestic life, while they preserve many traces of paganism. The best collections of them are those of Tchulkoff (St. Petersburg, 1770-74); Novikoff (Moscow, 1780-81); and Sakharoff (St. Petersburg, 1838-39). To popular literature belong the fanciful novels called *skazki*, which resemble somewhat the stories of the Fates. Their protagonists are strange beings created by the ardent popular fancy, *Baba-Iaga*, serpents with six or twelve heads, stags, horses, etc. The forces of nature are personified. At times the mythological element predominates in them entirely; and again it is blended with Christianity.

The oldest novels are characterized by their simplicity and by the repose of their recital. Some of them, like the one entitled "The Judgment of Shemjaka", are satirical compositions. Others are derived from Western novels, especially the Italian. The proverbs also belong to popular literature. They are called *poslovicy*, and are very abundant, the first complete collection of them having been made by D. Kniazhevitch in 1822. They are the spontaneous product of the wisdom, caustic spirit, and rudimentary culture of the Russian people, and reflect the various historical ages of Russia. Some of them date from pagan times, others emanate from the people's knowledge of Holy Scripture, and others originate in the events that produced the greatest impressions on the popular imagination. To popular literature belong also the enigmas or riddles (*zagadki*), collected by Khudiakoff (Moscow, 1861) and by Sadovinikoff (St. Petersburg, 1876); the incantations (*zagovory*), the conjurations (*zakliatia*), and the lullabies (*platchi*), which are most useful for the study of Russian folk-lore and primitive Russian life.

First Monuments of Russian Literature

The first written literature of Russia is coincident with the conversion of Russia to Christianity. Bulgaria was the first Slav educator of Russia, and the first translations of the Scriptures and the liturgies were Bulgarian. The most ancient monument of Russian literature, and at the same time of the ecclesiastical Palæoslavic language common to the primitive Slav Christians, is the Gospel called "Ostromirovo", written at Novgorod in 1056-57 by the Deacon Gregor, by order of Ostromir, first magistrate (*posadnik*) of the city. This valuable document was published by Vostokoff in 1843. Ancient Russian literature is of an eminently religious character.

The greater portion of its monuments are sermons, homilies, letters, lives of saints, pilgrimages; even the profane works, as chronicles and voyages, have a religious tone. On the other hand, owing to the fact that the Russians received their Christianity from Byzantium, their literature was openly Byzantine in character, the early Russians either translating the Byzantine works, or being inspired by the spirit of those works, and writing as if they were Byzantines. Primitive Russian literature, however, was subject also to other influences.

The Slav influence was due to the Bulgarians and Servians, who, until the fifteenth century, gave many cultured men to Russia, e. g., the Metropolitan Cyprian and Gregor Camblak. Greek influence lasted a longer time, and flourished in the seventeenth and eighteenth centuries. Russian literature in the beginning consisted of translations from the Greek and of original works. Its development was very slow, because the prices of codices were very high. The copying of books was considered not only a useful contribution to culture, but a supernatural work. The Princess of Polotsk, St. Euphrosyne (twelfth century), copied books, a work to which monks, and even bishops, devoted themselves. Russian monks were wont to go to Constantinople, or to Mount Athos, and there to become amanuenses and enrich the first Russian libraries by their work. The first books that were translated were those of the Holy Scriptures that were most used by the people (Psalms, the Gospels, Proverbs, Wisdom of Solomon, Ecclesiastes, Wisdom of Jesus the son of Sirach).

There were also collections of extracts from the Holy Scriptures, called *Paremii.* The translation of all the books of the Holy Scriptures in a single codex was made in 1499, by order of Gennadius Gonzoff, Archbishop of Novgorod (1484-1504). Simultaneously with the Holy Scriptures, the writings of the Fathers of the Church were greatly in vogue, especially those of St. John Chrysostom. Highly esteemed also were the doctrinal explanations of St. Cyril of Jerusalem, the canons of St. Basil, the homilies of St. Theodore the Studite, the discourses of St. Athanasius against Arianism, the discourses of St. Gregory of Nazianzus, the "Klimax" of St. John Climacus, and the works of St. Isaac the Syrian, St. Ephraem the Syrian, and

St. John Damascene. Until the seventeenth century, the theological writings of St. John Damascene were the sources of Russian Orthodox theology.

The great popularity of the works of the Fathers gave rise to the formation of collections of extracts from their discourses, and to annotated copies, with explanations, for the study of their writings, called *sborniki*, of which there are several: "Zlatoust", a collection of moral sermons and homilies (112), mostly from St. John Chrysostom; "Margarit", another collection from St. John Chrysostom, included in the monologue of the Metropolitan Macarius, and published for the first time at Ostrog in 1596; "Izmaragd", a collection of sermons and homilies from St. Basil, St. John Chrysostom, St. Ephraem, St. Gregory the Great, and St. Cyril of Alexandria; "Andriatis", a collection of the homilies recited by St. John Chrysostom at Antioch; "Zlataia ciep" (golden chain), a collection of discourses on the moral virtues, taken from the Fathers of the Church and from Russian writers; the "Ptchely" (bees), a collection of the literary flowers of St. Maximus the Confessor.

The famous "Sbornik" of Sviatoslaff Yaroslaffitch, Prince of Tchernigoff, which was translated in Bulgaria from the Greek, for the Tsar Simeon, in 1073, also has texts from the Fathers and from profane writers. The Greek *synaxaria*, the *Patereka* of Sinai and Jerusalem, translated in the twelfth and thirteenth centuries, and the "Patericon" of the Petcherskaia Shrine of Kieff, which is very valuable for the study of primitive Russian hagiology, are of a sacro-historical character. The Greek *synaxaria* took in Russian the name of *Prologos*. Collections of discourses in honour of the feasts of Our Lord, of the Blessed Virgin, and of the saints received the name of "Torzhestvenniki". An historical compendium of the Old Testament, called "Palei", from *palaia diatheke*, dates from the earliest times of Russian Christianity.

The oldest codices of the "Palei" are of the fourteenth century, but their origin is much older. To sacred and profane literature belong the so-called *chronographoi*, collections and transformations of writings of Byzantine chroniclers, especially of Malala, Amartolos, Manasses, and Zonaras, as also the Slav version of the "Christian Topography" of Cosmas Indicopleustes. Partly to sacro-profane and partly to profane literature belong many novels and stories translated from Byzantine, Servian, and Bulgarian writings, in the sixteenth and seventeenth centuries.

One of the most famous novels, taken from the literature of Constantinople, is the history of Barlaam and Josaphat. At the end of the sixteenth century, the influence of Polish literature helped to spread in Russia two works that were much in vogue in the West, the "Gesta Romanorum", and the "Speculum Magnum." The apocryphal books of the Old Testament (story of Adam and Eve; story of the Tree of the Cross; story of the Just Enoch, etc.), and those of the New Testament (story of Aphroditian on the miracles in Persia; dispute of Christ with the Devil; conversation of Adam and Lazarus in Limbo, etc.) were also widely disseminated in the literature of that time.

There were also translated into Palæorussian the "Elucidarium sive dialogus de summa totius religionis christianæ", attributed to Honourius of Autun by Migne; books of magic and books of astrology ("Gromnik", "Molnianik", "Koliadnik", etc). Under the influence of this literature, religious songs were created that became very popular with the people (*Dukhovnye stikhi*). These little poems or songs treat of the most varied subjects, and it is very difficult to divide them into different classes.

They are of a moral and religious character, referring to the Creation, to St. Michael the Archangel, to the sufferings of the damned, to the birth or passion of Jesus Christ, to the Russian saints, etc. And beside these poetical productions sprang up the hagiological legends, of which the best known refer to St. Nicholas of Myra, St. Parasceve, and St. Cassian. The deep researches of Arkhangelski and Sobolevski throw a great deal of light on the Russian versions of the Fathers and of the Byzantine writings.

Literature from The Eleventh to The Thirteenth Centuries

Q5. Bring out the features of Russian literature with respect of various annotations adopted in various centuries.

Russian literature, properly so called, from the period of the advent of Christianity in Russia to the time of Peter the Great, comprises discourses, instructions, and letters that are intended to infuse Christian sentiments, and to draw the people from pagan practices; polemical works, directed at first against the Latins, and later against the first Russian heresies; lives of saints, chronicles, and historical Works, pilgrimages and voyages, and juridical monuments. There is almost a total absence of poetry. The first centres of culture were Kieff and Novgorod; in the sixteenth century, Moscow.

Among the writers who left a name for sacred eloquence in the period from the eleventh to the thirteenth centuries, mention is made of Luke Zhidiata, Archbishop of Novgorod (1035-59), whose discourse is a brief recapitulation of the truths of the Faith; St. Hilarion, Metropolitan of Kieff in 1051, whose discourses contain very valuable data for the early history of Russian Christianity; the Blessed Theodosius Petcherski, who wrote discourses for the people and the monks; Nicephorus, Metropolitan of Kieff (1104-20), whose discourses and letters, written in Greek were translated later into Russian; Cyril of Turoff (1171-82), a brilliant writer who, on account of his natural and vigourous eloquence, resembling that of St. John Chrysostom, is called the Chrysostom of Russia. His discourses, homilies, writings on monastic life, and prayers are among the most important monuments of the ancient ecclesiastical literature of Russia.

The polemics against the Latins found almost their only exponents among the Greeks who in the beginning governed the Russian dioceses. Leontius, metropolitan (992-1008), wrote against the Arians; George, metropolitan (1065-73), wrote a "Dispute with a Latin", in which the various pretended innovations of the Roman Church are attacked; Ivan II (1186-89) is the author of a letter to Clement III, in which the Latins are reproved only on account of the insertion of the *Filioque* in the Creed. The letter on the Faith of the Vareghi (or *Variazhskoi vierie*), which by some is attributed, although without strong arguments, to St. Theodosius Petcherski, is believed by some to be of Russian origin. Among the first Russian hagiologists mention should be made of Jacob, a monk of the Petcherskaia hermitage, who wrote an account of the martyrdom of Sts. Boris and Glieba, and the panegyric of St. Vladimir; of Nestor, the most famous of the ancient Russian writers, a monk of the hermitage of Kieff, who died in 1114. He is the author of the lives of Boris and Glieba of the Blessed Theodosius, and of a chronicle ("Lietopis") The original of the chronicle of Nestor has not come down to us; the most ancient copy of it is that of the monk Lawrence, made in 1377 for Demetrius Constantinovitch, Prince of Suzdal. Nestor was not the first Russian chronicler.

Other chroniclers, whose names and works have not been handed down to our times, wrote before him at Novgorod. The national and literary importance of the chronicle of Nestor is very great. The Russians rightly consider it as an epic history, warm with the love of country. It finishes with the year 1110, but was continued by other writers, under various names, as "Chronicle of Kieff", "Chronicle of Volhynia", "Chronicle of Suzdal", etc. They are of an eminently religious character, and abound in texts from the Scriptures and in ascetic considerations. Another important work in which the Russian national sentiment predominates is the journey of the *higumeno* Daniel (thirteenth century) to the Holy Places: before the Holy Sepulchre he prays "for all the land of Russia". Anthony, Archbishop of Novgorod, visited Constantinople four years after the taking of that city by the Latins (1204), and left a short but very important description of its churches and monasteries.

To profane literature belong the "Testament" Vladimir Monomachus, written in 1099, in which its author gives a recital of his enterprises; and the celebrated account of the battle of Igor ("Slovo" or "Polku Igorevie"), which was found in 1795 in the library of Count Musin Pushkin. It is the only poetical work of the Russia of the princes, and relates the military expedition of Igor Sviatoslavitch, Prince of Novgorod-Sieverski, against the Polovcy (1185).

It is characterized by the grandeur of its poetical sentiment, the beauty of its descriptions, and love of country. In the twelfth century was written the discourse of Daniel Zatotchnik (*Captivus*), who, imprisoned in the Government of Olonetz, writes to a prince to ask for his liberty, making a great display of his learning. Among the juridical monuments of that age we may cite the "Russkaia Pravda" (Russian code) of Prince Yaroslaff I, and the Greek *Nomocanon*, translated in the earliest times of Russian Christianity, and qualified with the epithet of *Kormtchaia kniga*, corresponding to the Greek *pedalion*. To the *nomocanon* were added the "Ecclesiastical Regulations" ("Cerkovnye ustavy") of Vladimir and Yaroslaff, which however are not of those princes, at least in the form in which they have been transmitted to us in codices of the thirteenth century.

The monasteries were centres of the literary culture of Russia in the eleventh and twelfth centuries; and the Greco-Russian clergy laboured for the diffusion of it. From the Greek clergy came the polemical works, and the hatred of the Latins that became fixed in the hearts of the Russian people. The first Greek polemics who lived in Russia spread the most absurd calumnies against the Latins, and anathematized as heretical the most simple liturgical customs: the Metropolitan George enumerated twenty-seven points of divergence between the Greeks and Latins. The thirteenth century is very poor from the standpoint of literature.

The Tatar invasions stopped the progress of culture, and prevented intellectual work. Among the literary monuments of that century are cited a letter of Simon, Bishop of Vladimir (1215-26), to Polycarp, a monk of the Petcherskaia hermitage; the life of Abraham of Smolensk, a most important historical document; the sermons of Serapion, Bishop of Vladimir (1274-75), and a synodal and canonical decision of Cyril II,

Metropolitan of Kieff (1243-80), which is inserted in the *Kormtchaia kniga.*

Literature from The Fourteenth to The Sixteenth Centuries

In the period from the fourteenth to the sixteenth centuries, literary culture, paralyzed by Tatar oppression in the region of Kieff, continued to flourish at Novgorod and Pskof, and from there was carried to other centres, viz., Vladimir, Rostoff, Murom, Yaroslaff, Tver, Ryazan, and finally Moscow, which received the name of the Third Rome. In the fourteenth century sacred sermons were written by various authors, among whom were Peter, Metropolitan of Moscow; Alexei, another metropolitan of Moscow (1293-1377) who, in a codex of the Gospel which he transcribed, corrected the ancient Slav version in many points, by the Greek original; Matvei, Bishop of Sarai; the Metropolitan Cyprian (1376-1406), a Servian by birth, who also left various letters and translated the Psalter, the Missal (*Sluzhebnik*), the *Nomocanon*, etc.; the Blessed Cyril, founder of the monastery of Bielozero, the author of several letters to the sons of Prince Demetrius Donskoi; Basil, Archbishop of Novgorod (1331-1352), who wrote a letter to Feodor, Bishop of Tver, to convince him of the existence of a terrestrial paradise.

Brief descriptions of Constantinople and its churches in the fourteenth century were left by Stephen, a monk of Novgorod, by Ignatius, a deacon of Smolensk, and by Alexandr D'jak ("judge", "magistrate"). Among the novels special mention should be made of the "Zadonshina", written by Sofronio or Sofonio of Ryazan, an epic story that relates the military acts of Prince Demetrius Donskoi, who vanquished the Tatars at Kulikovo (1380). In the fifteenth century the beginning of heresies in Russian Christianity, which originated in the decadence of monastic asceticism as well as in the gross ignorance of the clergy and laity, opened up new fields to Russian religious polemics.

Photius, Metropolitan of Moscow (1410-31) and Gregor Camblak, Metropolitan of Kieff (1416) composed letters and moral sermons; Gennadius, Archbishop of Novgorod (1485-1504), wrote against the sect of the Judaizers, which originated in that city about 1471; the *higumeno* Josef Sanin of Polotsk assailed the same sect in his tedious work "Prosvietitel" ("the illuminator"). Nil Sorski (1433-1508), founder of a hermitage on the banks of the Sora River, is the author of writings that were directed towards the reformation of the ideals and the life of Russian monasticism. Among the travellers of this period Zosimus, hiero-deacon of the hermitage of St. Sergius, and a merchant, Basil, left accounts of their pilgrimages to the Holy Land. Simeon, hiero-monk of Suzdal, accompanied Isidore, Metropolitan of Moscow, to the Council of Florence, and left an interesting recital of his voyage to Italy, and a short but important account of the council, which is one of the monuments of the Russian polemics against the Latins. Anthony Nikitin, a merchant of Tver, went to India through Persia in 1466, returned to his country in 1472, and in the account of his travels gave important information on the religious beliefs of the people of India. In historical literature, besides the valuable sketch of the Council of Florence, there should be mentioned the account of the foundation and the taking of Constantinople, which was very popular among the Russians.

The sixteenth century, as Porfiréff rightly states, was one of criticism and restoration. Its literature, always eminently religious, proposed to revive the ancient customs, and the ancient traditions, and to restore religion and the family. The most famous and most learned champion of these reforms was Maximus the Greek, born at Arta, in Albania, and educated in Italy. He entered monastic life on Mount Athos, and in 1518 repaired to Russia, where he took an active part in the religious life of the country, and in the correction of the liturgical books; he suffered a painful imprisonment in various monasteries, from 1525 to 1553, and died at the hermitage of St. Sergius in 1556.

A most learned theologian, he wrote polemical works against the Gentiles, the Jews, the Judaizers, the

Mohammedans, and the Latins, especially in opposition to the supremacy of the pope and to the *Filioque;* he combatted astrology, and wrote short works and discourses on moral subjects. Among the Russian prelates of the sixteenth century, Daniel, elected Metropolitan of Moscow in 1522, acquired fame. He was the author of sixteen discourses that prove him to have read assiduously, and to have had a profound knowledge of patristic literature. The most important monument of the literature of the sixteenth century is the "Domostroi", attributed to Sylvester, a priest who was the contemporary of Ivan the Terrible; Sylvester was, however, the compiler rather than the author of the work. It is a book of a moral character, in which are propounded the rules for living according to the precepts of the Faith and Christian piety, the duties of man as a member of the family, and the way to govern the home well and to care for domestic economy.

The "Domostroi", therefore, is a compendium of the duties of a Christian man, and at the same time a true picture of the social and domestic organization of Russia in the sixteenth century. Another great work, which had remained unpublished until now but which the Archæographical Commission of St. Petersburg is now bringing to light, is the "Tchet'y Minei" of the Metropolitan Macarius of Moscow (1542-64). From the beginnings of its literature, Russia possessed lives of saints, the number which increased from century to century.

The Metropolitan Macarius collected into a vast work the lives of all the saints of the Greco-Russian Church, adding panegyrics and discourses in their honour, and also whole books of Scripture, with commentaries, writings of the Fathers, and *synaxaria,* so that his menologies are almost a complete répertoire of the ancient literature of Russia, rather than a simple hagiological collection.

To the same century belong the hagiological legends, which are lives of the saints, or episodes in them, embellished by popular fancy, examples of which are the legends of the Tsarevitch Peter (thirteenth century), of St. Mercurius, of

Martha and Mary, of Prince Peter of Murom, and of his consort, Febronia. Prince Andrew Kurbski, a warm defender of the Orthodox Church, translated the dialectics and the *Pege gnoseos* of St. John Damascene, and wrote a brief history of the Council of Florence and a history of Ivan the Terrible, with whom he was in correspondence; these letters are preserved to our day. An important work of religious polemics was written by the monk Zinovii of Otna, who refuted the heretical and Judaistic doctrines of Kosoi. The title of the work is "Istiny pokazanie" (demonstration of the truth), and it consists of fifty-six chapters. Of the sixteenth century there are also two small works, written in refutation of Protestantism, which at that time was beginning to spread in Russia. Among the Russian pilgrims who visited the Holy Places and who wrote an account of their travels the most distinguished are Trifon Korobeinikoff and George Grekoff, who went to Jerusalem in 1583.

Literature of Little Russia and Great Russia in The Seventeenth Century

The seventeenth century witnessed the Renaissance of Little Russia, which became the instructor of Great Russia. Under Catholic and Polish influence Little Russia drew near to the West, assimilated Western science, and modelled its schools upon those of the Latins.

The "Union" of Brest in 1596 gave an efficient impulse to Orthodox culture. Confraternities were established to open schools and printing-offices for the publication and dissemination of polemical works; among them those of Lemberg, Vilna, and Kieff were famous. Scholastic theology and philosophy entered into and dominated the Russian academies and seminaries. Latin became the official language in the teaching of theology.

Peter Mogilas, Metropolitan of Kieff, transformed into a superior school of theology the school established by the Confraternity of the Church of the Apparition of the Lord. The works of St. Thomas Aquinas exercised a great influence on Orthodox theology, and in the academy of Kieff the Immaculate Conception was upheld.

The literature of the religious polemics against the Latins, to which the Union of Brest gave rise, is very rich. In 1597 was published the "Ekthesis", or Orthodox history of the Union of Brest; Kristofor Bronski, under the pseudonym of Filalete, wrote the "Apokrisis" against Peter Skarga, and later the "Perestroga" (admonishment). Meletius Smotricki, Archbishop of Polotsk (died 1633), wrote the "Threnos" and other works of religious polemic, and finally embraced Catholicism; in 1622 Zacharias Kopystenski wrote the "Palinodia", the most important work in this polemical literature. The writings of Meletius Smotricki in defence of Catholicism, which he had on other occasions so strenuously opposed, were confuted by Andrew Muzkilovski, by Job Borecki, Metropolitan of Kieff, and by Gelasius Diplic. Joannikius Galiatovski, rector of the academy of Kieff (died 1688), wrote several works against the Catholics, one of them against the *Filioque*, confuted the Hebrews in his work

"The True Messias", and also wrote several works in refutation of the Koran. Another polemic against the Latins was Lazarus Baranovitch, Archbishop of Tchernigoff (died 1694); in a work that was directed against the Jesuit Boyme, he opposed the supremacy of the pope and the Procession of the Holy Ghost from the Son.

The first Orthodox catechisms appeared in the seventeenth century, written by Laurence Zizanii and by Peter Mogilas; the latter, in the work *Lithos* (attributed to him), defends the Orthodox Church against the charge of Protestantism; he is considered to be the author of the famous Orthodox Confession of the Eastern Church, approved by the special Council of Jassy in 1643. Among the preachers whom the sacred orators of the East sought to imitate, mention may again be made of Joannikius Galiatovski, who wrote a treatise on the art of oratory, entitled "Kliutch razumienia"; Anthony Radivilovski, *higumeno* of the hermitage of Kieff; and Lazarus

Baranovitch. In 1591 there was published at Lemberg the first Slavo-Greek grammar; Lawrence Zizanii wrote a Slav grammar in 1596, and the grammar of Meletius Smotricki was published in 1619. Zizanii added a small Slav dictionary to his grammar, but the first Slavo-Russian lexicon was published by Berynda, hiero-monk of Kieff, in 1627. Western influence is revealed also in the poetry of the academy of Kieff. Besides the sacred cantata, the "Mysteries" were introduced to the schools and colleges; these "Mysteries" were sacred plays, modelled upon those of the Jesuit colleges. Among the historical works of Little Russia, mention should be made of the "Synopsis" of the history of Russia by Innocent Gizel, Archimandrite of Kieff, the "Enegesis" or history of the school of Kieff, and the"Paterikon" of the Petcherskaia hermitage by Sylvester Kossoff, Metropolitan of Kieff (died 1657). From Kieff Western culture was carried to Moscow, to which city masters and learned men of Little Russia were called to organize schools, compose works, and print books; but they did not receive a friendly welcome.

Their orthodoxy was suspected; the more so since several of the most illustrious theologians of Kieff admitted with the Latins the dogmatic truth of the Immaculate Conception, and the efficacy of the words of consecration alone to effect Transubstantiation.

The suspicion against the purity of their theological teachings became so strong that the Russians turned to the Greeks for masters. In 1685 the Greek school was established at Moscow, and in time took the name of Greco-Slav-Latin Academy. Its first masters were the Greek hieromonks Joannikius and Sophronius Likhudes, who had studied in Italy, and who taught Greek literature at Moscow from 1685 to 1694.

They wrote many polemical works against the Latins, against Protestants, and against the theologians of Little Russia who leaned towards the Latins, especially against Sylvester Medviedeff. In ecclesiastical literature the most distinguished authors were Epiphanius Slavinecki, the first of Russian bibliographers; Arsenius Sukhanoff, author of "A Voyage to the Holy Land" ("Proskynitarion"); Simon Polocki (of Polotsk), author of one of the first systematic treatises on Orthodox theology ("Vienec viery"), and also of sermons that are highly prized, of sacred poems, and of sacred plays; St. Demetrius of Rostoff (1651-1709), one of the most illustrious bishops of the Russian Church, a theologian, historian, poet, polemic, and hagiologist. He was the author of two Orthodox catechisms, of a very strong work against the Raskolniki ("Rozysk"), of a diary of his life, the "Tcheti minei" (menologies), a work upon which he spent twenty years; many sacred discourses that are appreciated for the simplicity of their style and for their depth of religious sentiment, and, finally, of several sacred plays, one of the most interesting of which is the "Birthday". Epiphanius Slavinecki and an unnamed priest of Orel were also distinguished as sacred orators.

The former rendered a great service to Patristic literature by translating into Russian a great many of the writings of the Fathers (St. Justin, St. Gregory of Nazianzus, St. Basil, and St. John Damascene). One of his scholars, Eutimius, wrote a polemical work, called "Osten", against the theories of Sylvester Medviedeff, who sided with the Latins in the question of the Epiklesis.

Against the Raskolniki, besides St. Demetrius of Rostoff, there wrote Simeon of Polotsk in 1666 ("Zhely pravlenija"); in 1682 the Patriarch of Moscow, Jacob ("Uviet dukhovnii"); likewise, the Metropolitan of Siberia, Ignatius, and George Krizhanitch. The latter, who was a student of the Greek College of St. Athanasius at Rome (1640), became famous on account of his theories of the cause of the schism between East and West, which he attributed to politics and the antagonism between Greeks and Latins, due to Panslavist ideas and political doctrines.

The Learned Sergius Bielokuroff devoted four volumes to the life and works of Krizhanitch. In the seventeenth century there began to be published the first Greco-Latin lexicons, and also the first scientific books, arithmetics and geographies. Historical literature is represented by the chronicle of the

Patriarch Nicomachus, which is brought down to 1631; by the chronicle called "Voskresenski", after the monastery where it was written, of which the relation finishes with the year 1560; and by several special chronicles, as the account of the siege of the Shrine of St. Sergius by the Poles in 1610, by Abraham Polycin, and by others of the *diak* Feodor Griboiedoff, of the deacon Timothy Kamevevitch Rvovski, of Andrew Lyzloff, a priest of Smolensk, and of Sergius Kubasoff.

Russian Literature of The Time of Peter The Great

Under Peter the Great there began a new period in Russian literature. The foundation of St. Petersburg put Russia in more direct contact with the West. Peter the Great, by violence and absolutism, dragged Russia out of her isolation, and directed her upon a new way. A new and more simple alphabet took the place of the old Slav alphabet, the new characters being adapted from the Latin.

The first book that was printed with the new characters is a treatise on geometry (1708). In arithmetical books, Arabic figures were substituted for the Slav letters that represented numerals (1703). Schools of navigation, of military science, and of medicine were established. Peter the Great determined to establish an academy of sciences at St. Petersburg, and Catherine I carried out his project in 1726. Many foreign books were translated into Russian, and the most intelligent students were sent to foreign countries to complete their studies. Russian literature lost its ecclesiastical character and assumed a lay form; and in ecclesiastical literature itself there was effected a transformation towards the modern, due to the reforms of Peter the Great.

The first period of this new literature begins with Peter the Great, and closes with Lomonosoff and Sumarokoff. In the realm of sacred literature there became famous Stephen Javorski (1658-1723), patriarchal vicar and Metropolitan of Ryazan, and Theophanus Procopovitch, Archbishop of Novgorod. (1681-1736). The former, in his "Kamen viery" (Rock of Faith), wrote a most learned refutation of

Protestantism, taking much from Bellarmine; the second, who was the author of the "Ecclesiastical Regulations" of Peter the Great, wrote a voluminous course of Orthodox theology in Latin, and acquired fame as a man of letters and orator. In profane literature the influence of the French entirely predominated. There began the period of the new Russian poetry, the rules of which were propounded by Tredianovski (1703-69), who translated into Russian the "Ars Poetica" of Horace, and the work bearing the same title by Boileau. Prince Antiochus Dmitrievitch (1708-44), a Rumanian in the service of Russia, inaugurated the era of classicism in Russian poetry with his satires, which are often servile imitations of Horace, Juvenal, and Boileau.

Michael Vasilevitch Lomonosoff (1711-65) deserves to be called the Peter the Great of Russian literature on account of his versatility, of the multiplicity of his works, and of his great literary influence: he wrote a treatise on Russian poetry (1739), on rhetoric (1748), on grammar (1755); he composed an epic poem on Peter the Great, two tragedies (Tamira and Salim, and Damofonte); he translated the Psalms into verse and wrote lyric poems, among which the ode to the Empress Elizabeth has remained famous.

Alexander Petrovitch Sumarokoff composed many tragedies, some of them with Russian subjects (Yaropolk and Dimisa, Vysheslaff, Demetrius, Mstislav); he founded the national Russian drama, wrote the comedies "Opekun" (The Tutor), and "Likhoimec" (The Concussionist), composed satires, and in 1759 established the first Russian literary periodical, the "Trudoliubivaia Ptchela" (The Working Bee). Among the prose writers, Ivan Pososhkoff (1670-1725), in his "Zavieshanie otetcheskoe" (testament of the Fatherland), shows the necessity of well-ordered reforms in Russia, and in his book on poverty and wealth ("Kniga o skudosti i bogatstvie") he develops in an original way his theories on political and social economy. Basil Nikititch Tatishsheff (1685-1750) gathered the chronicles, the *synaxaria,* and the historical documents, and subjecting them to critical analysis, wrote the

"History of Russia".

The academician Schlötzer spent forty years elucidating the origin and the historical problems of the primitive national chronicles of Russia. In 1728 the Academy of Sciences began the publication of the "S. Petersburgskija Viedomosti", under the direction of the academician Müller, who in 1755 also founded the first scientific-literary periodical, called the "Ezhemiesatchnyja sotchinenia".

Literature of Russia in The Eighteenth Century

During the reign of Catherine II French influence upon Russian literature became greater instead of decreasing. The writings of the French Encyclopedists and materialist philosophy became popular; Voltaire and Rousseau were much esteemed, and Catherine II became entirely imbued with a Voltairean spirit. She did not limit herself to favouring scientific institutions, and to creating new ones, but aspired to literary laurels. She wrote spelling-books,, stories for children, letters on education, comedies, newspaper articles, and several volumes of memoirs in French, in which, with a cynical simplicity of style, she relates some of the ugliest episodes of her unchaste life. During her reign many literary publications were established.

The empress herself did not disdain to contribute to the "Vsiakaja vsiatchina" (General Miscellany). Dionysius Ivanovitch Fonvizin (1744-92) wrote comedies which, like the "Brigadier", and the "Nedorosl" (Pupil), became popular in Russia. Gabriel Romanovitch Derzhavin (1743-1816), of Tatar origin, assimilated the classical and modern Literatures, and as a lyric poet sought to rise to the height of Horace and Pindar. His encomiastic odes are an apotheosis of the reign of Catherine II.

In his religious songs, with his "Ode to God" (1784), which the Russians regard as the most beautiful monument of their national poetry, he perhaps attains sublimity of inspiration.

His moral and philosophical odes and his Anacreontic verses reveal in him a great poetical genius. His tragedies "Pozharski", "Tiemnji" and "Euprassia" do not join dramatic quality to their elegance of form. Mikhail Matveievitch Kheraskoff, of Wallachian origin, by his poems "Rossiada" and "Vladimir", which have been forgotten, deserves the title of the Virgil or the Homer of Russia.

Ippolit Feodorovitch Bogdanovitch (1743-1803), in his poem "Dushenka", imitated La Fontaine's "Amours de Psyché et de Cupidon". Basil Ivanovitch Maikoff (1728-78) distinguished himself as a writer of comic poetry; Kniazhnin (1742-91) wrote tragedies and comedies; "Iabeda" (The Calumny), a comedy by Kapnist (1757-1828), was also among the plays that became popular. The scientific movement was greatly promoted by the Academy of Sciences of St. Petersburg, by the University of Moscow, and by the Russian Academy, which was opened in 1783. Among those who distinguished themselves in historical work or in the study of the social and political conditions of Russia were Shsherbatoff (1733-90), who wrote six volumes of a "History of Russia"; Boltin (1735-92), whose learned volumes of "Observations on the History of Russia", edited by Leclerc, were much praised by Soloveff; Radishsheff (1749-1802), whose "Journey from St. Petersburg to Moscow", describing the miseries of the peasants and the abuses of the Russian bureaucracy cost its author an exile of ten years in Siberia.

The archpriest of Moscow, Alekseieff, wrote the first ecclesiastical encyclopedia, while the Bishop Damascenus Rudneeff, who died in 1795, published his "Russian Library", which contains an account of Russian literature, from its origin to the eighteenth century. Tchulkoff and Mikhail Popoff collected the monuments of the popular literature of their country.

Literature of Russia in The Nineteenth Century

In the nineteenth century, Russian literature freed itself little by little from the yoke of foreign imitation, perfected the language, making it a most adequate means for the expression of the highest conceptions of the mind and the most delicate affections of the heart, and through a number of men of genius, won a place of honour in the history of universal literature.

The merit of this transformation, of this new direction of Russian thought, is in great measure due to Nikolai Mikhailovitch Karamzin (1766-1826), who acquired a great fame in his country through his letters on travels that he made in Europe, his novels, and the part that he took in the establishment of the periodicals "Moskovski Zhurnal" and the "Viestnik Europy" (Courier of Europe). But his greatest claim to glory is the "Istorija gosudarstva rossiiskago" (History of the Russian Empire), a masterpiece of style, exposition, and eloquence, which contributed more than anything else to the formation of Russian prose. Historical criticism may find more to say of this work, but the literary merit of it will never be eclipsed.

The work formed a literary school, to which belong Ivan Ivanovitch Dmitrieff (1760-1837), an exponent of elegance in poetry, author of poetical stories, satires, and fables; and Izmailoff, who became famous through his "Journey in Southern Russia" etc. In the realm of dramatic poetry, there became famous Ozeroff, by his tragedy "Œdipus in Athens" (1804); "Fingal" (1805); "Dmitri Donskoi" (1807), and "Polissena" (1809); the most noted satirists were Gortchakoff and Nakhimoff. But the greatest poetical glory of this period was Vassili Andreievitch Zhukovski (1783-1852), the master of romanticism in Russia, author of the Russian national hymn "Bozhe, carja Khrani", and an indefatigable translator of Homer, Schiller, Goethe, Bürger, Uhland, Rükkert, Byron, and Scott. His elegies are full of passion and sentiment; his ballads, imitations of the German, became popular; they reveal in him a vivid poetical imagination. Ivan Andreievitch Kryloff (1768-1844) owes his celebrity rather to his comedies than to his fables, which, it is true, are imitations of La Fontaine, but are written with so much simplicity, elegance, and richness of style, with such variety of rhythm and expression, that they form a veritable literary jewel, the value of which can be appreciated only by those who have a thorough knowledge of Russian. His comedies, "Modnaja lavka" (The Custom Shop) and "Urok dotchkam" (A Lesson to Girls), are of less literary merit. As a writer of comedy, Alexander Sergeievitch Griboiedoff (1790-1829) rose to the pinnacle of the art in a play that is the masterpiece of Russian theatrical composition, "Gore ot uma" (The Misfortune of Having Talent), a work which is full of pessimism on the social conditions of Russia and civilization generally; many of its verses have become proverbs.

The epoch of Nicholas I, which was one of fierce absolutism, was nevertheless one of glory in the development of Russian literature. Russian genius being oppressed, withdrew within itself, and revealed to the world the treasures of the æsthetic sentiments of the Russian soul.

Among the greatest poets of this period there stands pre-eminent Alexander Pushkin (1799-1837), whose career was brought to an end in a duel, when his genius was at its height. Melchior Vogüé rightly considers him one of the greatest poets that ever lived. He began his literary career at the age of fifteen, when he was a student in the lyceum of Tsarskoye Selo. His first lyric poems bear the date of 1814, and are a revelation of his genius. He adopted Byron and Zhukovski for his models. Among those lyric poems his invective against the calumniators of Russia ("K klevetnikam Rossii"), written in 1831, is famous. Of his epic works we may cite the famous "Rusalka, the Prisoner of the Caucasus" ("Kavkazski pliennik") in 1821; the "Fountain of Bakhtchiserai" (1822-23); the "Tzigani" (1824); "Poltava" (1828), one of Pushkin's most perfect poems, written in glorification of Peter the Great; "Eugene Oniegin" (1823-31), an original imitation of Byron's "Childe Harold", admirable on account of the freshness of its inspiration and of its exquisite versification; and finally "The Hussar" (1833).

Among his romances, three became popular at once, the "Dubrovski (1832-33), "The Daughter of the Captain" (1833-36), and "Pikovaja dama" (The Queen of Spades), a work that is admirable on account of the subtility of its psychological analysis. In the realm of dramatic poetry Pushkin gave to his country a great masterpiece, the tragedy "Boris Godunoff" (1825-31), and in that of drama, "Skupoi rycar" (The Avaricious Knight), "Mozart and Saléry", and "Rusalka". Among his works in prose, mention should be made of the "Outlines of the History of Peter the Great", and of the "History of the Sedition of Pugatcheff". Pushkin was the first great original poet of Russia, and the one who excelled in classic style. At the same time he was the author of a school that has among its members Ivan Ivanovitch Kozloff, author of two most touching poems, "Tchernec" (The Monk) and "Natalia Dolgorukaja"; Delvin (1798-1831); Jazykoff (1803-46), and Eugene Baratynski (1800-44).

Nikolai Vassilievitch Gogol (1808-52), a native of Little Russia, was another genius of the Russian literature of the nineteenth century. His comedy, "The Reviser", published in 1836, is one of the masterpieces of the Russian theatre, a true portrait of the malversations of the bureaucracy. Among his romances and novels, he acquired merited fame through "Taras Bul'ba", an historical romance of Southern Russia, "The Dispute between Ivan Ivanovitch and Ivan Nikiforovitch", "The Portrait", "The Arabesques", "Koliaska" (The Calash), "Zapiski sumasshedshago" (Memoirs of a Madman), and lastly "Mertvyja dushi" (The Dead Souls), in two parts, a masterpiece in the romantic literature of Russia, which makes its author the rival of Cervantes and Lesage.

It is a suggestive and faithful picture of Russian society: a vast theatre in which the most varied types of the Russian people are in action. Mikhail Yurievitch Lermontoff (1814-41) is also of the school of Pushkin and Byron. He was one of the most delicate lyric poets of modern Russia, whose lyric poetry, tinged with sadness, touches the deepest chords of the heart, and exhibits the soft melody of the literary language of Russia in its fullness.

The most famous of his epic poems are "The Demon", which is based upon a Georgian legend, and in which the beauties of the Caucasus are described in admirable verses

"Ismail Bey"; "Khadzhi-Abrek, the Boyard Orsha", an episode of the times of Ivan the Terrible; "Mcyr", a legend of the Caucasus. Lermontoff is the author of the very popular romance "Geroi nashego vremeni" (A Hero of our Times), which reveals him as one of the masters of Russian prose, and as having a profound knowledge of the human heart. He died at the age of twenty-seven years, and like Pushkin, in the plenitude of his intellectual activity. Alexei Vasilievitch Kolcoff (1809-42) also distinguished himself as a lyric poet of the school of Pushkin and Lermontoff. He was the poet of the peasants and of nature, and the inventor of a special kind of poems (*Dumy*), in which a question to be resolved is proposed and is answered. Other poets who also were ornaments of Russian literature, although they did not attain the height of those already mentioned, were Odoevski, Count Sollogub, Marlinski, Weltmann, Polevoi, and Kukolnik, a prolific writer of historic dramas. History, philology, and critical studies had a period of growing prosperity during the reign of Nicholas I. Pogodin, Butkoff, Ivanoff, Venelin, Grigor'eff, and Muravieff worked to defend the Russian chronicles against the charge of lack of authenticity, to throw light on the origin of the Russian nation, and to investigate the historical past of Russia and the various European nations.

In the study of the ancient Slav language, and of the primitive literature of Russia, and in the collection of ancient texts, fundamental works that are yet esteemed were written by Kalaidovitch, Vostokoff, Undolski, Kliutchareff, Maximovitch, Certeleff, Snegireff, Sakharoff, and Bodianski. This class of studies were greatly promoted by the Society of Russian History and Antiquities, established at Moscow in 1814 and still flourishing. Eugene Bolkhovitinoff, Metropolitan of Kieff, prepared two historical lexicons of the clerical and lay writers of Russia; Polevoi, Shevyreff, and Nikitenko wrote histories of Russian literature; while Prince A. Viazemski, Nadezhdin, and especially Bessarion Grigorievitch Bielinski (1810-48) were the chief literary critics.

Literary and scientific progress was assisted by the periodicals "Viestnik Evropy", "Russki Viestnik", "Syn

Otetchestva" (The Son of the Fatherland), "Sievernaja Ptchela" (The Bee of the North), "Russki Invalid", and "Otetchestvennyja zapiski" (Memoirs of the Fatherland). During the reign of Alexander II the literary genius of Russia continued to shine brightly, and to assume always a more national character, although the influence of foreign writers, especially of Dickens, George Sand, and Balzac, was felt. There appeared the school of Slavophils, the most illustrious representatives of which are the two Kireievski (Ivan and Peter), Khomiakoff, Valueff, Konstantin and Ivan Aksakoff, Kosheleff, Elagin, Tiuttcheff, Grigorieff, Strakhoff, and Danilevski. This school was dominated by a spirit of stingy patriotism; it invaded the domain of theology, preached the superiority of Orthodoxy over Catholicism, and in the person of their theological legislator, Alexei Khomiakoff, a genial poet, historian, and philosopher, it proclaimed that Orthodoxy is the expression of the religious ideal of Christianity. The religious and political paradoxes of the Slavophils found their opponents in the school of the Occidentalists (*Zapadniki*). The philosopher Tchaadaeff, in his philosophical letters published in 1836, wrote of Russian barbarity, and proclaimed Catholicism to be the only means of bringing Russia into the civilization of the nations of the West.

The most illustrious representatives of this school, which had not many followers, were Hercen (1812-70), who became one of the leaders of Nihilism; the poet Ogareff, Granovski, Soloveff, Kavelin, Kalatchoff, and Pavloff, illustrious names in the realms of Russian history and Russian philosophy.

The most famous writer of the time of Alexander II was Ivan Sergeievitch Turgenieff (1818-83), the magician of Russian prose. As a poet his title to fame rests on the poems "Parasha", "Yakoff Pasynkoff", "Rudin", "Faust", "Asja", "A Nest of Nobles". In 1862 he published one of the most famous of Russian novels, "Otcy i dieti" (Fathers and Sons). Among the other novels of Turgenieff, the most successful were "Zapiski Okhotnika" (Memoirs of a Huntsman), rich in admirable descriptions of nature; "Dym" (Smoke); "Nov" (Virgin Soil);

and among his stories: "Lear of the Steppe", "Waters of Spring", "The Brigadier", "The Dream", "The Story of Father Alexis", "The Song of Triumphant Love", "The Desperado" etc. He enriched Russian literature with several plays, among which the most beautiful is called "Zavtraku predvoditelja" (The Collation with the Marshal of the Nobility). Ivan Alexandrovitch Gontcharoff (1812-91) acquired no less fame as a novelist through his novels "Obyknovennaja istorija" (A Simple Story), "Oblomoff", which personifies the want of initiative and semi-fatalism of the Russian character, and "Obryff" (The Precipice), which was considered a decadent production. Greater fame was acquired by Feodor Mikhailovitch Dostoievski (1822-81), whose first novel, "Biednye liudi" (Poor People), published in 1846, made its author famous, at once, by the depth of its psychological analysis. After four years of a most painful imprisonment and exile to Siberia, he wrote the "Zapiski iz Mertvago Doma" (Memoirs of the House of the Dead), in which he describes the tortures of the exiles with a most effective vigour of style; the famous novel "Prestuplenie Nakazanie" (Crime and Punishment), a psychological masterpiece, "The Idiot", "Biezy" (The Possessed), and "The Brothers Karamazoff". To romantic literature also belong Dimitri Vassilievitch Grigorovitch, an imitator of George Sand, and a faithful portrayer of the sufferings of the lower classes, in his romances and novels, among which we will mention "Derevnia" (The Village), "Anthony Goremyka", "The Valley of Smiedoff", "The Fishermen", and "The Colonists".

In other novels he described the life and condition of the middle and higher classes, as in "Neudavshaajasja zhizn" (An Uneventful Life), "Suslikoff the Kapelmeister", "The School of Hospitality", etc. The naturalist school was represented by Alexei Teofilaktovitch Pisemski (1820-81). In the novel "Bojarshshina" (The Time of the Boyars), he preached free love: the censorship prohibited the circulation of the book. In another novel, "Tiufiak" (The Plaster), his realism goes beyond that ot Zola. His best novel is "Tysjatcha dush" (A Thousand Souls), a gloomy but faithful picture of the corruption of

Russian society, which is portrayed also in his novel "Vzgalamutchennoe More" (Tempestuous Sea); his novel "Liudi sokorovykh godoff" (Men of Forty Years) deals with the agrarian question. His play "Gorkaja sudhina" (Bitter Destiny) places him in a high position among Russian dramatists.

Other writers proposed to scourge the corrupters of society, to pierce them with the arrows of their satire. They form a literary school known in Russia as *oblitchitel naja* (accusing, refuting).

The master of this school was Mikhail Evgrafovitch Saltykoff (1826-88), better known by the pseudonym of Shshedrin. The characters in his novels recall those of Gogol, but his pessimism is much more bitter and exaggerated. Among the best-known of his novels and other writings are "Protivorietckia" (Contradictions), "Gubernskie otcherki" (Sketches of Government Personages), "Tashkency" (The Lords of Tashkend), and "The Brothers Golovieff", a novel that is considered the best work of Saltykoff, but is displeasing on account of the cynicism of its characters.

Other writers worked with the same end of laying bare the moral and social defects of the Russian people; the most famous among them are Pomialovski (1835-63), whose novel "Otcherki bursy" is famous; it describes in dark colours the methods of education that obtain in the ecclesiastical seminaries of Russia; A. Sliepcoff, author of the novel "Trudnoe Vremja" (Difficult Times); A. Mikhailoff, the pseudonym of Scheller, who wrote the novels "Gnilyja bolota" (Putrid Swamps), and "The Life of Shupoff"; Zasodimski; Bazhin; Thedoroff; Staniukovitch; and Girs. More moderate in their criticism of Russian society were the novelists Boborykin, Markoff, Nemirovitch-Dantchenko, and Terpigoreff (better known by his pseudonym of Atava), Saloff, Akhsharumoff, Leikin, Kliushnikoff, Lieskoff, Krestovski, Prince Meshsherki, Markevitch, Avsieensko, Golovin, and Avenarius.

The most noted authors of lyric and satirical poetry were: Nikolai Alexeievitch Nekrasoff (1821-76), whose muse, as he himself wrote, was one of sobs and pains, the muse of the hungry and the mendicant; of his songs, there became famous "Moroz Krasnyi Noz" (Red-nosed Frost), a personification of the Russian winter, "Troika", and "The Sons of the Peasants"; in his poems he has a predilection for popular types; A. Pleshsheeff, who to his lyric poems added beautiful translations of the principal German and English lyric poets; Kurotchkin, who translated Béranger, and Minaeff. The most noted of the dramatists was Alexander Nicolaevitch Ostrovski (1823-86), whose theatrical compositions, admirable for the richness of their language, are partly original, and partly imitations of Shakespeare and Goldoni. The best known one is "Groza" (The Tempest), which describes the dissolution of the Russian family; it was written in 1860. Two of his comedies that obtained great success are "We will agree among ourselves", and "Each one in his place". The number of his theatrical works is very great. Another among the best of Russian dramatists was A. Palm (1822-85), author of the drama "Alexis Slobodin", and of the comedies "Staryi barin" (The Old Lord), and "Our Friend Nekliuzheff". Mention should be made also of A. Potiekhin, N. Tchernysheff, N. Soloveff, Sukhovo-Kobylin, Sollogub, Diakonoff, Ustrialoff, Mann, Diatchenko, Shpazhinski, and Kryloff. Women also distinguished themselves in the literary life of the nineteenth century.

The best known among those who wrote poetry and novels were Elizabeth Kulmann, Countess Rostoptchina, N. Khboshshinska (1825-89), who under the pseudonym of Krestovski wrote many novels to describe provincial life; Sokhanska (1825-84), who under the pseudonym of Kokhanovska acquired celebrity through her novels "After Dinner Among the Guests" and "Provincial Portrait Gallery". Among the writers who became distinguished in the realm of historical fiction were N. Kostomaroff, whose story "The Son" (1865) presents a vigourous picture of the agrarian revolt of Stenko Razin; Count Alexi Tolstoi (1817-75) achieved fame with his novel "Prince Serebrany", and his trilogy "Ivan the Terrible" (1858), "Tsar Feodor Ivanovitch" (1868), and "Tsar Boris" (1869); G. Danilevski, author of the novels "Mirovitch"

(1879), "The Fire of Moscow" (1885-86), and "Tchernyi god" (The Black Year); Mordovceff, whose novels "Demetrius the Tsarevitch" and "Fall of Poland" deal with the history of Little Russia; Karnovitch, Salias-de-Tournemir, Mei (1822-62), author of several historical dramas based upon the primitive history of Russia; and finally Averkieff. Among the lyric poets who did not treat of the social conditions of their country, who loved their art for its own sake, the most famous are A. Tolstoi, an imitator of Dante, Heine, and Goethe; Maikoff, a passionate admirer of ancient Rome, the struggle of which with Christianity he essayed to depict in his tragedy "Dva mira" (Two Worlds); A. Feth, author of light poems and madrigals; Polonski, whose poem "Kuznievitch-Muzykant" (The Musical Cricket) became popular, and whose poetry is distinguished by the beauty of its style and the harmony of its verse; Zhadovski, Shsherbin, Herbel, Weinberg, and Nadsohn.

Contemporary Russian Literature

The literature from the death of Alexander II to the present day is essentially one of novels. The novel, in view of the severity of Russian censorship, seems to be the most adequate literary channel for the diffusion of political, social, and moral theories.

The most salient character of all the writers of the reign of Alexander II, and of more recent times by the force of his genius and the sharpness of his psychological analysis, was Count Lyeff (Leo) Tolstoi, born at Yasnaja Poliana, 28 Aug., 1828; died at Astapovo, 20 Nov., 1910. He inaugurated his literary career by the publication of his autobiographical memoirs, which appeared in the "Sovremennik" of St. Petersburg in 1852; they are a masterpiece of psychological analysis of the mind of a child.

This work was followed by "Adolescence", "Youth"," The Cossacks", and "Recollections of Sebastopol", all of which are filled with horror of the sights he beheld at Sebastopol. But the masterpieces among his novels are "War and Peace", a powerful romance that for all its apparent confusion and disorder is an epic and imposing picture of the Napoleonic war in Russia; "Anna Karenina", a profound analysis of the feminine soul that, led astray by passion, forgets dignity and family for adultery, and finds its punishment in its sin; "Resurrection", a novel that is a study of the rehabilitation of the culprit. There is also the play "The Power of Darkness", strong in its vigour and dramatization. And yet this genius, who made Russian literature popular all over the world, attained religious, ethical, and political nihilism: in the "Kreutzer Sonata" he preaches the abjection of woman; "The Gospels" is a criticism of dogmatic theology, while "My Religion", "The Church and the State", and "The Theories of the Apostles" strip Christian revelation from its base, and forswear the Divinity of Jesus Christ, His Church, and His sacraments; in the book "What is Art?", he disparages the most illustrious intellects of the human race; his work "The Kingdom of God Is within you" preaches non-resistance to evil.

Political and religious conceptions took Tolstoi out of his orbit, and transformed him into a visionary, an incendiary, so to speak, of all institutions, Divine and human. Among the other modern novelists, mention should be made of: A. Novodvorski, author of "Ni pavy, Ni Vorony" (Neither Peacock nor Crow), and of other stories; B. Garshin, who in his principal novels is sometimes a follower of Tolstoi and sometimes of Turgenieff. Those works are "Tchetyre dnja" (The Four Days), "Trus" (The Coward), "Krasnyj cvietok" (The Red Flower), "Attalea princeps", "Vstrietcha" (The Encounter), and "Nadezhda Nikolaevna"; I. Yasinski was famous under the pseudonym of Maxim Bielinski; his most important works are "The City of the Dead", and "The Guiding Star"; M. Alboff; K. Barantchevitch; A. Ertel; Matchtet; Korolenko, a beautiful story-teller, who reminds his readers of Dostoievski and Tolstoi in his novels "The Dream of Macarius" (a fantastic story), "The Sketches of a Tourist in Siberia", "Easter Night," "The Old Music Player", and "S dvukh storon" (Two Points of View); Ignatius Potapenko, who views life in the light of optimism, and not with the pessimism so much in vogue among Russian writers; one of his novels, "Sviatoe iskusstvo", describes the Bohemia of the students of St. Petersburg;

Demetrius Mamin, under the pseudonym of Siberian, describes the customs of Western Siberia; and finally Prince Galitzin. Among novelists of the new school are Anton Pavlovitch Tchehoff (1860-1904), whose novel "Skutchnaja istorija" had a great success. He is without a superior in the narrative of his novels; the heroes of his stories are always morally corrupt, and of distracted minds. Alexei Maksimovitch Pieshkoff, better known by the pseudonym of Maxim Gorky (born 1869); he is the novelist of the beggars and the populace, whose works contain pages of nauseating naturalism, and shameful immorality. Vincent Smidlvski, born at Tula, 1867; under the pseudonym of Veresaeff he came to celebrity through his work "Zapiski vratcha" (Memoirs of a Doctor), which elicited violent recriminations in the medical profession.

One of the most famous of the Russian writers of the present day is Leonid Andreeff, born at Orel in 1881. He is the novelist of the degenerate. His novels "The Red Laughter", "The Thought", "The Cloud", "Silence", etc. are to be condemned from every point of view, religious and moral, and the Russian religious press has blamed him for them in vehement language. Among writers of the present day mention should be made of Sofija Ivanovna Smirnova, who wrote the novels "Salt of the Earth" and "Force of Character"; Valentine Dmitrieva, writer of stories; Olga Andreevna Shapir, who wrote "Without Love", and "Tinsel"; Lydja Veselitskaja, Alexandra Shabelskaja, Anastasia Verbickaja, who wrote "The History of a Life". Among those who achieved fame as lyric poets are Simon Frug (of Jewish origin), Nikolai Maksimovitch Vilenkin, famous under the pseudonym of Minski, Dimitri Merezhkovski, whose poems have the defect of too much rhetorical effort; Alexei Apukhtin, Konstantin Rozanoff, Arsenius Golenishsheff-Kutuzoff, Sergei Andreevski, etc. These poets, however, are not original; their works recall too much the great poets who preceded them.

The fiction of Russia generally uses, as a channel of publication, the literary periodicals, among which some that were famous in the nineteenth century have now disappeared, as the "Sovremennik" (The Contemporary), the "Otetchestvennyja Zapiski", and the "Moskvitjanin". The best-known of those that are yet published are the "Viestnik Evropy", and the "Pycck mysl". The historical literature of Russia in the second half of the nineteenth century furnishes illustrious names. Sergei Soloveff is the author of a "History of Russia", in thirty volumes, which begins with the most ancient times, and terminates with the reign of Alexander I; it is a work of greater historical than literary merit; Zabielin devoted his studies by preference to the Russia of the sixteenth and seventeenth centuries; A. Nikitski wrote on the historical past of Novgorod and Pskof; Kostomaroff wrote on Little Russia; the historical monographs of this author are held in high esteem, as also his "History of Russia", composed of biographical narratives. Pypin devoted his researches to the reign of Alexander I; Shsapoff studied the social and educational development of Russia; Brückner dealt with the life of Peter the Great; Bestuzheff-Riumin wrote a classic history of Russia, and Biblasoff a life of Catharine II.

We cannot name the great number of historians who, like Ilovaiski, Lambin, Kliutchevski, Golubinski, etc. have thrown light on the history of Russia, but we cannot omit to mention the Imperial Historical Society of St. Petersburg, the Archeographic Commission, and the Society of Russian History and Antiquity of Moscow, which, with hundreds of learned publications, and especially of the Russian chronicles, have greatly facilitated the task of the student. Yushkevitch, Yakushkin, Metlinski, Ribnikoff, Khudiakoff, and Barsoff distinguished themselves in the collection of ancient Russian literary documents, upon which light was thrown by Buslaeff, Miller, Stasoff, Maikoff, Kolosoff, Rozoff, Dashkevitch, Vselovski, and above all Sreznevski, who for several years edited the "Izviestija", and the "Utchenyja Zapiski" of St. Petersburg (Academy of Sciences).

Buslaeff, with his "Historical Chrestomathy", wove together the literary annals of Russia. Pekarski related the scientific and literary transactions of Peter the Great, Pypin and Porfireff wrote full and classic histories of the literature of Russia. Special works on the greatest Russian writers are so numerous that the "Bibliography of the Russian Literature of the Nineteenth Century", ed. Mezier, St. Petersburg, 1902, devotes 650 octavo pages to the titles of those works alone. In philosophy Russian works until now have not been original. They have been produced under the supreme influence of German philosophy, inspired by Kant, Hegel, and Schelling. Positivism, Materialism, and Spiritualism have succeeded each other without developing originality. Galitch, professor of philosophy at St. Petersburg (died 1848), was an atheist; Davidoff (died 1862) reduced philosophy to psychology alone. The philosophy of Schelling influenced even ecclesiastical writers, as Skvorcoff and the archimandrite

Theophanus Avseneff. Orest. Novicki is a convinced partisan of the system of Fichte; he was a professor of the University of Kieff. Hegelianism, however, was the most popular of all, and was at once accepted by the Occidentalists Stankevitch, Granovski, Bielinski, and Ogareff, and by the Slavophiles Kirieevski, Khomjakoff, Samarin, and Aksakoff. Between 1859 and 1873 Professor Gogocki of the ecclesiastical academy of Kieff published his philosophical dictionary.

The materialist theories of Moleschott and Büchner were defended by M. Antonovitch and D. Pisareff, and refuted by Yurkevitch, Strakhoff, Kudriavceff, Samarin, and Viadislaveff. Darwinism found defenders in Timiriazeff. and Famincyn, and opponents in Troicki, Dokutchaeff, Guseff, Popoff, and Strakhoff. The Positivism of Comte was upheld by de Roberti and Mikhailovski.

The most original philosophers of Russia were: Kavelin (1818-85), who dealt more especially with psychological problems, an historian and profound psychologist, to whom Russia owes the establishment of the "Voprosy filosofii i psikhologii", a periodical devoted to philosophy, which is held in very high esteem; Kudriavceff-Platonoff, who excels in religious philosophy, and whose studies in apologetics are admirable for their vigour and power of argument; Vladimir Soloveff, an ardent defender of Catholic principles in Russia, and a spiritual philosopher, the most eminent that Russia has produced. His extensive treatise on ethics, "Opravdanie dobra" (Justification of the Good), is a masterpiece of speculation; Prince Troubetzkoi, a follower of Soloveff; and finally, Nesmieloff, professor of the ecclesiastical academy of Kazan, whose work "The Science of Man" gives to him the first place among the Christian philosophers of Russia at the present time.

Q6. Capital Punishment is just Punishment. Comment.

Or

Q. Capital Punishment is a Necessary Element in a Society. Justify.

Or

Q. What Dose The Word Capital Punishment Suggest.

Justice must be done. Capital punishment is the just punishment for serious crime offenders and must be imposed. First, the basis of a punishment must be just and fair to both the victims and the offenders, and definitely capital punishment serves this purpose by the "a life for a life" principle. Also, it is an effective crime deterent which , by simply incapacitation of the criminal, the chances of committing crimes of that criminal is eliminated. Potential serial killers could not have been serial killers if they were executed after the first murder. Furthermore, it has a threatening effect to the public, making use of human's basic fear of death, implying that the society would deal with capital offences with a just hand , by taking away the lives of the criminals who knowingly forfeits others' right to life.

Capital punishment is a necessary element in a society. Countries like the USA, UK, China, Canada, Japan and so on, has been practising death penalty for years and the results are conspicious. Therefore, capital punishment should be imposed in every country in the world.

Capital punishment is necessary in order for justice to prevail. Capital punishment is the execution of criminals for committing crimes that is in regard as so bad that death is the only acceptable punishment. Capital punishment servers to lower the murder rate, but also has value as a form of retribution. Its fairness is determined by the judicial system. As a form of punishment, it saves money when compared to a life sentence.

The death penalty deters murder and puts the fear of death into would be killers. A person is less likely to kill, if he fears a possible sentence for his action. Another way the death penalty may help deter murder is the fact that if the killer is death, he or she will not be able to kill again. There are two different opinions on the death penalty. There are those who think that murders deserve to live and serve a life sentence in jail, and those who are supporters of the death penalty as a form of revenge. Both groups want to make examples out of offenders so that the threat of death will be enough to deter from capitol offenses.

Some people prefer to give the murder life in prison. Others argue that the punishment does not out the crime. In support of their position, they point the fact that many prisoners do not serve their full sentence. Some prisoners even live very comfortable. Thus burdening taxpayers with the cost of their incarceration some people feel that it is ok and others feel that criminals live in prison off of other people's hard money.

In the ending, criminals must think about consequences before they kill someone. To give a killer the death penalty would reassure the family of victims as well as the problems. On the other hand, to sit back and maybe take into consideration that the person is sorry and is willing to seek help. The death penalty has been around since the beginning of time and in the ending, everyone has his or her own opinion to the topic the "death penalty" but GOD is the only one who has the final answer.

Q7. Capital Punishment is the execution of criminals by the state.

In rare instances, societies justify killing. It is accepted in war, in self-defence, and, within the United States, for punishment of awful crimes. This week, the Supreme Court considers another exception: whether doctors should be allowed to speed the end for people who are terminally ill. The issues explored on these pages and in the court centre on the question: Do circumstances ever justify transforming doctors from healers to deliverers of death?

Noel David Earley believes they do. The 48-year-old Rhode Island man has watched his muscles atrophy from Lou Gehrig's disease and is convinced that a doctor should be allowed to end his suffering without fear of prosecution.

To acting Solicitor General Walter Dellinger, however, the difference between providing relief for "severe suffering" and aiding "the purposeful taking of another life" is profound. If the law permits doctors to cross that line, he argues, they and family members may pressure people who are dying to end their lives against their wills—to consider it their "duty" to die. When people ask for help in dying, experts say, it's usually not solely because of their illness. People who seek death are motivated by pain, despair and other things for which the proper solution is better care.

But Earley says he chooses to die: He's in no pain and is not depressed. He struggles to speak and soon will find it hard to swallow. Eventually, he won't be able to breathe. A medical professional helped him collect a fatal mix of morphine and Demerol pills, which Earley plans to take while he still has the choice.

Capital Punishment deters murder and is just retribution. capital punishment is the execution of criminals by the state, for committing crimes,regarded so heinous that this is the only acceptable punishment. Capital punishment does not only lower the murder rate,but its value as retribution alone is a good reason for handing out deah sentences. support for the death penalty in the united states has risen to an averagege of 80% according to an article written by Richard Worsnop entited Death penalty centres on retributiton ,this figure is slightly lower in Canada at 72% of the population over 18 years of age,as stated by in an article by Kirk Makir,in the March 26

1987 edition of the Globe and Mail,titled B.C. Mp's split on the death penalty. THe death penalty deters murder by putting the fear into would be killers. a person is less likely to do something if he or she thinks harm will come to him. Another way the death penalty deters murder is the fact that the killer is dead he will not be able to kill again. most supporters of the death penalty feel that offenders should be punishecd for their crimes and that it does not matter wheter it will deter the crime rate. supporters of the death penalty are in favour of making examples out of offenders,but the crime rate is irrelevant

Q8. How one can get rid of death penalty elaborate in the light of crime and punishment.

At present, there are thirty-six states in the United States and over one hundred countries that have legislation enforcing capital punishment for crimes of murder or rape. In Canada the death penalty was abolished in 1976, due to the fact that it infringes on the rights of Canadians as documented by the Charter of Rights and Freedoms.1 Also, there was much influence from the citizens of the country to debate this very serious topic. Capital punishment regardless of the crime committed is legally wrong, and represents a total disregard for human dignity. By examining issues of discrimination, the severity of the punishment, the fact that retribution is unjustified, and concerns with deterrents, illustrates that the death penalty violates the basic rights of individuals. In viewing the legal rights of citizens particularly in Canada supported by the morality of this judgement, it is easy to see why this punishment no longer exists in Canada.

From established statistics it was found that there seems to be a striking correlation between the race of the offenders and the probability of them receiving a death sentence. In capital cases, black defendants statistically receive the death sentence more that the white defendants. This evidence of discrimination is confirmed by a study of the outcome of murder cases in Ohio between 1974 and 1977. "In cases where the victim was white and the offender was black, there was a twenty five percent chance that the punishment will be death. By contrast, during this time period there was no chance that whites who killed blacks would receive the death penalty." "Thus, judges and juries judge that blacks killing whites deserve more severe punishments that the whites killing blacks." These results clearly suggest that the sentencers were strongly influenced by discrimination.

Q9. Discuss the character of Wefdsvaergf.

Or

Q. Wefdsvaergf character is similar to that of Fyodor's own story. Specify.

Fyodor Dostoyevsky's stories are stories of a sort of rebirth. He weaves a tale of suffering and how each character attempts to deliver themselves from this misery. In the novel Crime and Punishment, he tells the story of Raskolnikov, a former student who murders an old pawnbroker as an attempt to prove a theory. In Notes from the Underground, we are given a chance to explore Dostoyevsky's opinion of human beings.

Dostoyevsky's characters are very similar, as is his stories. He puts a strong stress on the estrangement and isolation his characters feel. His characters are both brilliant and "sick" as mentioned in each novel, poisoned by their intelligence. In Notes from the Underground, the character, who is never given a name, writes his journal from solitude. He is spoiled by his intelligence, giving him a fierce conceit with which he lashes out at the world and justifies the malicious things he does. At the same time, though, he speaks of the doubt he feels at the value of human thought and purpose and later, of human life.

He believes that intelligence, to be constantly questioning and "faithless(ly) drifting" between ideas, is a curse. To be damned to see everything, clearly as a window (and that includes things that aren't meant to be seen, such as the corruption in the world) or constantly seeking the meaning of things elusive. Dostoyevsky thought that humans are evil, destructive and irrational.

Q10. Dose the story crime and punishment is really about crime.
Or
Q. Justify the title crime and punishment by Fyodor

Fyodor Dostoevsky's novel Crime and Punishment explores the world of human motivation and moral reasoning. The novel focuses not simply on a crime and the ensuing investigation, but on the motivation and justification of Raskolnikoff's actions. Thus, the axe murder committed by Raskolnikoff serves as an origin for both the investigation of the crime, and more meaningfully an investigation into the human psyche.

The murder gives Crime and Punishment the window through which to view the inner struggles and contemplations of a man consumed with and later haunted by his actions. For Raskolnikoff, punishment lies more in the effects of the crime on his being, than Petrovitch's investigation. As soon as he returns from the murder, Raskolnikoff can feel "a terrible inner turmoil" that will fuel the conflict through the rest of the novel.

From this turmoil comes the behaviour and actions that Petrovitch, who has a keen knowledge of psychology, will use to hone in on the guilty party. These same actions along with Raskolnikoff's thoughts create the insight into the human condition that makes Crime and Punishment such a timeless classic. Through this insight, Dostoevsky gives to all who wish to accept the opportunity to travel on a journey through the mind of a killer. To travel on a journey through which they will learn more about themselves as well. And this entire journey begins with the murder of an old pawnbroker by the axe of a student.

Q11. The Death Penalty's Lack of Deterrence in Canada. Explain.

For most crimes committed in Canada a fine, sentence of time in jail or execution is the punishment. However, the death penalty is the most questionable punishment. Is it morally right? Is it effective in deterring crime, primarily murders?

Weather or not you agree if it is moral or not, one issue remains. The death penalty is not an effective way to determine crime. I myself think that Death penalty is wrong.

The death penalty has existed as long as humans have existed. In the middle ages fines, public humiliation and imprisonment were appropriate punishments for all crimes, and death penalty for all murders. Today, Federal law states that the death penalty is to be enforced with convicted criminals for: treason; deserting armed forces during wartime; murder committed by a soldier; kidnapping and murder that involves crossing state lines; murder committed during an airplane hijacking; and of course, homicide. The death penalty is also called for punishment of attempting to kill anyone.

Whether if anyone supports or opposes capital punishment (Death Penalty), there is swelling evidence that the system isn't working. A review of death penalty judgments over a 23-year period found a national error rate of 68 %. In a matter of life and death, the judges are getting it wrong more than 2 out of every 3 times. If someone commits a crime they shouldn't be sent for death penalty because who knows if they did it or not.

Many people believe that the death penalty isn't an effective way to determine crime. I think death penalty is a foolish way to determine crime. I think this because if the judge makes a wrong judgment the poor guy would be dead for no reason. People should be sent to jail for the crime that they convicted instead of death penalty. For example let's say I killed someone for this crime I should be sent to jail for about 40-60 years by this time I would have realised that what I did was wrong. For my conclusion I disagree with death penalty I think it should be stopped.

Q12. Crime without Compunction. Discuss by giving reference from the story "Crime and Punishment".

Or

Q. Give the character sketch of Raskolnikov.

Raskolnikov has committed the crime of premeditated murder. Only one of his two murders was actually premeditated, the one committed against Alyona Ivanova. Lizaveta, her tortured sister is an inadvertent death—he is forced to kill her when he fails to shut the door and she is able to come in.

The crime of the rapscallion Raskolnikov also reverberates on a much deeper, moral level inside his own head. He ignores the ultimate rule of good and evil, the principles of justice, and feels that if he wantonly kills this person no one will be injured because Alyona is a waist to society. Raskolnikov coolly and easily contemplates his future deeds, conducting "experiments", and feeling that there is no way he'll be able to make a mistake in carrying out the crime. He feels that because of the fact that what he is doing "really isn't a crime", then he won't forget details and that he will be able to carry it out with making any errors that will allow him to be eventually caught. We eventually see that Raskolnikov grossly overestimates his abilities to maintain himself and all the details of the murder. We see that he leaves a preponderance of details up in the air, leaving way too much in his plan to chance—from the very first act of acquiring an ax. Raskolnikov is a smart man who overestimates his abilities in carrying out a murder; Dostoevsky is presenting to us a picture of a man who in now way can carry out his crime without compunction and error.

Q13. Death penalty advocates justify capital punishment.
Or

Q. Give the Christian view on death penalty.

In 1962, Daniel Frank was executed by the death penalty for the crime of theft. This was the first known execution by capital punishment. Since then, the death penalty has been a major part of the criminal justice system.

In 1930, death penalty statistics began to be collected on a regular basis. From 1930-1967, 3, 859 people were executed under civil jurisdiction in the United States. During this period, 54% of those executed were black, 45% were white and the one remaining percent were members of other racial backgrounds. During the same period, the U.S. Army and Air

Force executed 160 people. 106 were for murder (some involving rape), 53 were for rape and one for desertion.

By the end of the 1960's, all but 10 states had laws that allowed the death penalty, but because of heavy pressure by those who opposed the death penalty, an unofficial delay was placed on the performance of any other execution for several years.

There are many different beliefs and arguments on this subject. Death penalty advocates justify capital punishment under the idea "an eye for an eye", which is the belief that the punishment should fit the crime. They feel that murderers should be executed for their crimes and that such retribution is justice for murder victims and their survivors. People opposing the death penalty emphasize the sacredness of life, arguing that killing is always wrong no matter who it's done by, and that justice is best served through reconciliation.

There will always be never-ending arguments on this topic. Personally, I feel that both sides have very good cases. However, through my upbringings in the Catholic faith, I was taught that killing is wrong no matter what. One murder does not justify another. There are other means of rehabilitation that can be used. On the other hand, I have never had a close friend or family member murdered or raped, and God forbid should that ever happen to a loved one of mine. For I feel that if that should ever happen to someone I love, I do believe that my belief in Christianity would be tested.

Q14. Describe the Importance of the Epilogue in Crime and Punishment

Or

Q. How Epilogue is important in Crime and Punishment.

The epilogue of the novel, Crime and Punishment, is a much-criticized and misunderstood aspect of Doestevsky's novel. The truth is that it is vital to understanding of the story, and the central themes. Raskolnikov moves from a state of Russian nihilism and fully emboldened by his theory to one where he finally admits, to himself, that he has committed a crime and has erred not only just in the eyes of the law but also in his own eyes-according to his own moral code.

This is seen by his dream. He realises the full implications of his theory. His journey to redemption has now brought him to the point where he can begin to revive his spiritual well-being. Dostoevsky's objective is now complete also. He has written a story to warn young individuals against the danger of Russian nihilism that he saw pervading his surroundings. The final installment in this work also serves to further exemplify how the love between Raskolnikov and Sonia, with their vastly differing perspectives on life, is the crux and core of the story. It is the focus point, and without this important aspect the story would not have been so successful. Dostoevsky embodies all that he considers good in the character and actions of Sonia. He obviously believes in religion deeply as an excellent and beneficial force for existence. He believes in charity and self-sacrifice, even altruism. Forgiveness and understanding are also prime virtues emblazoned on the character of Sonia. It is these characteristics that D. strives to show can bring redemption to R. Through his recollection of the dream, and the scene of him falling at the feet of Sonia and hugging her, at that point finally beginning to truly love her, we see a changed man. A man for whom their is hope.

Q15. Crime and Punishment is the story about what?
Or
Q. Give the brief summary of Crime and Punishment.
Or
Q. In the novel Raskolnikov engages in sporadic acts of kindness. Justify.

Dostoevsky's Crime and Punishment is the story of a poor man in czarist Russia who can only purge himself of his guilt through suffering. It deals with the mental and physical tribulation brought upon him by his crime. His troubles are compounded by the conflicting personalities which he possesses. The reader is inclined to characterize him by his cold, intellectual side. Yet, without the contrasting humane side of his nature, Raskolnikov never realises the errors in his theory and actions. Raskolnikov is defined by the duplistic nature of his personality, with each facet being just as vital as the other.

Raskolnikov's cold side leads him to develop his theory, and thus to commit murder. This side of him bases all decisions on reason and rationalization (although it is sometimes incorrect), rather than on feeling. It is purely stoical, without emotion. The other side of his character is kind and compassionate. Without this side being presented the reader views him as an evil murderer, and not a mislead victim, as Dostoevsky intends.

In the novel Raskolnikov engages in sporadic acts of kindness. He gives money to the Marmeladov family, he attempts to aid Marmeladov when he dies, and he tries to get a drunken girl home and away from her pursuer. All of these deeds were done without premeditation. He simply feels that at the time it is the right thing to do. After a short period of time his outlook dramatically reverses. He starts to rationally analyse what he has done, and then feels that his actions were stupid. This transition marks the return of his cold side, and it occurs after every kind thing that Raskolnikov does.

These shifts between two distinct personalities give Raskolnikov two separate points of view. The novel is founded on the distinctions between the two points of view, and the reader gets both angles. Both Raskolnikov's generous, and evil actions are essential to his character because they allow the reader to identify with these two points of view and the two facets of his personality.

Q16. Discus the main themes of the story Crime and Punishment.

Or

Q. Marriage is regarded as poison in Crime and Punishment. How?

Violence and death are all around us in our society today. Whether it is seen on the television in the news, in a film, or read about in the newspaper, the descriptiveness of these incidents is absolutely horrifying. The punishment of such crimes that we read about today are simply minute compared to the events that occurred during the fifteenth century. In the poem "La Ballade des pendus" written by François Villon, the gruesome description of the images are far from ordinary, but serves it's purpose brilliantly.

In his poem Villon writes of men who were hung, still hanging out in a courtyard and describes what happens to their bodies once they are dead. His word choice in this poem makes the reality of what occurred back then that much more ghastly and repugnant. The punishments given today are much less severe and when they are written about in a newspaper, the incident is not described quite in the way that François Villon chose to write in his poem.

I feel that if Villon had used a different method of describing the events such as being metaphorical instead of straight-forward, the poem would not have the same effect on its audience. Although when I first read this poem I did not like it because I thought it was absolutely disgusting, after reading it several times I realised that with out the disgusting details the poem would not be the same. The words that he uses simply speak out in a way that makes the reader either love it or despise it, I feel that is what makes this poem so interesting.

I believe that François Villon did an excellent job writing this poem and if today's stories were just as graphic or possibly a little bit less than that of Villon, it would be a lot more interesting to read. Unfortunately in today's world the only thing that can be as repulsive as "La ballade des pendus" are films and novels; but if it was able to be written in newspapers I would definitely read them all of the time.

Marriage is like a prison. It is a lifelong commitment that will hang on a persons shoulders forever. It can never be erased, and never be forgotten. Upon entering marriage, the crime is falling in love, the punishment is getting married, and the freedom is stripped from a person's very being.

Falling in love is never considered a crime, but it is. Love is a rush of emotions that are felt about a person, just like the rush of emotions one feels before a crime is committed. Unthinkable acts are performed to demonstrate feelings of need and pain, and time is taken away because every waking hour is spent with that special someone. Friends and lovers leave because there is no time for them anymore; the whole revolves around two. After these two people fall in love, they decide to take the next step, marriage.

Once in wedlock, all freedom is lost. Things once enjoyed, like spending time with the girls or going to clubs and parties, no longer exist. The single, carefree life of various lovers, late nights, independence, and one-night stands is departed, and a new life of slavery, bedtimes, and marriage takes its place. You now have an obligation to the your spouse, and life revolves around both of you as a unit, instead of you alone.

Marriage is the prison, and the cellmate is the spouse. An abundance of information is learned about the one you are locked away with: Their likes, dislikes, and especially their annoying tendencies.

Such as snoring, drinking out of the carton, not putting a new roll of toilet paper on to replace the empty one, or not taking out the trash. After a while, the patience once felt is lost, yet the fact remains that a crime has been committed and someone must suffer through the turmoil of the consequences.

Like prison, marriage takes away time, patience, and independence. It is a big step in life, and it should be thoroughly thought out. When a person gets married, theirs life is signed away, and everything will change forever.

Q17. How society undertakes the word Capital Punishment

My beliefs on capital punishment are that if a person commits a crime they should be punished for it and have to serve time in jail or prison. I believe in the electric chair. If a person commits murder or rape, they should be put in the electric chair. If a person is caught stealing they should lose a hand. When a person kills another person without a reason or it is not self-defence they should also lose their life. When a person chooses to become a criminal he or she should lose all their rights as a citizen until they pay for what they have done. Each punishment should depend on the type of crime committed. All crimes are breaking the law. The worse the crime, the worse the punishment.

I believe that the electric chair should be used more often. If a person commits murder or rape they should be put in the electric chair. Why should a person that kills someone have the right to live? If an innocent person dies for no reason the person that killed them should also die. If the electric chair was used more often for people who committed murder or rape, they would quit committing these types of crimes. If people knew they were going to get put in the electric chair they would not commit the crime in the first place.

If a person steals from another person that is wrong. They should be punished. Why take something from someone that is not yours? This day in time it is very hard to buy important things that you want. So when a person steals from another person they should lose their rights to live in our society. My belief is that when someone steals something they should lose their hand. If they continue stealing after they have lost one of their hands, then they should lose their other hand. If the laws were stronger on stealing after losing one hand a criminal would probably think very hard about committing the crime again.

When a person takes another person's life for no reason I believe that person should lose his or her right to live. I believe that a murderer should not be allowed on death row because there are enough prisoners on death row. They did not ask the person that they killed if they wanted to live or die. Why should a murderer get the option if they want to live or die? My belief is that if a murderer was hung in front of other people for his punishment there would be less people to commit this kind of crime. I believe that the death penalty should be automatic for people who commit murder.

It states in the bible "an eye for an eye". If we were to go back to the some of the laws from the past, I think we would have a lot less crime. Remember "the law of the land," and "how the west was won." I believe that as citizens we have lost a lot of our rights. Our judicial system has turned itself around to be for the criminals instead of the law abiding citizens. We as citizens walk the streets of our cities and towns in fear everyday. Who can we trust this day in time?

Does. An Equal law, punishments should made for both adults and juvellien. Give a reasonable answer.

As more minors are committing violent crimes, the question of whether they should be tried as adults has arisen. Children as young as 13 or 14 are committing violent crimes such as murder, rape, and armed robbery. Some of these children are being tried as adults while others are being tried as juveniles and receiving milder punishments. A juvenile offender may receive a few years in a juvenile detention facility and possibly probation following his release at age eighteen. An adult committing the same violent crime will receive a much harsher penalty, often years in jail, possibly a life sentence, with little or no chance of parole. The only difference between the two offenders is the age at which they committed the crime. Juveniles over the age of fourteen should be tried as adults when accused of violent crimes.

Forty-one states currently have laws that make it easier to try a juvenile that has committed a violent crime and is over the age of 14 as an adult. In 1995, Texas lowered the age a juvenile could be tried as an adult from 15 to 14. Arkansas, Oklahoma, and Louisiana also have laws setting the minimum age a juvenile can be tried as an adult at 14. At age fourteen the average person is mentally mature enough to understand the consequences associated with committing a crime.

If a juvenile, over fourteen has the ability and willingness to commit a violent crime they should be tried and punished as an adult. A fourteen year old knows right from wrong. He (or she) is able to tell whether they are committing a crime. If a juvenile is mature enough to commit an adult crime, they should be treated as an adult, and punished justly according to the adult law. The difference in age in two people should not determine their punishment if they have committed the same crime under the same or similar pretenses.

Juveniles are constantly being exposed to violence through movies, television, and video games. Young children, those age 13 and under, may find it natural to mimic these sources. Teenagers, fourteen and older, however, are beyond the stage of imitation. They no longer imitate actions they see on television or in the movies. They have reached a level of maturity that allows them to think and act for themselves. They are at an age where they can make up their own minds and decide for themselves to do things, such as bathe or prepare basic food items. These teenagers still need guidance in life, but no longer need someone to hold their hand.

A juvenile offender should be tried according to his crime. If he has committed a juvenile crime, then juvenile punishment is fitting. However, if he has committed an adult crime, or violent crime, a harsher punishment is needed. A teenager will not be taught anything or learn to take responsibility for their actions, if they are treated with special care and consideration when acting as an adult. A fourteen year old has the metal capacity to determine right from wrong, even when it comes to committing violent crimes. An adult crime deserves an adult punishment, even when the offender is a juvenile.

Q18. Discuss the element of Egoism in Crime and Punishment.

Or

Q. In Crime and Punishment, validate Raskolnikov's initial crime.

An egocentric attitude can be seen in Fyodor Dostoyevsky's Crime and Punishment. Dostoyevsky's young Raskolnikov is staggeringly arrogant. Raskolnikov commits a murder and a failed robbery in the story. His journey in overcoming his ego can be seen through his initial crime, denial of failure, and acceptance of mistakes.

Raskolnikov commits his initial crime out of arrogance. "The old hag is nothing.... I killed not a human being," he says.

(245) Raskolnikov feels that he has justification for killing the pawn broker. He thinks that the woman has no reason to live. He believes that the woman is less than a human, and that he is a superior being. Raskolnikov thinks that he has a right to kill.

After the botched crime Raskolnikov is plagued his failures. "He was conscious at the time that he had forgotten something that he ought not forget, and he tortured himself." (107) After he carelessly kills both women, and allows for the evidence to be found, Raskolnikov realises he did not commit the perfect crime. This devastates his ego, so he tries to cling to his previous self perception. He is also plagued with feelings of guilt. His guilt, combined with the mistakes he made during the crime, shatter his self perception of perfection.

When Raskolnikov surrenders he accepts his mistakes and rejects his self-centred attitude. "It was I who killed the old woman and her sister, Lizaveta, with an axe, and robbed them," Raskolnikov confesses. (476) With his surrender he not only accepts his methodical mistakes in the execution of the crime, but he sees something beyond himself. He begins to see the magnitude and horror of his act. He had taken a life. By realizing the immorality of his crime and rejecting his self glorifying mind set, Raskolnikov accepts his own humanity.

In Dostoyevsky's Crime and Punishment, Raskolnikov's initial crime, failure, and acceptance of mistakes are his road to overcoming his ego, as well as self discovery. It is after all this that Raskolnikov realises his own humanity and the humanity of others. In the end, Raskolnikov conquered his ego and began to see others as equals. Egoism truly is one of the world's greatest problems. Pride spurs wars and conflict. Superiority complexes prevent the understanding of others, and often result in isolation from others and a narrow world view. As J. Petit-Senn said, "In all that surrounds him the egotist sees only the frame of his own portrait."

Q19. Establish the relation between "The Bible and Crime and Punishment"

Dosteovsky's novel Crime and Punishment depicts the Biblical account of Jesus' path to crucifixion burdened with a wooden cross through the character of Raskolnikov. After committing a cold-blooded murder he experiences mental anguish, and in a defeated state, confesses, and accepts the consequences of his crime.

Although the novel begins by focusing on the crime itself, the majority of the book discusses Raskolnikov's struggle through denial and redemption after the murder has been committed. His own "greatness" leads to his denial of God, and his attempt to suppress his conscience causes insanity and sickness. However these negative consequences force him to acknowledge his rectitude and realise his need for confession.

The prostitute, Sonya, helps Raskolnikov take a step toward redemption by discussing with him the Biblical account of Lazarus' revival from death. This scene depicts his inability to comprehend Sonya's God, and epitomizes his refusal to cling to a higher being. Raskolnikov's incessant pursuit of hindering Sonya's faith characterized the frustration and struggle he experienced because of spiritual issues. However, his path to confession progressed during their conversation because of his hidden desire to understand Sonya's faith. With her aid, he took a step toward redemption foreshadowing her action in raising him from the "dead." Sonya pleads with him to wear her cross and confess to his heinous crime. However, he refuses to accept this burden. This directly parallels with Jesus' refusal to die before his proper time.

The climax of the novel takes place after Raskolnikov's realization and acceptance of his consequences. He visits Sonya and receives her cross. Through this action, he accepts punishment and ironically, his life. This gift's benefactor, Sonya, carries significance in this allusion to the Bible. Sonya, a sinner through the world's eyes, bestows her cross on Raskolnikov. In addition, she gives him the strength to live again. Jesus was given the cross to carry by the people, sinners by definition of the Bible. By his actions, he gave life back to the people that condemned him to death.

Raskolnikov's tread to police headquarters for confession paralleled Jesus' trudge to crucifixion with his cross. By kissing the ground before he confessed, Raskolnikov showed humility just as Jesus did on his journey to Calvary adorned in a crown of thorns.

Raskolnikov's confession causes a transformation in his character. Through his suffering, the burden of greatness lifts off of his shoulders, enabling him to recover and move on with his life. Jesus lay exanimate in his tomb for three days before he was alive again; Raskolnikov's recovery also took time, and months passed before he was vibrant and fully "raised from the dead."

Q20. Confer the "Theories of Porfiry" in Crime and Punishment.

Raskolnikov commits a murder. He has a theory. Porfiry is an investigator. He too has a theory. Porfiry's is getting closer and closer to winning. Porfiry Petrovich believes many things about criminal nature—and therefore he believes these things will happen to Raskolnikov, the man that he has pinned as the perpetrator or the murder. He uses the comparison of a butterfly moving closer to a candle, the fact that if he lets the criminal wallow in mixed freedom and terror he will be able to complete a mathematical proof of the crime, and that the criminal's best move is to tell the truth, during which endeavor he will ultimately lie and fumble his plan. Perhaps Porfiry Petrovich is an excellent wax maker. He also has some very powerful and resilient matches. He uses these skills to light and let burn a candle that keeps Raskolnikov coming to him, so far twice, on the naive pretense of seeing about his father's watch. We know that Raskolnikov no longer has any care for things in the material world. He deposits all that he stole under a rock. He gave Katerina's family 25 roubles. Money and goods are not a concern for Raskolnikov. He is there because of the undeniable force of the light which Porfiry is relentlessly shining on him. Raskolnikov fits this aspect of Porfiry's theory expertly. Unlike Porfiry did to Raskolnikov's theory, Raskolnikov can find no holes to pick in Porfiry's.

Descartes believed that mathematics was the only thing that really existed with certainty besides his own existence, his own mind. Porfiry strongly believes in the benefit of having a "mathematical" proof in order to determine the guilty nature of a suspect. Like Descartes, Porfiry is able to doubt all things, such as circumstantial evidence and inclination, in order to await the completion and realization of a "mathematical formula" that leads directly to the true perpetrator of the crime. Porfiry's equation though is not yet balanced.

This is why Raskolnikov is still spared for a time. The eventual arrival of Nikolay disrupts this drive to develop a concrete mathematical theory for Porfiry. Porfiry believes that a criminal best defence is to continue telling the truth in all matters that he may without giving away everything. He holds that this is a benefit to the criminal for a time, until he slips up, lies, and must double back on what he has said. Then this policy becomes an advantage for the investigator. Porfiry then has the upper hand. All of these things make up the crux of Porfiry's theory with which he pursues the truth about Raskolnikov.

Resurrection of Lazarus in Crime and Punishment

In Dostoevsky's Crime and Punishment, Raskalnikov undergoes a period of extreme psychological upheaval. By comparing this death and rebirth of Raskalnikov's psyche to the story of the resurrection of Lazarus, Dostoevsky emphasizes not only the gravity of his crimes, but also the importance of acceptance of guilt.

From the moment when Raskalnikov murders the old woman, his personality begins to change drastically. Dostoevsky challenges the reader to understand the madness which ensues by first demonstrating that the ideas and convictions to which Raskalnikov clung died along with the women. While the reader struggles with this realization,

Dostoevsky incorporates the Biblical legend of Lazarus as a symbolic mirror for Raskalnikov's mind. By connecting the two, the reader encounters the foreshadowing of a rebirth of morals and beliefs, though what form this may assume remains cryptic. As references to Lazarus continue to occur, the feeling of parallelism increases in intensity. Just as Raskalnikov slowly struggled through madness, Lazarus lay dying of a terrible disease. When Lazarus eventually dies, Raskalnikov mimes this by teetering on the edge of insanity, the death of the mind.

Eventually Sonya begins to pull Raskalnikov back to reality by relieving a portion of his guilt. As his Christ figure, she accomplishes this by providing the moral and spiritual sturdiness which Raskalnikov lost after his debasement during the murders. Sonya affects him not by active manipulation, but via her basic character, just as Christ personified his beliefs through the manner in which he lived his life. No matter what Raskalnikov says or does to her, she accepts it and looks to God to forgive him, just as Jesus does in the Bible. This eventually convinces Raskalnikov that what he did was in fact a crime and that he must repent for it and" seek atonement".

Through this realization, Raskalnikov decides he must redeem himself not only in the eyes of the law, but in the eye of God as well. By foreswearing his old philosophy and accepting his guilt, Raskalnikov again mirrors Lazarus's acceptance of Jesus as his savior. While Lazarus accepts his new life through his rebirth, Raskalnikov acknowledges his guilt and therefore allows his mind to begin life anew.

Raskalnikov's symbolic gesture of accepting Sonya's cross reinforces and clarifies his link to Lazarus. Raskalnikov's final realization of his love for Sonya summarizes the moral of the Christian philosophy that through love of Christ comes eternal life. This final act allows a definite conclusion to both the tale of Lazarus and the story of Raskalnikov. By withholding the ultimate destination of Raskalnikov's life, Dostoevsky keeps the foreshadowing mostly obscure until both the reader and Raskalnikov are prepared to accept all of its ramifications.

Q21. Analyse the term Capital Punishment with reference to Crime and Punishment.

Putting to death people judged to have committed certain extremely terrible crimes is a practice of ancient standing, but in the United States in the second half of the twentieth century, it has become a very controversial issue. Changing views on this difficult issue led the Supreme Court to abolish capital punishment in 1972 but later upheld it in 1977. Although capital punishment is what the people want, there are many voices raised against it. People all over the country debate this issue quite frequently. They question the deterrent effect, morality, executions of innocents, and many more. I have heard a lot about the death penalty and feel that the arguments against it are not at all convincing.

Some people argue that capital punishment is morally wrong. They feel that killing some one for their crime is murder. In any dictionary it states that murder is the unlawful act of killing. Since capitol punishment is within the law it is not murder. Also if an execution is murder then prison is kidnapping and charging taxes is extortion. There is a difference between crime and punishment. Are police officers wrong for speeding to enforce the speeding laws? No. They also say that we should value all human life. Even the most despicable. It is because we value human life so much that we put such a terrible consequence for taking it.

One argument states that the death penalty does not deter people from murdering. To abolish capital punishment on this basis would be way off base. You would also have to get rid of prisons because they do not keep people from committing crimes also. Texas A&M University collected data and the results are horrifying. In 1960 there were 56 executions and 9,140 murders. In 1964 there were 15 executions and 9, 250 murders. In 1969 there were no executions and 14,590 murders. Seven more years without executions and there was 20,510 murders. As you can see the deterrent effect is there and works very well.

As you can see the death penalty is for the common good and it saves lives. People out there say that the death penalty is wrong, but usually they do not have all of the facts. They have only looked at the "good" parts instead of the whole picture. To do this is wrong. In order to form an opinion one must look into the facts themselves and form their own opinion instead of someone else's. A crime is only as severe as the punishment that follows it. As Edward Koch once said, "It is by exacting the highest penalty for the taking of human life that we affirm the highest value of human life."

Q22. The Rejection of Svidrigailov in Crime and Punishment. Explicate.

Crime and Punishment Raskolnikov would reject Svidrigailov because he knows that this man has designs against his sister. Dounia has been his main concern for the past couple chapters-he hounds Svidrigailov not because he enjoys his company, but he worries endlessly about his intentions. Svidrigailov and Raskolnikov at the bar engage in a conversation about Dounia and the interactions of her and he at the house of Marfa Petrovna. Raskolnikov is eventually duped by the base Svid., and he lets him be after he has jumped on a carriage and is speeding down the road-he is not going to the Islands though, he is coming back and has a meeting scheduled with Dounia. Svidrigailov, like Porfiry, employs tacit and devious tactics. Raskolnikov realises this, and he resents Svidrigailov for this. There is another very important reason why Raskolnikov hates Svid. As Hobbes pointed out, if a person knows that another man knows the truth about a lie he is telling, or is in the position to find out such information, he will subsequently hate that person no matter what previous relation they were in. This hate and dislike can be repressed, but even then it still has the ability to come out in a deluge of rejection.

Raskolnikov, so far, has been able to repress his anger towards Svidrigailov and also Porfiry. He does scream at Porfiry to either arrest him or let him be, but he is much less outwardly forceful with his anger. Does Svidrigailov represent Raskolnikov's evil side? Does he embody the ideas and philosophies of Raskolnikov? Perhaps it is easy to say yes-to simplify this great work of a philosophy and psychological writing. It is much better to steer away from the trap though of simply saying that he is the representation of R.'s evil side. The story is much deeper than that. Svidrigailov molests, irks, and bothers young women who do not wish to be associated with him. He panders to their weakness and self-admittedly uses deception to win them for his own. This is not Raskolnikov. Raskolnikov is the man who conceives a theory-a theory that actually had the better of society as its aim-Svid. simply exists in a nihilistic atmosphere of vice and wanton behaviour. Raskolnikov's actions, no matter how immoral, are at least thought out and conceived with care. These discrepancies prevent us from seeing Svid. as truly a manifestation of Raskolnikov's evil side. Svid. plays a much more important role. He serves to highlight Raskolnikov's good side. He serves to highlight the fact that Raskolnikov cares about his sister and is still worried about her, even though he realises his fate is practically sealed. Raskolnikov must reject Svid. because he is evil-not because he represents the evil of Svidrigailov.

Q23. Clarify The Character of Dounia.

Dounia's commitment to her brother is unfaltering. Even when she is presented with the ultimatum of Luzhin, she continues to endure in her dedication and loyalty to her irritable and rascally brother. She realises that making sure Raskolnikov is there will probably secure her fate in that she will not marry Luzhin. She refuses to do so though if he does not accept his brother. Dounia's commitment and loyalty can be seen in her calm nature about the letter, her loyal response to it, and her actions when she goes to visit her brother—she regards his gestures and words with guarded skepticism, but realises that he is at least "unfeigned" when grasping her hand. When Pulcheria shows Dounia the letter she doesn't let her emotions go awry, but she reads the letter like a military sergeant on the battle field, simply carrying out the next order in an entire chain. She decides that she must talk to Raskolnikov before answering Luzhin or making her decision. She stands calm and collected in face of the massive divide and rift that has now been created in her life—she has been presented with a dilemma, she is going to be forced to choose between the one she loves and the one she feels "esteems her". In the small garret of Raskolnikov, Pulcheria and Advotya go to see and confer with the now "well" Rodya. Dounia's main purpose is to give Raskolnikov the option of whether he would like to come to their house when Luzhin is there. When her brother responds that it is essentially the women's choice, Dounia is firm in her commitment that he must be there. She wishes to convince him that she is not doing it purely for his sake—but rather for her own.

Raskolnikov's chastising of her is ironic because she is only doing less blatant forms of actions he has already committed. Dounia, even after admitting that her marriage to Luzhin will help her very much, still loyally insists that Raskolnikov must be present for the meeting. She is willing to risk what she has professed is simply for her own sake. Her physical actions when she goes to visit her brother are an amalgam of compassion and skepticism. She is intelligent enough to realise that the things Raskolnikov is saying seem feigned, as if he had a script written for him. Could Razumihin be an aspiring playwright? The scenic continues to unfold with Raskolnikov taking the hand of Dounia and the two engage in a quiet, passionate rapture and recovering of their differences from the previous day. Dounia is a loving character and is extremely considerate and giving to her brother. We see in these chapters, primarily from her responses from the letter, that all of her previously perceived qualities are further confirmed.

Q24. Critically Examine The Fyodor's Work and Russian Literature.

KANT'S AESTHETICS IN DOSTOEVSKY'S NOTES FROM UNDERGROUND

by David A. Goldfarb

When we consider Dostoevsky, we tend to think first of a literature of existential despair, alienation, and a resulting amoralism. Nothing seems further from Dostoevsky than either the Idealistic aesthetics or the strict ethics of Immanuel

Kant, who is the direct object of the narrator's contempt in Dostoevsky's *Zapiski is podpol'ia*. Critics have tended to read the Underground Man's rant as a direct expression of the author's view, though it contains so many contradictions that it cannot be said to express any view, directly. I would like to step back from the text, set aside the problem of the author's intention,and read the text anew as fiction, to ask, despite the Underground Man's frequent jibes at Kant's theory of "the sublime and the beautiful" in Dostoevsky's *Notes from Underground* , is there a more profound sense in which Dostoevsky affirms Kant's theory?

Dostoevsky and Kant seem strange bedfellows, because Dostoevsky's supreme man of ressentiment, who admits of chance as a motive for action, and acts out of "spite" rather than adherence to a rigid moral imperative, appears to be the antithesis of the follower of Kant's *Groundwork of the Metaphysic of Morals*. The fundamental principle of the categorical imperative, recall, is this: "Act on that maxim which can at the same time have for its object itself as a universal law of nature" (Kant, *Groundwork*)While Kant has traditionally been criticized for the rigidity of this standard of universality, particularly in cases where seemingly universalizable beliefs come into conflict, we should note that Kant's placement of adherence to law as the highest principle embodies a regard for others that is not entailed by moral skepticism. The skeptic allows no adjudication of conflicting moral principles, because they are rooted in private sentiment, and not facts that could be subject to reason. Kant's test demands that moral principles be universalizable in form.

There seem to be two motivational principles for action suggested in the *Notes from Underground*. The one that leads us to the familiar existentialist reading is the moral skepticism of the principle, declared by the narrator to Liza in part II, that "the world can go to hell, as long as I can always have my tea". The underlying tenet here is the Humean claim that there is no rational argument against such a view, because morals are matters of sentiment rather than of fact. This is precisely the sort of ethical claim to which Kant was responding, when he proposed the test that one must "Act always on that maxim whose universality as a law you can at the same time will" (Kant, *Groundwork*). If the belief that "the world can go to hell, so long as I can always have my tea" were universal, no one would get any tea.

We cannot take this principle as stated at face value, if we want to come up with a consistent reading of the Underground Man's beliefs. If the Underground Man actually believed that "the world can go to hell, so long as I can always have my tea," he would, after all, really be Chernyshevsky's egoistic man, always directed by the motive of vygoda, "advantage," "comfort" or "pleasure." It is clear that Dostoevsky's polemic toward the end of Part I is directed against Chernyshevsky's view, so we would have to take this declaration of utilitarian egoism as a case of the narrator "lying," something he admits to having done frequently, "out of spite", or as what Mikhail Bakhtin calls the "loophole" that allows the Underground Man to contradict himself, turning his monologue into dialogue (Bakhtin). The narrator is taking up Chernyshevsky's position, here, for the purpose of beating it down elsewhere. This fact does not yet entail an acceptance of Kantian ethics, but we can certainly see that Kant and Dostoevsky have a common enemy in utilitarianism.

The Underground Man is also motivated by an aesthetic principle. If morality were the only motivation for action, after all, we would not need to worry about it. The masochistic idea that the Underground Man would break out of Chernyshevsky's "crystal palace" merely for the sake of doing so, is highly consistent with Kant's aesthetic notion that the feeling of the sublime is produced by violating the boundaries of the elegant and the useful, and that the pleasure of the sublime is one wholly unto itself, serving no other function. As Kant states it in the *Critique of Judgement*:

> The beautiful in nature is connected with the form of The object, which consists in having [definite] boundaries. The sublime, on the other hand, is to be found in a formless object, so far as in it or by occasion of it boundlessness is represented,

and yet its totality is also present to thought. Thus the beautiful seems to be regarded as the presentation of an indefinite concept of understanding, the sublime as that of a like concept of reason. Therefore the satisfaction in the one case is bound up with the representation of quality, in the other with that of quantity (Kant, *Judgement*).

The aesthetic principle of the sublime in the context of Dostoevsky has clear ethical consequences, we shall see, blurring the distinction between ethics and aesthetics.

The narrator seems to launch a direct attack against the "sublime and the beautiful," but the reader will again have to gauge whether he is "lying out of spite." In the narrator's most protracted lampoon involving Kant's aesthetic, he imagines himself having become a sentimental critic, "drinking to everything beautiful and sublime." "I would have sought out the beautiful and sublime in the nastiest, most indisputable trash," he says.

I would have become as tearful as a wet sponge. An artist, for example, has painted a portrait of. At once I drink to the artist who painted that portrait of Ge because I love everything beautiful and sublime.... I'd demand respect for myself in doing this, I'd persecute anyone who didn't pay me any respect. I'd live peacefully and die triumphantly—why, it's charming, per fectly charming! And what a belly I'd have grown by then, what a triple chin I'd have acquired, what a red nose I'd have developed.

The object of satire here is hardly Kant's theory, but the imperiousness of certain critics and their insipid appropriation of German Romantic aesthetics as a marker of unrelated social status. Notice that the expression "beautiful and sublime" in these satiric referencesappears always as hendiadys, "i prekrasnoe i vysokoe" where the items do not describe an opposition of quality and quantity, but a single sublimely beautiful thing. It seems as if, for the moment, the narrator does not even understand that there is a difference.

The narrator must be "lying," adopting a pose here, however, because his strongest argument is saved for the very

Kantian notion of a "pleasure of despair", or a masochistic, sublime pleasure in pain. For Kant,

> The feeling of the sublime is... a feeling of pain arising from the want of accordance between the aesthetical estimation of magnitude formed by the imagination and the estimation of the same formed by reason. There is at the same time a pleasure thus excited, arising from the correspondence with rational ideas of this very judgment of the inadequacy of our greatest faculty of the sense, in so far as it is a law for us to strive after these ideas (Kant, *Judgement* , my emphasis).

This feeling is once removed from the objects in question. The pain does not result from the immensity of nature itself, but the inconsistency of the imagination and reason. The pleasure results from our sense of our potential to comprehend that inconsistency. It is a feeling in the mind that results from a representation in the mind removed from reality, like Dostoevsky's dialogue itself, which Bakhtin describes as "a word about a word addressed to a word" (Bakhtin).

The difficulty that the comparison of Dostoevsky to Kant reveals is not between these two thinkers, but between Kant's ethics and Kant's aesthetics themselves: It seems that the pursuit of sublimity somehow sets aside morality. The sublime is a purely subjective feeling, while morality demands universalization in Kant. Kant compares the sublime and the beautiful, thus:

> We must seek a ground external to ourselves for the beautiful of nature, but seek it for the sublime merely in ourselves and in our attitude of thought (Kant, *Judgement*).

The feeling of the sublime is entirely internal, the painful pleasure of the apprehension (within the mind) of inconsistency between reason and imagination (within the mind). Kantian morality entails the application of will beyond the self, and the imagination of others inflicting that will onto the self in turn, externally.

Dostoevsky posits painful pleasure as a response to nature in the opposition to "consciousness" or reason. The moans of a toothache, for instance, "express the sufferer's enjoyment," the narrator says. Particularly they "express all the aimlessness of the pain which consciousness finds so humiliating, the whole system of natural laws about which you really don't give a damn, but as a result of which you're suffering nonetheless, while nature isn't". The humiliation of consciousness in the face of nature's limitlessness is exactly Kant's description of the feeling of the sublime. The sublime is the pain resulting from the failure of reason to comprehend the immensity of quantity in nature.

This feature of the sublime might in turn explain Dostoevsky's idea of the conflict between free will and "arithmetic." On the one hand, the Underground Man is making a straightforward argument that the relation of human desires to interests cannot be understood mechanistically when he states:

> You'll shout at me (if you still choose to favour me with your shouts) that no one's really depriving me of my will [in Chernyshevsky's Crystal Palace]; that they're merely attempting to arrange things so that my will, by its own free choice, will coincide with my normal interests, with the laws of nature, and with arithmetic.

But having anticipated the question, he asks in response to his imagined interlocutors, "But gentlemen, what sort of free choice will there be when it comes down to tables and arithmetic, when all that's left is two times two makes four? Two times two makes four even without my will. Is that what you call free choice?". The narrator's observation that , "Two times two makes four even without my will" really has nothing to do with the belief that desires could be rationalized. Either the Underground Man is reading Chernyshevsky too literally and becoming incoherent, or "arithmetic," here, is no longer a metaphor for the mechanistic understanding of desire, but rather the expression of an opposition between human quantities and the infinite.

"Even if man turned out to be a piano key, even if this could be demonstrated to him by natural science and pure mathematics," the narrator claims, "even then he still won't become reasonable; he'll intentionally do something to the contrary, simply out of ingratitude, merely to have his own way". That is to say, if human desires could be reduced to small rational numbers and simple ratios, the desire for sublimity would impel us to reach beyond the bounds of the known for a glimpse of the infinite. How could the rational even have meaning if we could not imagine the irrational?

Though a detailed analysis of the second part of the *Notes from Underground* is beyond the scope of this paper, we might observe that we can read it as a demonstration of the Kantian pursuit of the sublime. Each event in succession—the attempt to get thrown out of a bar, the clash with the officer on the Nevsky Prospekt, the confrontation building to the challenge of Zverkov to a duel, the abuse of Apollon, the servant, and finally the sentimental seduction of Liza that results in a treacherous rape—pushes the limits of violence and humiliation further and further. In each case the the object of the Underground Man's offense is increasingly helpless, while his psychological relation to his object is closer, increasing the depth of possible shame. He has constructed a sequence of events in which, as he states earlier, "each thing will be more repugnant than the last".

This sequential and additive violation of the moral boundaries might be taken as the moral enactment of dialogue. Each scene entails a boundary to be violated through its loophole. The state of continuous violation is a way of remaining suspended in the sublime, and in the end, the Underground Man indicates that he really does know the difference between the "beautiful and sublime," when he asks, "Which is better: cheap happiness or sublime suffering?".

Taking this problem into consideration, the Underground Man might be seen as acting not out of "spite" as he claims, but from a maxim that one ought assert the freedom of the will for its own sake, even doing harm to oneself in a world where good action would be universally regulated by appeal to Chernyshevsky's "advantage" or "self-interest." Stated this way, the problem suggests the solution that perhaps the feeling of the sublime is the source of judgement in the assessment of maxims that might serve as "universal laws" in the way Kant suggests, and ironically, that the Underground Man exemplifies Kant's aesthetic-moral principle that "[I]t is just this freedom from dependence on interested motives which constitutes the sublimity of a maxim and the worthiness of every rational subject to be a law-making member in the kingdom of ends; for otherwise he would have to be regarded as subject only to the law of nature—the law of his own needs" (Kant, *Groundwork*). The Underground man's ironic "individualism" is not about satisfying his own needs, but fulfilling the maxim of individuality for its own sake, even when his own material needs are contradicted. It is individualism without egoism.

Chapter 13

Crime and Punishment with Various Annotations

There are perhaps no more valuable publishing houses on the planet than Great Britain's *Wordsworth Editions* and America's *Dover Thrift Editions*. In an era where literature is at a low ebb, these two houses have released great works of public domain classic literature at very affordable prices- usually at anywhere from 10-50% off the prices that the same titles can be gotten at larger publishing houses. Among the great titles that I was to get from Dover was Fyodor Dostoevsky's *Crime And Punishment*, the definitive 1914 Constance Garnett translation. So much has been written about this book that I find it difficult to comprehend how so much of it is wrong- and I'm not talking about whether it's a great piece of literature or not. I am talking about the misperceptions of the religiosity in the tale's morals and the very nature of the lead character's supposed ethical reclamation.

The novel is a very good one, and compared to the crap that passes as literature these days it is a classic, however, it is not a great piece of literature. The book has too many manifest flaws, such as being far too long, far too 'talky', and most of all, aside from the belief that it's a 'Christian tract', the biggest misread of the book is that it is somehow a work of 'social realism'. Nothing could be less true- it is primarily a work of symbolism. This is evident from its title, as the very *punishment* referred to is not that of the legal variety, but that of internal guilt. Yes, when it was first published, in pre-Freudian 1866, it may have seemed a work of psychological depth, but even compared to the fiction of Anton Chekhov, just a few decades later, it is utterly Neolithic in its approach to the human psyche.

Characterization

The best example of this is that its lead character, Rodion Romanovitch Raskolnikov, is not a realistic villain, but an archetype- and really a symbol. The sound of his name connotes his being a rascal or rapscallion, and in Russian *raskolnik* even means to be divided, or schismatic. His swings between guilt and mendacious evil are better seen as devices serving the drama of the narrative than as any true portrait of a sociopath- be it a modern serial killer, a gangster, or any other form. Raskolnikov has many seeming virtues- he loves his mother and sister, he has saved people from death, he protects a young girl from a would-be john, and treats the drunken Marmeladov and his clan with respect. Yet, he also views himself as above the law of man, perhaps because of these virtues, and his undoing and seeming acceptance of Christianity by tale's end has been seen as suggesting that he has submitted only to the higher law of God, one which even Napoleonic supermen, as he fancies himself to be, must give in to. This idea of the higher man has also led to a Nietszchean interpretation of the book, even though it preceded that philosophy. Critics who hold this point of view will point to such passages as this, from Part Three, Chapter Five:

'That wasn't quite my contention,' he began simply and modestly. 'Yet I admit that you have stated it almost correctly; perhaps, if you like, perfectly so.' (It almost gave him pleasure to admit this.) 'The only difference is that I don't contend that extraordinary people are always bound to commit breaches of morals, as you call it. In fact, I doubt whether such an argument could be published. I simply hinted that an 'extraordinary' man has the right ... that is not an official right, but an inner right to decide in his own conscience to overstep ... certain obstacles, and only in case it is essential for the practical fulfillment of his idea (sometimes, perhaps, of benefit to the whole of humanity). You say that my article isn't definite; I am ready to make it as clear as I can. Perhaps I am right in thinking you want me to; very well. I maintain that if the discoveries of Kepler and Newton could not have been made known except by sacrificing the lives of one, a dozen, a hundred, or more men, Newton would have had the right, would indeed have been in duty bound ... to *eliminate* the dozen or the hundred men for the sake of making his discoveries known to the whole of humanity. But it does not follow from that that Newton had a right to murder people right and left and to steal every day in the market. Then, I remember, I maintain in my article that all ... well, legislators and leaders of men, such as Lycurgus, Solon, Mahomet, Napoleon, and so on, were all without exception criminals....'

Raskolnikov has also been seen as something of a representative of the wrongheadedness of atheistic socialism, for much of the social utilitarianism that Raskolnikov tries to rationalize his murders with are easily compared to modern Leftist intellectuals' naïve and/or nihilistic dismissal of the horrors of Lenin, Stalin, and Mao. By book's end Raskolnikov still believes his murder of the pawnbroker was justified, even after he seemingly accepts Christianity. His perverse contempt for and admiration of the pedophilic Svidrigaïlov also suggests that there are levels to Raskolnikov that Dostoevsky either chose not to plumb, or simply was incapable of realizing, either within his own art or in the realities of his time, for much of the book reads as a complex morality play, rather than the realistic unfolding of a crime and its aftermath.

His love, Sonia, is the classic hooker with a heart of gold. Why she feels anything positive for Raskolnikov is never made clear, save the redemptive power of Christ, which she holds out to him, in the form of her cross. Dostoevsky also makes an interesting dramatic choice to portray her on a somewhat morally equivalent level with a murderer. This may have seemed realistic in its Victorian day, but now it can only be read symbolically, as her inhuman, in the best sense, decency-

from prostituting herself for her family, to her boundless forgiveness- makes her a symbol, not a character with any footing in reality. If she is a counterpart to Raskolnikov, so is Dounia, his sister. Where he is self-centred, cruel, and an intellectual boor, she is selfless, kind, and almost as compassionate as Sonia. She is, in fact, the only realistic major and female character in the novel. Only her brother's friend, Razumikhin, is nearly as realistically variegated- but only in his displays of intellect, not in his actions, and her marriage to him at the end of the book is therefore an appropriate and realistic love, unlike Raskolnikov's and Sonia's.

If the two younger women are counterparts of a sort to Raskolnikov, then Svidrigaïlov is both his doppelganger and mitigator. He is clearly the representation of an evil that Dostoevsky sees as even worse than his lead murderer's, which makes his eventual suicide the only way for his character to end, for even in death he needs to 'sin'. Yet, he is not as evil as Raskolnikov, for after Svidrigaïlov foresees a descent into irredeemable pedophilia, he does bring justice upon himself, while even after being imprisoned Raskolnikov still clings to his beliefs of his and others' possible superiority to man's laws, even as he mouths Christian banalities to the world and Sonia. We see this recapitulated even in their actions, as well. Svidrigaïlov acknowledges he will never have Dounia, after he gives up on raping her, while Raskolnikov clings to his belief that Alyona Ivanovna's murder is justifiable.

Themes

Many believe that the primary themes of *Crime And Punishment* are either the redemptive power of Christianity, or, more generally, faith in higher powers, while others contend that it is alienation. While I believe Dostoevsky primarily was attempting to work those themes within his allegory, clearly, since Raskolnikov is not redeemed fundamentally, there needs to be a reassessment of these two dominant claims. The very thinness of Raskolnikov's presumed prison conversion, in the epilogues, argues powerfully against the pro-religion posit for the book, but the alienation theme is harder to deny, so I shall not. I will only claim that alienation is not the primary theme. I would argue that the main theme of the book is the immutability of the fundaments of a human being. In short, none of the characters undergoes any significant growth in the novel. Raskolnikov seemingly becomes merely a more devious manipulator. Sonia becomes even more selfless, giving up her youth for her family, and the rest of her life to save a man she may not even truly love. Raskolnikov's mother is a rather underdeveloped character, but all the rest of the minor actors in the book are clearly either caricatures, or representative of a fundamental stasis that Dostoevsky- or, rather this work (as I would have to compare it to his other works)- subscribes to. Marmeladov is a drunk, and that's it. Alyona, despite being murdered, is correctly diagnosed by Raskolnikov as a social leech. Even Porfiry Petrovitch, the detective who hounds Raskolnikov, shows no subtlety.

Despite his failures, he continues to assail Raskolnikov by appealing to guilt, whereas Raskolnikov is finally undone by Sonia- but not for his guilt. Rather, he confesses to manifestly gain something- that is her loyalty and companionship, even though Lizaveta, the other murder victim, was a friend of hers. The epilogues make it abundantly clear that Raskolnikov is in the process of learning how to game the 19th Century Russian legal system to his advantage, and the love of Bible thumping woman, even an ex-prostitute, can do no harm. Only his sister, Dounia, and her eventual husband, Razumihin, show even the barest signs of personal growth- to borrow that modern buzz phrase. While alienation is a theme, it is unresolved at the book's end, as Raskolnikov is still scheming, whereas, since that is clearly his essential nature, the more powerful argument is that people are fixed into their essences at a certain age, and very little can be done to alter that state of being.

Psychology, especially in the almost proto-embryonic form that it is portrayed in this novel, is also seen as a major theme, given that, despite the title, the two titular nouns are separated by hundreds of pages of Raskolnikov's inner angst. The murders and their effects and ramifications to anyone other than Raskolnikov are of little concern to Dostoevsky. This is clear, as in this scene where Raskolnikov rationalizes to Sonia in Part Five, Chapter Four:

'Whether I can step over barriers or not, whether I dare stoop to pick up or not, whether I am a trembling creature or whether I have the right....'

'To kill? Have the right to kill?' Sonia clasped her hands.

'Ach, Sonia!' he cried irritably and seemed about to make some retort, but was contemptuously silent. 'Don't interrupt me, Sonia. I want to prove one thing only, that the devil led me on then and he has shown me since that I had not the right to take that path, because I am just such a louse as all the rest. He was mocking me and here I've come to you now! Welcome your guest! If I were not a louse, should I have come to you? Listen: when I went then to the old woman's I only went to try....You may be sure of that!'

'And you murdered her!'

'But how did I murder her? Is that how men do murders? Do men go to commit a murder as I went then? I will tell you some day how I went! Did I murder the old woman? I murdered myself, not her! I crushed myself once for all, for ever....But it was the devil that killed that old woman, not I. Enough, enough, Sonia, enough! Let me be!' he cried in a sudden spasm of agony, 'let me be!'

Having had intimate knowledge of the inner workings of many sorts of criminal minds, however, I can clearly state, with no fear of contradiction, that Raskolnikov is almost a laughably absurd mélange of criminal aspects, and clearly not a realistic character. More to the point he is a bunch of hypotheses tossed into a stew of a character. Yes, he doubts himself, reinforces, suffers fainting spells and deliria, and might be classed as a manic depressive or schizophrenic, given his desire to best Petrovitch and the others whom he feels are on to him, to prove his superiority, alternating with his great despair. Yet, Dostoevsky clearly posits the idea that Raskolnikov's guilt is a far greater punishment than that the legal system could dispense, for that is the raison d'être of the tale, and here is where Raskolnikov's schism and unreality as a character comes into play. Dostoevsky cannot seem to decide whether Raskolnikov is a good person with a conscience, who was merely misguided, or an amoral sociopath, and therefore ends up with a character who is convincingly neither.

By splitting the difference between the two possibilities he delivers a flawed character (literarily), not merely a character with flaws. This error in Dostoevsky's construction of Raskolnikov is manifested in the upsmanship games Petrovitch and Raskolnikov play. A true sociopath would fly by the claims and not be bothered in the least, yet a truly repentant individual would not have taken hundreds of pages to crack- albeit it is arguable whether that is the correct term, since he seems to be using both Sonia and the legal system to his advantage. Whether Dostoevsky would have conceived of and executed a more realistic protagonist/antihero were *Crime And Punishment* written today I do not know, but that, of course, has nothing to do with what must be dealt with in the actual novel.

PART I

CHAPTER 1

We meet Rodion Romanovitch Raskolnikov, a handsome college student in St. Petersburg, with a big ego, who is endebted to his landlady, Praskovya Pavlovna, and selling to an old pawnmistress, named Alyona Ivanovna. Much in the fashion of the later real life Leopold and Loeb, he plans the pawnbroker's murder, just to see if he could do it. Yet, he is repulsed by himself and goes to a bar.

CHAPTER 2

Raskolnikov meets Semyon Zakharovitch Marmeladov, who tells him he lost his job for drinking, but got it back. Marmeladov mentions his wife's beating a month ago by a man named Andrey Semyonovitch Lebeziatnikov, and admits he is afraid to go home and face his wife, Katerina

Ivanovna Marmeladov, for he drank all their money. He says their oldest daughter, Sofya Semyonovna Marmeladov (also called Sonia), has been forced into prostitution. Raskolnikov takes Marmeladov home and sees the family's low state. He leaves some money on their windowsill, despite his own debts.

CHAPTER 3

Raskolnikov goes to his flat. A maid, Nastasya Petrovna, tells him his landlady is filing a complaint because he owes rent. His mother, Pulcheria Alexandrovna Raskolnikov, writes him of his sister, Avdotya Romanovna Raskolnikov (also called Dounia). She worked as a tutor for the Svidrigaïlov clan. The father, Arkady Ivanovitch Svidrigaïlov, is an amoral cad, who tried to seduce Dounia, but failed, and may have been behind some deaths. Svdrigailov's wife, Marfa Petrovna Svdrigailov, spread rumors about Dounia about town, then recanted. Dounia will marry Pyotr Petrovich Luzhin in St. Petersburg, and she and Dounia will visit him soon. She wants Raskolnikov to work with Luzhin. Raskolnikov is not pleased.

CHAPTER 4

Raskolnikov decides he must stop Dounia's wedding. He thinks Dounia is prostituting herself to her future husband. He meets a drunken underage girl, approached by a man. He gets a cop to protect the girl, then decides to leave them be. Raskolnikov will visit an old college chum, Dmitri Prokofitch Razumihin.

CHAPTER 5

Raskolnikov delays his visit to Razumihin until after he murders the pawnbroker. He dreams he is seven, visiting his mother's grave with his father. Drunken peasants attack a wagon and kill a horse. Raskolnikov thinks this is about his murder plot. He is not deterred, though, and finds out when Lizaveta Ivanovna, Alyona's retarded sister who lives with her, will be gone.

CHAPTER 6

Raskolnikov rationalizes his coming crime by recalling a hypothetical where students he knew discussed the ethics of killing Alyona, to use her riches to do good. He reckons many good acts outweigh one crime and she and her kind prey off the vulnerable. Her money will aid him to become a man of consequence who will benefit humanity. Raskolnikov believes criminals get caught because of a 'disease of will' and he will not be weighed down by it. He gets to Alyona's apartment at 7:30 pm, later than planned. Despite his rationales, he is panicky.

CHAPTER 7

Raskolnikov murders Alyona with an ax. He tries to find money, to make it seem a robbery. But his lateness means Lizaveta returns and sees him. He kills her, too. He panics and tries to clean the scene. Two visitors ring the doorbell. The door is locked from the inside, so they leave to get help, allowing Raskolnikov's escape. He gets home and falls asleep.

Summary

Dramatically, we get a good portrait of a confused young man. But, in terms of real world psychology the portrait is hopelessly outdated and antiquated. Raskolnikov is clearly a psychopath, or sociopath, by modern nomenclature, and the acts he commits, yet his actions do not show this. Does he kill because he is amoral, or because of a twisted sense of morals? It is always stated in most criticism that he kills for a political or philosophical reason, yet it is just as plausible to posit that he kills to protect his sister. Later, in Part Five, Chapter Four, he tells Sonia, '*I will try to manage somehow to put it to my mother and sister so that they won't be frightened....My sister's future is secure, however, now, I believe....and my mother's must be too....Well, that's all.*' He does not want his sister to marry a man he disapproves of, and requires money to forestall that outcome. Thus, another motive for his killings, and one never touched upon in criticism. Yet, read this section describing the murder of Alyona, from Part One, Chapter Seven:

The old woman was as always bareheaded. Her thin, light hair, streaked with grey, thickly smeared with grease, was plaited in a rat's tail and fastened by a broken horn comb which stood out on the nape of her neck. As she was so short, the blow fell on the very top of her skull. She cried out, but very faintly, and suddenly sank all of a heap on the floor, raising her hands to her head. In one hand she still held 'the pledge.' Then he dealt her another and another blow with the blunt side and on the same spot. The blood gushed as from an overturned glass, the body fell back. He stepped back, let it fall, and at once bent over her face; she was dead. Her eyes seemed to be starting out of their sockets, the brow and the whole face were drawn and contorted convulsively.

He laid the axe on the ground near the dead body and felt at once in her pocket (trying to avoid the streaming body)—the same right-hand pocket from which she had taken the key on his last visit. He was in full possession of his faculties, free from confusion or giddiness, but his hands were still trembling. He remembered afterwards that he had been particularly collected and careful, trying all the time not to get smeared with blood....

Not only is there a schism in the lead character, as represented by his name, but there is a schism in Dostoevsky and his handling of the scene. Is he a sociopath (*He was in full possession of his faculties, free from confusion or giddiness....*) or is he a bumbling man with misguided morals? He clearly is one or the other, for they cannot be mutually coexistent, and a third choice is simply not dictated by the descriptions of Raskolnikov, nor modern criminal psychology. Here is also where some of the confusion comes in regarding the supposed later intervention of religion as an ameliorative. Clearly, although *Crime And Punishment* was written to seem realistic, as a work of art in the 21st Century we have to view it primarily on symbolic or mythic terms, for Raskolnikov is clearly not acting in believable and known human ways- normal nor aberrant. Another failure comes in Raskolnikov's conversation with Marmeladov- it is far too long, could have been pared to its essence, to give the illusion of 'reality' while coring into the offhand poetry that all people stumble upon on occasion.

This tendency to go on and on occurs in almost all the conversational scenes, and Dostoevsky's desire to hammer manifest points home to a reader is one of the great flaws of this book, and all Russian literature- this over-didacticism, and need to wallow in despair. Some say that Dostoevsky captures everyday speech patterns, and he does, at times- but a work of art is not reality, and he gives far too much of the banality and irrelevancy of the colloquial, when well-chosen nuggets would have sufficed. Yet, for every droning overly long unnecessary conversation that is boringly 'real', there is another that is almost Shakespearean in its soliloquizing. These are characters of the lowest classes, who cannot even make the most basic decisions for themselves, yet they are apt to spout apothegms clearly beyond their intellectual ability to grasp. This is more evidence that they are not meant to be 'real', merely act as symbols. Yet, the first section is by far the best in the book.

PART II

CHAPTER 1

Raskolnikov wakes and is angry with himself for his blunders and fears discovery. Nastasya comes into his room with a cop, and a summons. He thinks the summons is a trick to get him to confess, and mocks the interrogator at the station, who only wanted him to sign an IOU for the money owed his landlady. As he leaves he overhears a conversation about the murders and passes out. He wakes and feels they suspect him.

CHAPTER 2

Raskolnikov hides the stolen money under a large rock. He finally visits Razumihin, who offers him a translating job he turns down. Raskolnikov is in a daze and almost run down by a coach. An old woman pities him and gives him money. He tosses it away. Once home he thinks he hears Ilya Petrovich, a cop, beating his landlady. Nastasya tells him he is sick and hallucinating.

CHAPTER 3

Raskolnikov is febrile and forgets the murder. Razumihin is taking care of him, and some money comes from a stranger. Raskolnikov fears others know he is guilty, and considers leaving for America.

CHAPTER 4

A doctor, Zossimov, and police investigator, Petrovich, talk of the murder with Razumihin and Raskolnikov. Some house painters, Dimitri and Nikolai Dementiev, have been accused of the murders.

CHAPTER 5

Luzhin sees Raskolnikov. Raskolnikov dislikes him, but Luzhin ignores it. Luzhin has made arrangements for Dounia's and Pulcheria's visit. Raskolnikov hears all of Alyona's pawn customers are suspects. Razumihin claims the murderer was a novice. Raskolnikov and Luzhin argue violently and Luzhin takes offense.

CHAPTER 6

Raskolnikov leaves his apartment despite illness. He reads newspapers and meets Alexander Grigorievitch Zametov, a cop and friend of Razumihin, who agrees an amateur committed the murders. Raskolnikov then talks of the perfect execution of the murder and theft, the way he did it. He asks Zametov if he could be the murderer, but Zametov does not believe it. Raskolnikov takes off and sees a woman attempt to drown herself. He aims to confess and heads to the police station.

CHAPTER 7

On his way to the police station, Raskolnikov finds Marmeladov run over by a carriage. Raskolnikov brings him back to his apartment and calls for a doctor. Sonia comes in dressed as a prostitute, and Marmeladov dies in her arms. Raskolnikov gives Katerina twenty rubles and asks Polenka Marmeladov, the youngest daughter, to pray for him. The doctor, Zossimov, believes Raskolnikov might be insane. Raskolnikov goes home, and his mother and sister are waiting for him.

Summary

This section documents Raskolnikov's recovery from his depravity. The cracks are already beginning to appear in his rationalizations, and his actions are clearly that of a guilty person. There are some nice touches within this section, but paring is needed.

PART 3

CHAPTER 1

Raskolnikov says he won't allow Dounia to marry Luzhin. She's grateful to Razumihin for helping Raskolnikov. Razumihin and Zossimov find Dounia attractive.

CHAPTER 2

Razumihin visits Dounia and Pulcheria. He tells them of Raskolnikov's life. They show him a letter from Luzhin requesting Raskolnikov not be present at their first meeting.

CHAPTER 3

Dounia and her mother visit Raskolnikov, and find him offputting. Raskolnikov realises he can't speak freely without confessing his crime. Raskolnikov believes Dounia is a prostitute and demands she dump Luzhin.

CHAPTER 4

Sonia asks Raskolnikov to come to Marmeladov's funeral. Dounia and Luzhin argue. She and her mother leave. Raskolnikov tells Razumihin he wants to speak with Petrovich the detective. Sonia leaves and a man follows her to her place.

CHAPTER 5

Petrovich tells Raskolnikov he knows of his life and asks Raskolnikov about an article he wrote about crime. Raskolnikov believes there is a difference between ordinary men who must obey the law, and extraordinary men who can break it under certain circumstances, what he calls 'bloodshed by conscience.' Petrovich tries to trick Raskolnikov into an admission.

CHAPTER 6

Raskolnikov and Razumihin discuss Petrovich. A stranger tells Raskolnikov he knows Raskolnikov is the murderer. Raskolnikov rationalizes the murder, and dismisses the stranger's claim. He dreams he tries to kill Alyona but she does not die, and laughs at him. He wakes, and Svidrigaïlov is standing in his doorway.

Summary

The guilt starts to spread, and more of Raskolnikov's past comes to life. His claims of 'bloodshed by conscience' have led many to view the novel as a pre-Nietzschean document, even though the claims of classist superiority long predated the book. Too much backgrounding of minor characters occurs, and this causes the novel to lose its focus at times, with no counterbalance of enhanced realism, nor narrative depth.

PART IV

CHAPTER 1

Svidrigaïlov appears to Raskolnikov to be that extraordinary man he wants to be. Svidrigaïlov came to St. Petersburg because of Dounia. He offers to pay her 10,000 rubles if she won't marry Luzhin.

CHAPTER 2

Luzhin and Dounia break up. Razumihin defends Dounia.

CHAPTER 3

Raskolnikov leaves responsibility for his family to Razumihin. He has found the right man to take care of his family.

CHAPTER 4

Raskolnikov goes to Sonia, and taunts her. Sonia's faith emerges in the narrative. She reads of Lazarus in a Bible Lizaveta gave her. Raskolnikov tells her he knows who committed the murder. Svidrigaïlov eavesdrops.

CHAPTER 5

Raskolnikov and Petrovich again play a game of wits. Petrovich almost gets a confession from Raskolnikov, but is interrupted.

CHAPTER 6

Nikolay, a house painter at Lizaveta's and Alyona's home, confesses to the murder, along with his partner Dimitri. Raskolnikov learns the witness Petrovich had was the stranger who accused him of the murders. Petrovich was bluffing.

Summary

This section is the one, above all others, which has led to misinterpretations of the novel. The long conversations with Svidrigaïlov, Sonia, and Petrovich, have led to much of the imbuing of religion and amorality into the work. Seen symbolically, though, the conversations are little more than plot devices to move along what is, in essence, not a whodunit, but a willhegetawaywithit. They could be trimmed severely to benefit the novel's power.

PART V

CHAPTER 1

Luzhin gives ten rubles to Marmeladov's family. Lebeziatnikov compliments Luzhin on his kindness.

CHAPTER 2

Katerina has a funeral banquet and invites everyone she knows. She feels insulted by who shows up and argues with her landlady.

CHAPTER 3

Luzhin accuses Sonia of stealing a hundred rubles he plants on her. Lebeziatnikov proves Sonia's innocence. Luzhin leaves in disgrace. Katerina is evicted after her landlady gets involved in a melee.

CHAPTER 4

Raskolnikov confesses his crime to Sonia. Sonya asks him to ask for forgiveness but he refuses her cross and suggestion. She loves him and promises to follow him to Siberia. Svidrigaïlov eavesdrops again.

CHAPTER 5

Lebeziatnikov tells Sonia Katerina and her children are on the streets. Sonia finds them and Katerina collapses and dies. Svidrigaïlov offers financial help. Raskolnikov is still haunted and learns Svidrigaïlov knows his secret.

Summary

This section strays too much from the main character, Raskolnikov, as Dostoevsky attempts to widen his 'realistic' palette. Unfortunately, given the symbolism throughout, this section really adds little to the book, and a good editor would have excised it, and scattered the few key moments through the preceding and proceeding sections. Save for Raskolnikov's confession, and Svidrigaïlov's manipulations, this section is a totally needless digression.

PART VI

CHAPTER 1

Raskolnikov again asks Razumihin to look after his family. Dounia gets a letter from Svidrigaïlov and goes to meet him. Petrovich confronts Raskolnikov, who remains calm.

CHAPTER 2

Petrovich again tries to ensnare Raskolnikov by explaining why Nikolay and Dimitri could not have committed the crime and offers him a chance to confess.

CHAPTER 3

Raskolnikov leaves Petrovich and sees Svidrigaïlov drinking with a prostitute. He threatens Svidrigaïlov not to see Dounia.

CHAPTER 4

Raskolnikov and Svidrigaïlov converse. Svidrigaïlov tells Raskolnikov about his wife Marfa, his lustful obsession with Dounia, possible pedophilia, and other crimes.

CHAPTER 5

Svidrigaïlov tricks Dounia into going to his apartment. He tells her Raskolnikov is the murderer and tries to blackmail her- his silence for her body. Dounia is shocked, and tries to leave. Svidrigaïlov has locked the door and threatens to rape her. She takes a gun and shoots him twice, but misses. The third time, at close range, she refuses to kill him. Svidrigaïlov realises she'll never love him, and lets her go.

CHAPTER 6

Svidrigaïlov gives money to Sonia for her trip to Siberia with Raskolnikov, then has a perverse sexual dream about a five year old girl. He decides to kill himself before his descent to evil is complete.

CHAPTER 7

Raskolnikov confesses to Dounia. He goes to Sonia, then confesses his crimes in public.

CHAPTER 8

Raskolnikov accepts Sonia's cross. He asks forgiveness of God and confesses his crimes to the police. Sonia sticks by him.

Summary

This section is seen as a bolster to the idea that the book is a paean to the redemptive power of religion- specifically Christianity, but really this section serves as a sort of mitigation of Raskolnikov vis-à-vis Svidrigaïlov, who even commits a sin, suicide, to escape his evil. Yet the two epilogues, which are mostly unnecessary, tying up ends of minor plot points, and very deleterious to the overall work, make it clear that Raskolnikov is not saved, and merely an actor, and a better one than even he might have suspected. He still does not accept that his murder of the pawnbroker was evil. He also is likely using Sonia, for he has already deemed her a moral suicide for her prostitution, despite her faith, which means using her is not a transgression. They also demean much of the superior portions of the novel by trivializing it with specious moralizing, as well the discussed flaws in its attempt to delve into the mind of a murderer.

Assessment

If Dostoevsky's novel can be considered great, by some, it is not because of the things he intended within it that manifest its greatness, but that which was unwitting, and beyond him at the time, such as the real key to understanding the work, its great insight, that people do not change at a fundamental level. I was recently watching the *Up* documentary film series, by Michael Apted, on DVD, and those films are premised on the very notion that *Crime And Punishment* is, the Jesuit saying of '*Give me the child till he is seven, and I shall give you the man.*' We do not glimpse Raskolnikov at seven, but given what we know becomes of him it is not difficult to extrapolate that he was as amoral then as his twenty something self appears in the book. If Dostoevsky intended this work to be an allegory on Christianity's redemptive power he clearly failed, so I posit that that was not his intent at all, and that the psychological and ethical stasis of most human beings was his major theme.

Regardless, the book is not a great piece of art. It contains great moments, some brilliant writing, and is a *very good* work of art, however primitive, but it is certainly not great. A modern reader can simply not ignore all its manifest flaws, such as the awkward and heavy-handed symbolism, the stilted and unrealistic dialogue, which reinforces the truth of the characters' symbolism, as it veers between mawkishness during some of the death scenes and Raskolnikov's several confession scenes, and preachiness in many of the philosophical engagements. Again, these characters are uneducated plebes, for the most part, yet they often speak like high philosophes. This undermines the claims to realism in the novel. More problems arise with the over-usage of 'coincidence' to propel the plot along, as if it were a fifth rate soap opera. Just how many times do people overhear things accidentally, or eavesdrop, or dramatically appear to someone out of the dark? Here is the first such instance:

> There are chance meetings with strangers that interest us from the first moment, before a word is spoken. Such was the impression made on Raskolnikov by the person sitting a little distance from him, who looked like a retired clerk. The young man often recalled this impression afterwards, and even ascribed it to presentiment. He looked repeatedly at the clerk, partly no doubt because the latter was staring persistently at him, obviously anxious to enter into conversation.

This is rather well written, and a canny observation that holds true. But, this is from Part One, Chapter Two. The dozen or more times such encounters subsequently occur stretch the realistic point past breaking. Such wanton over-usage of coincidence is a sure sign that there is an over-reliance on plot over characterization. Another problem is the typically Russian overuse of meditation on a small or single event or thing. Like Tolstoy, Dostoevsky tends to go far too deeply into minor things, while American writers, even the past Masters, tend to skim surfaces- a happy medium is needed in these classics. Of the major Russian Masters, only Chekhov seemed to learn the value of concision. The book could easily lose 150 of the few pages in my volume, and not lose a single scene. In short, most of the writing has flab that is inessential. Dostoevsky's shifts between first person subjective and third person omniscient narration also drag the plot down, and reveal far too much extraneous information that a first person subjective narrative could not have revealed, for the better.

On the minor side, Dostoevsky also makes a big error in his use of character names. First, rather than merely using the characters' first names he uses their first, middle, surnames, and familiar names in different combinations, as well as multiple nicknames, which often confuse readers into not knowing who is doing what, since many of the names are similar, or exactly the same, even if the characters are not related.

Secondly, while the use of symbolism for the main character is fine, Dostoevsky goes overboard in the use of symbolism for minor characters. Among the many examples are Razumihin (intellect or reason), Zametov (he who notices), Marmeladov (which connotes a sort of candy or marmalade), and Luzhin (from *luzha,* which means a puddle). Svidrigaïlov is apparently the name of a wicked medieval prince from a Russian fairy tale.

Another problem with the work, one not in the actual work, but in its willful misinterpretation by critics with axes to grind, is that, aside from the confusion over the literary value of the work, all the poor theories regarding psychology and the fundaments of criminality have somehow found their way into pop culture, and done much to lead people astray in their ideas of true good and evil. Yet, the many fundamental questions that Raskolnikov deals with are never directly addressed, and are only used as a flawed premise for the main action of the novel to go off on.

Raskolnikov ponders why those who have power or mass murder in war are labeled heroes, gain fame and respect, have paeans and monuments made for them while the low born, who have to struggle with and against each other, are jailed if they kill. In Part Five, Chapter Four, he rationalizes not confessing to the murders by using this defence: 'What wrong have I done them? Why should I go to them? What should I say to them? That's only a phantom.... They destroy men by millions themselves and look on it as a virtue.

They are knaves and scoundrels, Sonia! I am not going to them. And what should I say to them- that I murdered her, but did not dare to take the money and hid it under a stone?' he added with a bitter smile. 'Why, they would laugh at me, and would call me a fool for not getting it. A coward and a fool! They wouldn't understand and they don't deserve to understand. Why should I go to them?'

This is a philosophically legitimate point, yet, instead of plumbing this, and applying it to the social caste he exists within, Raskolnikov flies off into mere pop sociological dementia with his ideas on supermen and exceptionalism, never realizing that exceptionalism in one or two fields, no matter how exceeding, brilliant, nor gifted, does not imply any sort of reciprocal ethical exceptionalism.

Yet, throughout the book, despite moments of brilliance, whenever Dostoevsky gets too close to the core, the nub of what the book is really about, he backs away. Whether because he lacked the answer or lacked the desire to deal with its clash with his own belief systems I do not know. But it is a flaw, and one that results in banal and bland sermonizing, such as that which ends the book in a very trite Hollywood film fashion:

He did not know that the new life would not be given him for nothing, that he would have to pay dearly for it, that it would cost him great striving, great suffering.

But that is the beginning of a new story- the story of the gradual renewal of a man, the story of his gradual regeneration, of his passing from one world into another, of his initiation into a new unknown life. That might be the subject of a new story, but our present story is ended.

To end, *Crime And Punishment* is certainly a milestone work in the development of both Dostoevsky and the art of the novel, but a work's cultural or artistic import is not equivalent to its artistic excellence. Therefore, while it may be a great representation of its time, artistically and culturally, it is not a great book- neither as a social tract nor as a novel. It reads more like a mid-stage version of better models to come, which is exactly what it really is. The very fact that such gross misreadings of it has taken root is a testament to the laziness of most readers, and the unwillingness of most to think for themselves. It is this problem with readers, their own anomic stasis, writ into the larger society, that Dostoevsky actually deals with. Raskolnikov, however, still smiles.

Chapter 14

Important Chapters from the Text

PART I

CHAPTER 1

On an exceptionally hot evening early in July a young man came out of the garret in which he lodged in S. Place and walked slowly, as though in hesitation, towards K. bridge.

He had successfully avoided meeting his landlady on the staircase. His garret was under the roof of a high, five-storied house and was more like a cupboard than a room. The landlady who provided him with garret, dinners, and attendance, lived on the floor below, and every time he went out he was obliged to pass her kitchen, the door of which invariably stood open. And each time he passed, the young man had a sick, frightened feeling, which made him scowl and feel ashamed. He was hopelessly in debt to his landlady, and was afraid of meeting her.

This was not because he was cowardly and abject, quite the contrary; but for some time past he had been in an overstrained irritable condition, verging on hypochondria. He had become so completely absorbed in himself, and isolated from his fellows that he dreaded meeting, not only his landlady, but anyone at all. He was crushed by poverty, but the anxieties of his position had of late ceased to weigh upon him. He had given up attending to matters of practical importance; he had lost all desire to do so. Nothing that any landlady could do had a real terror for him. But to be stopped on the stairs, to be forced to listen to her trivial, irrelevant gossip, to pestering demands for payment, threats and complaints, and to rack his brains for excuses, to prevaricate, to lie—no, rather than that, he would creep down the stairs like a cat and slip out unseen.

This evening, however, on coming out into the street, he became acutely aware of his fears.

"I want to attempt a thing /like that/ and am frightened by these trifles," he thought, with an odd smile. "Hm... yes, all is in a man's hands and he lets it all slip from cowardice, that's an axiom. It would be interesting to know what it is men are most afraid of. Taking a new step, uttering a new word is what they fear most.... But I am talking too much. It's because I chatter that I do nothing. Or perhaps it is that I chatter because I do nothing. I've learned to chatter this last month, lying for days together in my den thinking.. of Jack the Giant-killer. Why am I going there now? Am I capable of /that/? Is / that/ serious? It is not serious at all. It's simply a fantasy to amuse myself; a plaything! Yes, maybe it is a plaything."

The heat in the street was terrible: and the airlessness, the bustle and the plaster, scaffolding, bricks, and dust all about him, and that special Petersburg stench, so familiar to all who are unable to get out of town in summer—all worked painfully upon the young man's already overwrought nerves. The insufferable stench from the pot- houses, which are particularly numerous in that part of the town, and the drunken men whom he met continually, although it was a working day, completed the revolting misery of the picture. An expression of the profoundest disgust gleamed for a moment in the young man's refined face. He was, by the way, exceptionally handsome, above the average in height, slim, well-built, with beautiful dark eyes and dark brown hair. Soon he sank into deep thought, or more accurately speaking into a complete blankness of mind; he walked along not observing what was about him and not caring to observe it. From time to time, he would mutter something, from the habit of talking to himself, to which he had just confessed. At these moments he would become conscious that his ideas were sometimes in a tangle and that he was very weak; for two days he had scarcely tasted food.

CHAPTER 4

His mother's letter had been a torture to him, but as regards the chief fact in it, he had felt not one moment's hesitation, even whilst he was reading the letter. The essential question was settled, and irrevocably settled, in his mind: "Never such a marriage while I am alive and Mr. Luzhin be damned!" "The thing is perfectly clear," he muttered to himself, with a malignant smile anticipating the triumph of his decision. "No, mother, no, Dounia, you won't deceive me! and then they apologize for not asking my advice and for taking the decision without me! I dare say! They imagine it is arranged now and can't be broken off; but we will see whether it can or not! A magnificent excuse: 'Pyotr Petrovitch is such a busy man that even his wedding has to be in post-haste, almost by express.' No, Dounia, I see it all and I know what you want to say to me; and I know too what you were thinking about, when you walked up and down all night, and what your prayers were like before the Holy Mother of Kazan who stands in mother's bedroom. Bitter is the ascent to Golgotha.... Hm... so it is finally settled; you have determined to marry a sensible business man, Avdotya Romanovna, one who has a fortune (has /already/ made his fortune, that is so much more solid and impressive) a man who holds two government posts and who shares the ideas of our most rising generation, as mother writes, and who /seems/ to be kind, as Dounia herself observes. That /seems/ beats everything! And that very Dounia for that very '/seems/' is marrying him! Splendid! splendid!

"... But I should like to know why mother has written to me about 'our most rising generation'? Simply as a descriptive touch, or with the idea of prepossessing me in favour of Mr. Luzhin? Oh, the cunning of them! I should like to know one thing more: how far they were open with one another that day and night and all this time since? Was it all put into /words/, or did both understand that they had the same thing at heart and in their minds, so that there was no need to speak of it aloud, and better not to speak of it. Most likely it was partly like that, from mother's letter it's evident: he struck her as rude /a little/, and mother in her simplicity took her observations to Dounia. And she was sure to be vexed and 'answered her angrily.' I should think so! Who would not be angered when it was quite clear without any naïve questions and when it was understood that it was useless to discuss it. And why does she write to me, 'love Dounia, Rodya, and she loves you more than herself'? Has she a secret conscience-prick at sacrificing her daughter to her son? 'You are our one comfort, you are everything to us.' Oh, mother!"

His bitterness grew more and more intense, and if he had happened to meet Mr. Luzhin at the moment, he might have murdered him.

"Hm... yes, that's true," he continued, pursuing the whirling ideas that chased each other in his brain, "it is true that 'it needs time and care to get to know a man,' but there is no mistake about Mr. Luzhin. The chief thing is he is 'a man of business and /seems/ kind,' that was something, wasn't it, to send the bags and big box for them! A kind man, no doubt after that! But his /bride/ and her mother are to drive in a peasant's cart covered with sacking (I know, I have been driven in it). No matter! It is only ninety versts and then they can 'travel very comfortably, third class,' for a thousand versts! Quite right, too. One must cut one's coat according to one's cloth, but what about you, Mr. Luzhin? She is your bride.... And you must be aware that her mother has to raise money on her pension for the journey. To be sure it's a matter of business, a partnership for mutual benefit, with equal shares and expenses;—food and drink provided, but pay for your tobacco. The business man has got the better of them, too. The luggage will cost less than their fares and very likely go for nothing. How is it that they don't both see all that, or is it that they don't want to see? And they are pleased, pleased! And to think that this is only the first blossoming, and that the real fruits are to come! But what really matters is not the stinginess, is not the meanness, but the /tone/ of the whole thing. For that will be the tone after marriage, it's a foretaste of it. And mother too, why should she be so lavish? What will she have by the time she gets to Petersburg? Three silver roubles or two 'paper ones' as /she/ says.... that old woman... hm. What does she expect to live upon in Petersburg afterwards? She has her reasons already for guessing that she /could not/ live with Dounia after the marriage, even for the first few months.

The good man has no doubt let slip something on that subject also, though mother would deny it: 'I shall refuse,' says she. On whom is she reckoning then? Is she counting on what is left of her hundred and twenty roubles of pension when Afanasy Ivanovitch's debt is paid? She knits woollen shawls and embroiders cuffs, ruining her old eyes. And all her shawls don't add more than twenty roubles a year to her hundred and twenty, I know that. So she is building all her hopes all the time on Mr. Luzhin's generosity; 'he will offer it of himself, he will press it on me.' You may wait a long time for that! That's how it always is with these Schilleresque noble hearts; till the last moment every goose is a swan with them, till the last moment, they hope for the best and will see nothing wrong, and although they have an inkling of the other side of the picture, yet they won't face the truth till they are forced to; the very thought of it makes them shiver; they thrust the truth away with both hands, until the man they deck out in false colours puts a fool's cap on them with his own hands.

I should like to know whether Mr. Luzhin has any orders of merit; I bet he has the Anna in his buttonhole and that he puts it on when he goes to dine with contractors or merchants. He will be sure to have it for his wedding, too! Enough of him, confound him!

CHAPTER 7

The door was as before opened a tiny crack, and again two sharp and suspicious eyes stared at him out of the darkness. Then Raskolnikov lost his head and nearly made a great mistake.

Fearing the old woman would be frightened by their being alone, and not hoping that the sight of him would disarm her suspicions, he took hold of the door and drew it towards him to prevent the old woman from attempting to shut it again. Seeing this she did not pull the door back, but she did not let go the handle so that he almost dragged her out with it on to the stairs. Seeing that she was standing in the doorway not allowing him to pass, he advanced straight upon her. She stepped back in alarm, tried to say something, but seemed unable to speak and stared with open eyes at him.

"Good evening, Alyona Ivanovna," he began, trying to speak easily, but his voice would not obey him, it broke and shook. "I have come... I have brought something... but we'd better come in... to the light...."

And leaving her, he passed straight into the room uninvited. The old woman ran after him; her tongue was unloosed.

"Good heavens! What it is? Who is it? What do you want?"

"Why, Alyona Ivanovna, you know me... Raskolnikov... here, I brought you the pledge I promised the other day..." And he held out the pledge.

The old woman glanced for a moment at the pledge, but at once stared in the eyes of her uninvited visitor. She looked intently, maliciously and mistrustfully. A minute passed; he even fancied something like a sneer in her eyes, as though she had already guessed everything. He felt that he was losing his head, that he was almost frightened, so frightened that if she were to look like that and not say a word for another half minute, he thought he would have run away from her.

"Why do you look at me as though you did not know me?" he said suddenly, also with malice. "Take it if you like, if not I'll go elsewhere, I am in a hurry."

PART II

CHAPTER 2

"And what if there has been a search already? What if I find them in my room?"

But here was his room. Nothing and no one in it. No one had peeped in. Even Nastasya had not touched it. But heavens! how could he have left all those things in the hole?

He rushed to the corner, slipped his hand under the paper, pulled the things out and lined his pockets with them. There were eight articles in all: two little boxes with ear-rings or something of the sort, he hardly looked to see; then four small leather cases. There was a chain, too, merely wrapped in newspaper and something else in newspaper, that looked like a decoration.... He put them all in the different pockets of his overcoat, and the remaining pocket of his trousers, trying to conceal them as much as possible. He took the purse, too. Then he went out of his room, leaving the door open. He walked quickly and resolutely, and though he felt shattered, he had his senses about him. He was afraid of pursuit, he was afraid that in another half-hour, another quarter of an hour perhaps, instructions would be issued for his pursuit, and so at all costs, he must hide all traces before then. He must clear everything up while he still had some strength, some reasoning power left him.... Where was he to go?

That had long been settled: "Fling them into the canal, and all traces hidden in the water, the thing would be at an end." So he had decided in the night of his delirium when several times he had had the impulse to get up and go away, to make haste, and get rid of it all. But to get rid of it, turned out to be a very difficult task. He wandered along the bank of the Ekaterininsky Canal for half an hour or more and looked several times at the steps running down to the water, but he could not think of carrying out his plan; either rafts stood at the steps' edge, and women were washing clothes on them, or boats were moored there, and people were swarming everywhere. Moreover he could be seen and noticed from the banks on all sides; it would look suspicious for a man to go down on purpose, stop, and throw something into the water. And what if the boxes were to float instead of sinking? And of course they would. Even as it was, everyone he met seemed to stare and look round, as if they had nothing to do but to watch him. "Why is it, or can it be my fancy?" he thought.

At last the thought struck him that it might be better to go to the Neva. There were not so many people there, he would be less observed, and it would be more convenient in every way, above all it was further off. He wondered how he could have been wandering for a good half- hour, worried and anxious in this dangerous past without thinking of it before. And that half-hour he had lost over an irrational plan, simply because he had thought of it in delirium! He had become extremely absent and forgetful and he was aware of it. He certainly must make haste.

He walked towards the Neva along V- Prospect, but on the way another idea struck him. "Why to the Neva? Would it not be better to go somewhere far off, to the Islands again, and there hide the things in some solitary place, in a wood or under a bush, and mark the spot perhaps?" And though he felt incapable of clear judgment, the idea seemed to him a sound one. But he was not destined to go there. For coming out of V—— Prospect towards the square, he saw on the left a passage leading between two blank walls to a courtyard. On the right hand, the blank unwhitewashed wall of a four-storied house stretched far into the court; on the left, a wooden hoarding ran parallel with it for twenty paces into the court, and then turned sharply to the left. Here was a deserted fenced-off place where rubbish of different sorts was lying. At the end of the court, the corner of a low, smutty, stone shed, apparently part of some workshop, peeped from behind the hoarding. It was probably a carriage builder's or carpenter's shed; the whole place from the entrance was black with coal dust. Here would be the place to throw it, he thought. Not seeing anyone in the yard, he slipped in, and at once saw near the gate a sink, such as is often put in yards where there are many workmen or cab-drivers; and on the hoarding above had been scribbled in chalk the time-honoured witticism, "Standing here strictly forbidden." This was all the better, for there would be nothing suspicious about his going in. "Here I could throw it all in a heap and get away!"

PART III

CHAPTER 4

At that moment the door was softly opened, and a young girl walked into the room, looking timidly about her. Everyone turned towards her with surprise and curiosity. At first sight, Raskolnikov did not recognise her. It was Sofya Semyonovna Marmeladov. He had seen her yesterday for the first time, but at such a moment, in such surroundings and in such a dress, that his memory retained a very different image of her. Now she was a modestly and poorly-dressed young girl, very young, indeed, almost like a child, with a modest and refined manner, with a candid but somewhat frightened-looking face. She was wearing a very plain indoor dress, and had on a shabby old- fashioned hat, but she still carried a parasol. Unexpectedly finding the room full of people, she was not so much embarrassed as completely overwhelmed with shyness, like a little child. She was even about to retreat. "Oh... it's you!" said Raskolnikov, extremely astonished, and he, too, was confused. He at once recollected that his mother and sister knew through Luzhin's letter of "some young woman of notorious behaviour." He had only just been protesting against Luzhin's calumny and declaring that he had seen the girl last night for the first time, and suddenly she had walked in. He remembered, too, that he had not protested against the expression "of notorious behaviour." All this passed vaguely and fleetingly through his brain, but looking at her more intently, he saw that the humiliated creature was so humiliated that he felt suddenly sorry for her. When she made a movement to retreat in terror, it sent a pang to his heart.

"I did not expect you," he said, hurriedly, with a look that made her stop. "Please sit down. You come, no doubt, from Katerina Ivanovna. Allow me—not there. Sit here...."

At Sonia's entrance, Razumihin, who had been sitting on one of Raskolnikov's three chairs, close to the door, got up to allow her to enter. Raskolnikov had at first shown her the place on the sofa where Zossimov had been sitting, but feeling that the sofa which served him as a bed, was too /familiar/ a place, he hurriedly motioned her to Razumihin's chair.

"You sit here," he said to Razumihin, putting him on the sofa.

Sonia sat down, almost shaking with terror, and looked timidly at the two ladies. It was evidently almost inconceivable to herself that she could sit down beside them. At the thought of it, she was so frightened that she hurriedly got up again, and in utter confusion addressed Raskolnikov.

"I... I... have come for one minute. Forgive me for disturbing you," she began falteringly. "I come from Katerina Ivanovna, and she had no one to send. Katerina Ivanovna told me to beg you... to be at the service... in the morning... at Mitrofanievsky... and then... to us... to her... to do her the honour... she told me to beg you..." Sonia stammered and ceased speaking.

"I will try, certainly, most certainly," answered Raskolnikov. He, too, stood up, and he, too, faltered and could not finish his sentence. "Please sit down," he said, suddenly. "I want to talk to you. You are perhaps in a hurry, but please, be so kind, spare me two minutes," and he drew up a chair for her.

Sonia sat down again, and again timidly she took a hurried, frightened look at the two ladies, and dropped her eyes. Raskolnikov's pale face flushed, a shudder passed over him, his eyes glowed.

"Mother," he said, firmly and insistently, "this is Sofya Semyonovna Marmeladov, the daughter of that unfortunate Mr. Marmeladov, who was run over yesterday before my eyes, and of whom I was just telling you."

Pulcheria Alexandrovna glanced at Sonia, and slightly screwed up her eyes. In spite of her embarrassment before Rodya's urgent and challenging look, she could not deny herself that satisfaction. Dounia gazed gravely and intently into the poor girl's face, and scrutinised her with perplexity. Sonia, hearing herself introduced, tried to raise her eyes again, but was more embarrassed than ever.

"I wanted to ask you," said Raskolnikov, hastily, "how things were arranged yesterday. You were not worried by the police, for instance?"

"No, that was all right... it was too evident, the cause of death.. they did not worry us... only the lodgers are angry."

"Why?"

"At the body's remaining so long. You see it is hot now. So that, to-day, they will carry it to the cemetery, into the chapel, until to-morrow. At first Katerina Ivanovna was unwilling, but now she sees herself that it's necessary..."

"To-day, then?"

"She begs you to do us the honour to be in the church to-morrow for the service, and then to be present at the funeral lunch."

"She is giving a funeral lunch?"

"Yes... just a little.... She told me to thank you very much for helping us yesterday. But for you, we should have had nothing for the funeral."

All at once her lips and chin began trembling, but, with an effort, she controlled herself, looking down again.

During the conversation, Raskolnikov watched her carefully. She had a thin, very thin, pale little face, rather irregular and angular, with a sharp little nose and chin. She could not have been called pretty, but her blue eyes were so clear, and when they lighted up, there was such a kindliness and simplicity in her expression that one could not help being attracted. Her face, and her whole figure indeed, had another peculiar characteristic. In spite of her eighteen years, she looked almost a little girl—almost a child. And in some of her gestures, this childishness seemed almost absurd.

"But has Katerina Ivanovna been able to manage with such small means? Does she even mean to have a funeral lunch?" Raskolnikov asked, persistently keeping up the conversation.

"The coffin will be plain, of course... and everything will be plain, so it won't cost much. Katerina Ivanovna and I have reckoned it all out, so that there will be enough left... and Katerina Ivanovna was very anxious it should be so. You know one can't... it's a comfort to her... she is like that, you know...."

"I understand, I understand... of course... why do you look at my room like that? My mother has just said it is like a tomb."

"You gave us everything yesterday," Sonia said suddenly, in reply, in a loud rapid whisper; and again she looked down in confusion. Her lips and chin were trembling once more. She had been struck at once by Raskolnikov's poor surroundings, and now these words broke out spontaneously. A silence followed. There was a light in Dounia's eyes, and even Pulcheria Alexandrovna looked kindly at Sonia.

"Rodya," she said, getting up, "we shall have dinner together, of course. Come, Dounia.... And you, Rodya, had better go for a little walk, and then rest and lie down before you come to see us.... I am afraid we have exhausted you...."

"Yes, yes, I'll come," he answered, getting up fussily. "But I have something to see to."

"But surely you will have dinner together?" cried Razumihin, looking in surprise at Raskolnikov. "What do you mean?"

"Yes, yes, I am coming... of course, of course! And you stay a minute. You do not want him just now, do you, mother? Or perhaps I am taking him from you?"

"Oh, no, no. And will you, Dmitri Prokofitch, do us the favour of dining with us?"

"Please do," added Dounia.

Razumihin bowed, positively radiant. For one moment, they were all strangely embarrassed.

"Good-bye, Rodya, that is till we meet. I do not like saying good-bye. Good-bye, Nastasya. Ah, I have said good-bye again."

Pulcheria Alexandrovna meant to greet Sonia, too; but it somehow failed to come off, and she went in a flutter out of the room.

But Avdotya Romanovna seemed to await her turn, and following her mother out, gave Sonia an attentive, courteous bow. Sonia, in confusion, gave a hurried, frightened curtsy. There was a look of poignant discomfort in her face, as though Avdotya Romanovna's courtesy and attention were oppressive and painful to her.

"Dounia, good-bye," called Raskolnikov, in the passage. "Give me your hand."

"Why, I did give it to you. Have you forgotten?" said Dounia, turning warmly and awkwardly to him.

"Never mind, give it to me again." And he squeezed her fingers warmly.

Dounia smiled, flushed, pulled her hand away, and went off quite happy.

"Come, that's capital," he said to Sonia, going back and looking brightly at her. "God give peace to the dead, the living have still to live. That is right, isn't it?"

Sonia looked surprised at the sudden brightness of his face. He looked at her for some moments in silence. The whole history of the dead father floated before his memory in those moments....

"Heavens, Dounia," Pulcheria Alexandrovna began, as soon as they were in the street, "I really feel relieved myself at coming away—more at ease. How little did I think yesterday in the train that I could ever be glad of that."

"I tell you again, mother, he is still very ill. Don't you see it? Perhaps worrying about us upset him. We must be patient, and much, much can be forgiven."

"Well, you were not very patient!" Pulcheria Alexandrovna caught her up, hotly and jealously. "Do you know, Dounia, I was looking at you two. You are the very portrait of him, and not so much in face as in soul. You are both melancholy, both morose and hot-tempered, both haughty and both generous.... Surely he can't be an egoist, Dounia. Eh? When I think of what is in store for us this evening, my heart sinks!"

"Don't be uneasy, mother. What must be, will be."

"Dounia, only think what a position we are in! What if Pyotr Petrovitch breaks it off?" poor Pulcheria Alexandrovna blurted out, incautiously.

"He won't be worth much if he does," answered Dounia, sharply and contemptuously.

"We did well to come away," Pulcheria Alexandrovna hurriedly broke in. "He was in a hurry about some business or other. If he gets out and has a breath of air... it is fearfully close in his room.... But where is one to get a breath of air here? The very streets here feel like shut-up rooms. Good heavens! what a town!... stay... this side... they will crush you—carrying something. Why, it is a piano they have got, I declare... how they push!... I am very much afraid of that young woman, too."

"What young woman, mother?

"Why, that Sofya Semyonovna, who was there just now."

"Why?"

"I have a presentiment, Dounia. Well, you may believe it or not, but as soon as she came in, that very minute, I felt that she was the chief cause of the trouble...."

"Nothing of the sort!" cried Dounia, in vexation. "What nonsense, with your presentiments, mother! He only made her acquaintance the evening before, and he did not know her when she came in."

"Well, you will see.... She worries me; but you will see, you will see! I was so frightened. She was gazing at me with those eyes. I could scarcely sit still in my chair when he began introducing her, do you remember? It seems so strange, but Pyotr Petrovitch writes like that about her, and he introduces her to us—to you! So he must think a great deal of her."

"People will write anything. We were talked about and written about, too. Have you forgotten? I am sure that she is a good girl, and that it is all nonsense."

"God grant it may be!"

"And Pyotr Petrovitch is a contemptible slanderer," Dounia snapped out, suddenly.

Pulcheria Alexandrovna was crushed; the conversation was not resumed.

"I will tell you what I want with you," said Raskolnikov, drawing Razumihin to the window.

"Then I will tell Katerina Ivanovna that you are coming," Sonia said hurriedly, preparing to depart.

"One minute, Sofya Semyonovna. We have no secrets. You are not in our way. I want to have another word or two with you. Listen!" he turned suddenly to Razumihin again. "You know that... what's his name.. Porfiry Petrovitch?"

PART 4

CHAPTER I

"Can this be still a dream?" Raskolnikov thought once more.

He looked carefully and suspiciously at the unexpected visitor.

"Svidriga&#65533;lov! What nonsense! It can't be!" he said at last aloud in bewilderment.

His visitor did not seem at all surprised at this exclamation.

"I've come to you for two reasons. In the first place, I wanted to make your personal acquaintance, as I have already heard a great deal about you that is interesting and flattering;

secondly, I cherish the hope that you may not refuse to assist me in a matter directly concerning the welfare of your sister, Avdotya Romanovna. For without your support she might not let me come near her now, for she is prejudiced against me, but with your assistance I reckon on..."

"You reckon wrongly," interrupted Raskolnikov.

"They only arrived yesterday, may I ask you?"

Raskolnikov made no reply.

"It was yesterday, I know. I only arrived myself the day before. Well, let me tell you this, Rodion Romanovitch, I don't consider it necessary to justify myself, but kindly tell me what was there particularly criminal on my part in all this business, speaking without prejudice, with common sense?"

Raskolnikov continued to look at him in silence.

"That in my own house I persecuted a defenceless girl and 'insulted her with my infamous proposals'—is that it? (I am anticipating you.) But you've only to assume that I, too, am a man _et nihil humanum_... in a word, that I am capable of being attracted and falling in love (which does not depend on our will), then everything can be explained in the most natural manner. The question is, am I a monster, or am I myself a victim? And what if I am a victim? In proposing to the object of my passion to elope with me to America or Switzerland, I may have cherished the deepest respect for her and may have thought that I was promoting our mutual happiness! Reason is the slave of passion, you know; why, probably, I was doing more harm to myself than anyone!"

"But that's not the point," Raskolnikov interrupted with disgust. "It's simply that whether you are right or wrong, we dislike you. We don't want to have anything to do with you. We show you the door. Go out!"

Svidriga&#65533;lov broke into a sudden laugh.

"But you're... but there's no getting round you," he said, laughing in the frankest way. "I hoped to get round you, but you took up the right line at once!"

"But you are trying to get round me still!"

"What of it? What of it?" cried Svidriga&#65533;lov, laughing openly. "But this is what the French call _bonne guerre_, and the most innocent form of deception!... But still you have interrupted me; one way or another, I repeat again: there would never have been any unpleasantness except for what happened in the garden. Marfa Petrovna..."

"You have got rid of Marfa Petrovna, too, so they say?" Raskolnikov interrupted rudely.

"Oh, you've heard that, too, then? You'd be sure to, though.... But as for your question, I really don't know what to say, though my own conscience is quite at rest on that score. Don't suppose that I am in any apprehension about it. All was regular and in order; the medical inquiry diagnosed apoplexy due to bathing immediately after a heavy dinner and a bottle of wine, and indeed it could have proved nothing else. But I'll tell you what I have been thinking to myself of late, on my way here in the train, especially: didn't I contribute to all that... calamity, morally, in a way, by irritation or something of the sort. But I came to the conclusion that that, too, was quite out of the question."

Raskolnikov laughed.

"I wonder you trouble yourself about it!"

"But what are you laughing at? Only consider, I struck her just twice with a switch—there were no marks even... don't regard me as a cynic, please; I am perfectly aware how atrocious it was of me and all that; but I know for certain, too, that Marfa Petrovna was very likely pleased at my, so to say, warmth. The story of your sister had been wrung out to the last drop; for the last three days Marfa Petrovna had been forced to sit at home; she had nothing to show herself with in the town. Besides, she had bored them so with that letter (you heard about her reading the letter). And all of a sudden those two switches fell from heaven! Her first act was to order the carriage to be got out.... Not to speak of the fact that there are cases when women are very, very glad to be insulted in spite of all their show of indignation. There are instances of it with everyone; human beings in general, indeed, greatly love to be insulted, have you noticed that? But it's particularly so with women. One might even say it's their only amusement."

At one time Raskolnikov thought of getting up and walking out and so finishing the interview. But some curiosity and even a sort of prudence made him linger for a moment.

"You are fond of fighting?" he asked carelessly.

"No, not very," Svidriga&#65533;lov answered, calmly. "And Marfa Petrovna and I scarcely ever fought. We lived very harmoniously, and she was always pleased with me. I only used the whip twice in all our seven years (not counting a third occasion of a very ambiguous character). The first time, two months after our marriage, immediately after we arrived in the country, and the last time was that of which we are speaking. Did you suppose I was such a monster, such a reactionary, such a slave driver? Ha, ha! By the way, do you remember, Rodion Romanovitch, how a few years ago, in those days of beneficent publicity, a nobleman, I've forgotten his name, was put to shame everywhere, in all the papers, for having thrashed a German woman in the railway train. You remember? It was in those days, that very year I believe, the 'disgraceful action of the _Age_' took place (you know, 'The Egyptian Nights,' that public reading, you remember? The dark eyes, you know! Ah, the golden days of our youth, where are they?). Well, as for the gentleman who thrashed the German, I feel no sympathy with him, because after all what need is there for sympathy? But I must say that there are sometimes such provoking 'Germans' that I don't believe there is a progressive who could quite answer for himself. No one looked at the subject from that point of view then, but that's the truly humane point of view, I assure you."

After saying this, Svidriga&#65533;lov broke into a sudden laugh again. Raskolnikov saw clearly that this was a man with a firm purpose in his mind and able to keep it to himself.

"I expect you've not talked to anyone for some days?" he asked.

"Scarcely anyone. I suppose you are wondering at my being such an adaptable man?"

"No, I am only wondering at your being too adaptable a man."

"Because I am not offended at the rudeness of your questions? Is that it? But why take offence? As you asked, so I answered," he replied, with a surprising expression of simplicity. "You know, there's hardly anything I take interest in," he went on, as it were dreamily, "especially now, I've nothing to do.... You are quite at liberty to imagine though that I am making up to you with a motive, particularly as I told you I want to see your sister about something. But I'll confess frankly, I am very much bored. The last three days especially, so I am delighted to see you.... Don't be angry, Rodion Romanovitch, but you seem to be somehow awfully strange yourself. Say what you like, there's something wrong with you, and now, too... not this very minute, I mean, but now, generally.... Well, well, I won't, I won't, don't scowl! I am not such a bear, you know, as you think."

Raskolnikov looked gloomily at him.

"You are not a bear, perhaps, at all," he said. "I fancy indeed that you are a man of very good breeding, or at least know how on occasion to behave like one."

"I am not particularly interested in anyone's opinion," Svidriga&#65533;lov answered, dryly and even with a shade of haughtiness, "and therefore why not be vulgar at times when vulgarity is such a convenient cloak for our climate... and especially if one has a natural propensity that way," he added, laughing again.

"But I've heard you have many friends here. You are, as they say, 'not without connections.' What can you want with me, then, unless you've some special object?"

"That's true that I have friends here," Svidriga&#65533;lov admitted, not replying to the chief point. "I've met some already. I've been lounging about for the last three days, and I've seen them, or they've seen me. That's a matter of course. I am well dressed and reckoned not a poor man; the emancipation of the serfs hasn't affected me; my property consists chiefly of forests and water meadows. The revenue has not fallen off; but... I am not going to see them, I was sick of them long ago. I've been here three days and have called on no one.... What a town it is! How has it come into existence among us, tell me that? A town of officials and students of all sorts. Yes, there's a great deal I didn't notice when I was here eight years ago, kicking up my heels.... My only hope now is in anatomy, by Jove, it is!"

"Anatomy?"

"But as for these clubs, Dussauts, parades, or progress, indeed, maybe—well, all that can go on without me," he went on, again without noticing the question. "Besides, who wants to be a card-sharper?"

"Why, have you been a card-sharper then?"

"How could I help being? There was a regular set of us, men of the best society, eight years ago; we had a fine time. And all men of breeding, you know, poets, men of property. And indeed as a rule in our Russian society the best manners are found among those who've been thrashed, have you noticed that? I've deteriorated in the country. But I did get into prison for debt, through a low Greek who came from Nezhin. Then Marfa Petrovna turned up; she bargained with him and bought me off for thirty thousand silver pieces (I owed seventy thousand). We were united in lawful wedlock and she bore me off into the country like a treasure. You know she was five years older than I. She was very fond of me. For seven years I never left the country. And, take note, that all my life she held a document over me, the IOU for thirty thousand roubles, so if I were to elect to be restive about anything I should be trapped at once! And she would have done it! Women find nothing incompatible in that."

"If it hadn't been for that, would you have given her the slip?"

"I don't know what to say. It was scarcely the document restrained me. I didn't want to go anywhere else. Marfa Petrovna herself invited me to go abroad, seeing I was bored, but I've been abroad before, and always felt sick there. For no reason, but the sunrise, the bay of Naples, the sea—you look at them and it makes you sad. What's most revolting is that one is really sad! No, it's better at home. Here at least one blames others for everything and excuses oneself. I should have gone perhaps on an expedition to the North Pole, because _j'ai le vin mauvais_ and hate drinking, and there's nothing left but wine. I have tried it. But, I say, I've been told Berg is going up in a great balloon next Sunday from the Yusupov Garden and will take up passengers at a fee. Is it true?"

"Why, would you go up?"

"I... No, oh, no," muttered Svidriga&#65533;lov really seeming to be deep in thought.

"What does he mean? Is he in earnest?" Raskolnikov wondered.

"No, the document didn't restrain me," Svidriga&#65533;lov went on, meditatively. "It was my own doing, not leaving the country, and nearly a year ago Marfa Petrovna gave me back the document on my name-day and made me a present of a considerable sum of money, too. She had a fortune, you know. 'You see how I trust you, Arkady Ivanovitch'—that was actually her expression. You don't believe she used it? But do you know I managed the estate quite decently, they know me in the neighbourhood. I ordered books, too. Marfa Petrovna at first approved, but afterwards she was afraid of my over-studying."

"You seem to be missing Marfa Petrovna very much?"

"Missing her? Perhaps. Really, perhaps I am. And, by the way, do you believe in ghosts?"

"What ghosts?"

"Why, ordinary ghosts."

"Do you believe in them?"

"Perhaps not, _pour vous plaire_.... I wouldn't say no exactly."

"Do you see them, then?"

Svidriga&#65533;lov looked at him rather oddly.

"Marfa Petrovna is pleased to visit me," he said, twisting his mouth into a strange smile.

"How do you mean 'she is pleased to visit you'?"

"She has been three times. I saw her first on the very day of the funeral, an hour after she was buried. It was the day before I left to come here. The second time was the day before yesterday, at daybreak, on the journey at the station of Malaya Vishera, and the third time was two hours ago in the room where I am staying. I was alone."

"Were you awake?"

"Quite awake. I was wide awake every time. She comes, speaks to me for a minute and goes out at the door—always at the door. I can almost hear her."

"What made me think that something of the sort must be happening to you?" Raskolnikov said suddenly.

At the same moment he was surprised at having said it. He was much excited.

"What! Did you think so?" Svidriga&#65533;lov asked in astonishment. "Did you really? Didn't I say that there was something in common between us, eh?"

"You never said so!" Raskolnikov cried sharply and with heat.

"Didn't I?"

"No!"

"I thought I did. When I came in and saw you lying with your eyes shut, pretending, I said to myself at once, 'Here's the man.'"

"What do you mean by 'the man?' What are you talking about?" cried Raskolnikov.

"What do I mean? I really don't know...." Svidriga&#65533;lov muttered ingenuously, as though he, too, were puzzled.

For a minute they were silent. They stared in each other's faces.

"That's all nonsense!" Raskolnikov shouted with vexation. "What does she say when she comes to you?"

"She! Would you believe it, she talks of the silliest trifles and—man is a strange creature—it makes me angry. The first time she came in (I was tired you know: the funeral service, the funeral ceremony, the lunch afterwards. At last I was left alone in my study. I lighted a cigar and began to think), she came in at the door. 'You've been so busy to-day, Arkady Ivanovitch, you have forgotten to wind the dining-room clock,' she said. All those seven years I've wound that clock every week, and if I forgot it she would always remind me. The next day I set off on my way here. I got out at the station at daybreak; I'd been asleep, tired out, with my eyes half open, I was drinking some coffee. I looked up and there was suddenly Marfa Petrovna sitting beside me with a pack of cards in her hands. 'Shall I tell your fortune for the journey, Arkady Ivanovitch?' She was a great hand at telling fortunes. I shall never forgive myself for not asking her to. I ran away in a fright, and, besides, the bell rang. I was sitting to-day, feeling very heavy after a miserable dinner from a cookshop; I was sitting smoking, all of a sudden Marfa Petrovna again. She came in very smart in a new green silk dress with a long train. 'Good day, Arkady Ivanovitch! How do you like my dress? Aniska can't make like this.' (Aniska was a dressmaker in the country, one of our former serf girls who had been trained in Moscow, a pretty wench.) She stood turning round before me. I looked at the dress, and then I looked carefully, very carefully, at her face. 'I wonder you trouble to come to me about such trifles, Marfa Petrovna.' 'Good gracious, you won't let one disturb you about anything!' To tease her I said, 'I want to get married, Marfa Petrovna.' 'That's just like you, Arkady Ivanovitch; it does you very little credit to come looking for a bride when you've hardly buried your wife. And if you could make a good choice, at least, but I know it won't be for your happiness or hers, you will only be a laughing-stock to all good people.' Then she went out and her train seemed to rustle. Isn't it nonsense, eh?"

"But perhaps you are telling lies?" Raskolnikov put in.

"I rarely lie," answered Svidriga&#65533;lov thoughtfully, apparently not noticing the rudeness of the question.

"And in the past, have you ever seen ghosts before?"

"Y-yes, I have seen them, but only once in my life, six years ago. I had a serf, Filka; just after his burial I called out forgetting 'Filka, my pipe!' He came in and went to the cupboard where my pipes were. I sat still and thought 'he is doing it out of revenge,' because we had a violent quarrel just before his death. 'How dare you come in with a hole in your elbow?' I said. 'Go away, you scamp!' He turned and went out, and never came again. I didn't tell Marfa Petrovna at the time. I wanted to have a service sung for him, but I was ashamed."

"You should go to a doctor."

"I know I am not well, without your telling me, though I don't know what's wrong; I believe I am five times as strong as you are. I didn't ask you whether you believe that ghosts are seen, but whether you believe that they exist."

"No, I won't believe it!" Raskolnikov cried, with positive anger.

"What do people generally say?" muttered Svidriga&#65533;lov, as though speaking to himself, looking aside and bowing his head. "They say, 'You are ill, so what appears to you is only unreal fantasy.' But that's not strictly logical. I agree that ghosts only appear to the sick, but that only proves that they are unable to appear except to the sick, not that they don't exist."

"Nothing of the sort," Raskolnikov insisted irritably.

"No? You don't think so?" Svidriga&#65533;lov went on, looking at him deliberately. "But what do you say to this argument (help me with it): ghosts are, as it were, shreds and fragments of other worlds, the beginning of them. A man in health has, of course, no reason to see them, because he is above all a man of this earth and is bound for the sake of completeness and order to live only in this life. But as soon as one is ill, as soon as the normal earthly order of the organism is broken, one begins to realise the possibility of another world; and the more seriously ill one is, the closer becomes one's contact with that other world, so that as soon as the man dies he steps straight into that world. I thought of that long ago. If you believe in a future life, you could believe in that, too."

"I don't believe in a future life," said Raskolnikov.

Svidriga&#65533;lov sat lost in thought.

"And what if there are only spiders there, or something of that sort," he said suddenly.

"He is a madman," thought Raskolnikov.

"We always imagine eternity as something beyond our conception, something vast, vast! But why must it be vast? Instead of all that, what if it's one little room, like a bath house in the country, black and grimy and spiders in every corner, and that's all eternity is? I sometimes fancy it like that."

"Can it be you can imagine nothing juster and more comforting than that?" Raskolnikov cried, with a feeling of anguish.

"Juster? And how can we tell, perhaps that is just, and do you know it's what I would certainly have made it," answered Svidriga&#65533;lov, with a vague smile.

This horrible answer sent a cold chill through Raskolnikov. Svidriga&#65533;lov raised his head, looked at him, and suddenly began laughing.

"Only think," he cried, "half an hour ago we had never seen each other, we regarded each other as enemies; there is a matter unsettled between us; we've thrown it aside, and away we've gone into the abstract! Wasn't I right in saying that we were birds of a feather?"

"Kindly allow me," Raskolnikov went on irritably, "to ask you to explain why you have honoured me with your visit... and... and I am in a hurry, I have no time to waste. I want to go out."

"By all means, by all means. Your sister, Avdotya Romanovna, is going to be married to Mr. Luzhin, Pyotr Petrovitch?"

"Can you refrain from any question about my sister and from mentioning her name? I can't understand how you dare utter her name in my presence, if you really are Svidriga&#65533;lov."

"Why, but I've come here to speak about her; how can I avoid mentioning her?"

"Very good, speak, but make haste."

"I am sure that you must have formed your own opinion of this Mr. Luzhin, who is a connection of mine through my wife, if you have only seen him for half an hour, or heard any facts about him. He is no match for Avdotya Romanovna. I believe Avdotya Romanovna is sacrificing herself generously and imprudently for the sake of... for the sake of her family. I fancied from all I had heard of you that you would be very glad if the match could be broken off without the sacrifice of worldly advantages. Now I know you personally, I am convinced of it."

"All this is very na&#65533;ve... excuse me, I should have said impudent on your part," said Raskolnikov.

"You mean to say that I am seeking my own ends. Don't be uneasy, Rodion Romanovitch, if I were working for my own advantage, I would not have spoken out so directly. I am not quite a fool. I will confess something psychologically curious about that: just now, defending my love for Avdotya Romanovna, I said I was myself the victim. Well, let me tell you that I've no feeling of love now, not the slightest, so that I wonder myself indeed, for I really did feel something..."

"Through idleness and depravity," Raskolnikov put in.

"I certainly am idle and depraved, but your sister has such qualities that even I could not help being impressed by them. But that's all nonsense, as I see myself now."

"Have you seen that long?"

"I began to be aware of it before, but was only perfectly sure of it the day before yesterday, almost at the moment I arrived in Petersburg. I still fancied in Moscow, though, that I was coming to try to get Avdotya Romanovna's hand and to cut out Mr. Luzhin."

"Excuse me for interrupting you; kindly be brief, and come to the object of your visit. I am in a hurry, I want to go out..."

"With the greatest pleasure. On arriving here and determining on a certain... journey, I should like to make some necessary preliminary arrangements. I left my children with an aunt; they are well provided for; and they have no need of me personally. And a nice father I should make, too! I have taken nothing but what Marfa Petrovna gave me a year ago. That's enough for me. Excuse me, I am just coming to the point. Before the journey which may come off, I want to settle Mr. Luzhin, too. It's not that I detest him so much, but it was through him I quarrelled with Marfa Petrovna when I learned that she had dished up this marriage. I want now to see Avdotya Romanovna through your mediation, and if you like in your presence, to explain to her that in the first place she will never gain anything but harm from Mr. Luzhin. Then, begging her pardon for all past unpleasantness, to make her a present of ten thousand roubles and so assist the rupture with Mr. Luzhin, a rupture to which I believe she is herself not disinclined, if she could see the way to it."

"You are certainly mad," cried Raskolnikov not so much angered as astonished. "How dare you talk like that!"

"I knew you would scream at me; but in the first place, though I am not rich, this ten thousand roubles is perfectly free; I have absolutely no need for it. If Avdotya Romanovna does not accept it, I shall waste it in some more foolish way.

That's the first thing. Secondly, my conscience is perfectly easy; I make the offer with no ulterior motive. You may not believe it, but in the end Avdotya Romanovna and you will know. The point is, that I did actually cause your sister, whom I greatly respect, some trouble and unpleasantness, and so, sincerely regretting it, I want—not to compensate, not to repay her for the unpleasantness, but simply to do something to her advantage, to show that I am not, after all, privileged to do nothing but harm. If there were a millionth fraction of self-interest in my offer, I should not have made it so openly; and I should not have offered her ten thousand only, when five weeks ago I offered her more, Besides, I may, perhaps, very soon marry a young lady, and that alone ought to prevent suspicion of any design on Avdotya Romanovna. In conclusion, let me say that in marrying Mr. Luzhin, she is taking money just the same, only from another man. Don't be angry, Rodion Romanovitch, think it over coolly and quietly."

Svidriga&#65533;lov himself was exceedingly cool and quiet as he was saying this.

"I beg you to say no more," said Raskolnikov. "In any case this is unpardonable impertinence."

"Not in the least. Then a man may do nothing but harm to his neighbour in this world, and is prevented from doing the tiniest bit of good by trivial conventional formalities. That's absurd. If I died, for instance, and left that sum to your sister in my will, surely she wouldn't refuse it?"

"Very likely she would."

"Oh, no, indeed. However, if you refuse it, so be it, though ten thousand roubles is a capital thing to have on occasion. In any case I beg you to repeat what I have said to Avdotya Romanovna."

"No, I won't."

"In that case, Rodion Romanovitch, I shall be obliged to try and see her myself and worry her by doing so."

"And if I do tell her, will you not try to see her?"

"I don't know really what to say. I should like very much to see her once more."

"Don't hope for it."

"I'm sorry. But you don't know me. Perhaps we may become better friends."

"You think we may become friends?"

"And why not?" Svidriga&#65533;lov said, smiling. He stood up and took his hat. "I didn't quite intend to disturb you and I came here without reckoning on it... though I was very much struck by your face this morning."

"Where did you see me this morning?" Raskolnikov asked uneasily.

"I saw you by chance.... I kept fancying there is something about you like me.... But don't be uneasy. I am not intrusive; I used to get on all right with card-sharpers, and I never bored Prince Svirbey, a great personage who is a distant relation of mine, and I could write about Raphael's _Madonna_ in Madam Prilukov's album, and I never left Marfa Petrovna's side for seven years, and I used to stay the night at Viazemsky's house in the Hay Market in the old days, and I may go up in a balloon with Berg, perhaps."

"Oh, all right. Are you starting soon on your travels, may I ask?"

"What travels?"

"Why, on that 'journey'; you spoke of it yourself."

"A journey? Oh, yes. I did speak of a journey. Well, that's a wide subject.... if only you knew what you are asking," he added, and gave a sudden, loud, short laugh. "Perhaps I'll get married instead of the journey. They're making a match for me."

"Here?"

"Yes."

"How have you had time for that?"

"But I am very anxious to see Avdotya Romanovna once. I earnestly beg it. Well, good-bye for the present. Oh, yes. I have forgotten something. Tell your sister, Rodion Romanovitch, that Marfa Petrovna remembered her in her will and left her three thousand roubles. That's absolutely certain. Marfa Petrovna arranged it a week before her death, and it was done in my presence. Avdotya Romanovna will be able to receive the money in two or three weeks."

"Are you telling the truth?"

"Yes, tell her. Well, your servant. I am staying very near you."

As he went out, Svidriga&#65533;lov ran up against Razumihin in the doorway.

CHAPTER 2

It was nearly eight o'clock. The two young men hurried to Bakaleyev's, to arrive before Luzhin.

"Why, who was that?" asked Razumihin, as soon as they were in the street.

"It was Svidriga&#65533;lov, that landowner in whose house my sister was insulted when she was their governess. Through his persecuting her with his attentions, she was turned out by his wife, Marfa Petrovna. This Marfa Petrovna begged Dounia's forgiveness afterwards, and she's just died suddenly. It was of her we were talking this morning. I don't know why I'm afraid of that man. He came here at once after his wife's funeral. He is very strange, and is determined on doing something.... We must guard Dounia from him... that's what I wanted to tell you, do you hear?"

"Guard her! What can he do to harm Avdotya Romanovna? Thank you, Rodya, for speaking to me like that.... We will, we will guard her. Where does he live?"

"I don't know."

"Why didn't you ask? What a pity! I'll find out, though."

"Did you see him?" asked Raskolnikov after a pause.

"Yes, I noticed him, I noticed him well."

"You did really see him? You saw him clearly?" Raskolnikov insisted.

"Yes, I remember him perfectly, I should know him in a thousand; I have a good memory for faces."

They were silent again.

"Hm!... that's all right," muttered Raskolnikov. "Do you know, I fancied... I keep thinking that it may have been an hallucination."

"What do you mean? I don't understand you."

"Well, you all say," Raskolnikov went on, twisting his mouth into a smile, "that I am mad. I thought just now that perhaps I really am mad, and have only seen a phantom."

"What do you mean?"

"Why, who can tell? Perhaps I am really mad, and perhaps everything that happened all these days may be only imagination."

"Ach, Rodya, you have been upset again!... But what did he say, what did he come for?"

Raskolnikov did not answer. Razumihin thought a minute.

"Now let me tell you my story," he began, "I came to you, you were asleep. Then we had dinner and then I went to Porfiry's, Zametov was still with him. I tried to begin, but it was no use. I couldn't speak in the right way. They don't seem to understand and can't understand, but are not a bit ashamed. I drew Porfiry to the window, and began talking to him, but it was still no use. He looked away and I looked away. At last I shook my fist in his ugly face, and told him as a cousin I'd brain him. He merely looked at me, I cursed and came away. That was all. It was very stupid. To Zametov I didn't say a word. But, you see, I thought I'd made a mess of it, but as I went downstairs a brilliant idea struck me: why should we trouble? Of course if you were in any danger or anything, but why need you care? You needn't care a hang for them. We shall have a laugh at them afterwards, and if I were in your place I'd mystify them more than ever. How ashamed they'll be afterwards! Hang them! We can thrash them afterwards, but let's laugh at them now!"

"To be sure," answered Raskolnikov. "But what will you say to-morrow?" he thought to himself. Strange to say, till that moment it had never occurred to him to wonder what Razumihin would think when he knew. As he thought it, Raskolnikov looked at him. Razumihin's account of his visit to Porfiry had very little interest for him, so much had come and gone since then.

In the corridor they came upon Luzhin; he had arrived punctually at eight, and was looking for the number, so that all three went in together without greeting or looking at one another. The young men walked in first, while Pyotr Petrovitch, for good manners, lingered a little in the passage, taking off his coat. Pulcheria Alexandrovna came forward at once to greet him in the doorway, Dounia was welcoming her brother. Pyotr Petrovitch walked in and quite amiably, though with redoubled dignity, bowed to the ladies. He looked, however, as though he were a little put out and could not yet recover himself. Pulcheria Alexandrovna, who seemed also a little embarrassed, hastened to make them all sit down at the round table where a samovar was boiling. Dounia and Luzhin were facing one another on opposite sides of the table. Razumihin and Raskolnikov were facing Pulcheria Alexandrovna, Razumihin was next to Luzhin and Raskolnikov was beside his sister.

A moment's silence followed. Pyotr Petrovitch deliberately drew out a cambric handkerchief reeking of scent and blew his nose with an air of a benevolent man who felt himself slighted, and was firmly resolved to insist on an explanation. In the passage the idea had occurred to him to keep on his overcoat and walk away, and so give the two ladies a sharp and emphatic lesson and make them feel the gravity of the position. But he could not bring himself to do this. Besides, he could not endure uncertainty, and he wanted an explanation: if his request had been so openly disobeyed, there was something behind it, and in that case it was better to find it out beforehand; it rested with him to punish them and there would always be time for that.

"I trust you had a favourable journey," he inquired officially of Pulcheria Alexandrovna.

"Oh, very, Pyotr Petrovitch."

"I am gratified to hear it. And Avdotya Romanovna is not over-fatigued either?"

"I am young and strong, I don't get tired, but it was a great strain for mother," answered Dounia.

"That's unavoidable! our national railways are of terrible length. 'Mother Russia,' as they say, is a vast country.... In spite of all my desire to do so, I was unable to meet you yesterday. But I trust all passed off without inconvenience?"

"Oh, no, Pyotr Petrovitch, it was all terribly disheartening," Pulcheria Alexandrovna hastened to declare with peculiar intonation, "and if Dmitri Prokofitch had not been sent us, I really believe by God Himself, we should have been utterly lost. Here, he is! Dmitri Prokofitch Razumihin," she added, introducing him to Luzhin.

"I had the pleasure... yesterday," muttered Pyotr Petrovitch with a hostile glance sidelong at Razumihin; then he scowled and was silent.

Pyotr Petrovitch belonged to that class of persons, on the surface very polite in society, who make a great point of punctiliousness, but who, directly they are crossed in anything, are completely disconcerted, and become more like sacks of flour than elegant and lively men of society. Again all was silent; Raskolnikov was obstinately mute, Avdotya Romanovna was unwilling to open the conversation too soon. Razumihin had nothing to say, so Pulcheria Alexandrovna was anxious again.

"Marfa Petrovna is dead, have you heard?" she began having recourse to her leading item of conversation.

"To be sure, I heard so. I was immediately informed, and I have come to make you acquainted with the fact that Arkady Ivanovitch Svidriga&#65533;lov set off in haste for Petersburg immediately after his wife's funeral. So at least I have excellent authority for believing."

"To Petersburg? here?" Dounia asked in alarm and looked at her mother.

"Yes, indeed, and doubtless not without some design, having in view the rapidity of his departure, and all the circumstances preceding it."

"Good heavens! won't he leave Dounia in peace even here?" cried Pulcheria Alexandrovna.

"I imagine that neither you nor Avdotya Romanovna have any grounds for uneasiness, unless, of course, you are yourselves desirous of getting into communication with him. For my part I am on my guard, and am now discovering where he is lodging."

"Oh, Pyotr Petrovitch, you would not believe what a fright you have given me," Pulcheria Alexandrovna went on: "I've only seen him twice, but I thought him terrible, terrible! I am convinced that he was the cause of Marfa Petrovna's death."

"It's impossible to be certain about that. I have precise information. I do not dispute that he may have contributed to accelerate the course of events by the moral influence, so to say, of the affront; but as to the general conduct and moral characteristics of that personage, I am in agreement with you. I do not know whether he is well off now, and precisely what Marfa Petrovna left him; this will be known to me within a very short period; but no doubt here in Petersburg, if he has any pecuniary resources, he will relapse at once into his old ways. He is the most depraved, and abjectly vicious specimen of that class of men. I have considerable reason to believe that Marfa Petrovna, who was so unfortunate as to fall in love with him and to pay his debts eight years ago, was of service to him also in another way. Solely by her exertions and sacrifices, a criminal charge, involving an element of fantastic and homicidal brutality for which he might well have been sentenced to Siberia, was hushed up. That's the sort of man he is, if you care to know."

"Good heavens!" cried Pulcheria Alexandrovna. Raskolnikov listened attentively.

"Are you speaking the truth when you say that you have good evidence of this?" Dounia asked sternly and emphatically.

"I only repeat what I was told in secret by Marfa Petrovna. I must observe that from the legal point of view the case was far from clear. There was, and I believe still is, living here a woman called Resslich, a foreigner, who lent small sums of money at interest, and did other commissions, and with this woman Svidriga&#65533;lov had for a long while close and mysterious relations. She had a relation, a niece I believe, living with her, a deaf and dumb girl of fifteen, or perhaps not more than fourteen. Resslich hated this girl, and grudged her every crust; she used to beat her mercilessly. One day the girl was found hanging in the garret. At the inquest the verdict was suicide. After the usual proceedings the matter ended, but, later on, information was given that the child had been... cruelly outraged by Svidriga&#65533;lov. It is true, this was not clearly established, the information was given by another German woman of loose character whose word could not be trusted; no statement was actually made to the police, thanks to Marfa Petrovna's money and exertions; it did not get beyond gossip. And yet the story is a very significant one. You heard, no doubt, Avdotya Romanovna, when you were with them the story of the servant Philip who died of ill treatment he received six years ago, before the abolition of serfdom."

"I heard, on the contrary, that this Philip hanged himself."

"Quite so, but what drove him, or rather perhaps disposed him, to suicide was the systematic persecution and severity of Mr. Svidriga&#65533;lov."

"I don't know that," answered Dounia, dryly. "I only heard a queer story that Philip was a sort of hypochondriac, a sort of domestic philosopher, the servants used to say, 'he read himself silly,' and that he hanged himself partly on account of Mr. Svidriga&#65533;lov's mockery of him and not his blows. When I was there he behaved well to the servants, and they were actually fond of him, though they certainly did blame him for Philip's death."

"I perceive, Avdotya Romanovna, that you seem disposed to undertake his defence all of a sudden," Luzhin observed, twisting his lips into an ambiguous smile, "there's no doubt that he is an astute man, and insinuating where ladies are concerned, of which Marfa Petrovna, who has died so strangely, is a terrible instance. My only desire has been to be of service to you and your mother with my advice, in view of the renewed efforts which may certainly be anticipated from him. For my part it's my firm conviction, that he will end in a debtor's prison again. Marfa Petrovna had not the slightest intention of settling anything substantial on him, having regard for his children's interests, and, if she left him anything, it would only be the merest sufficiency, something insignificant and ephemeral, which would not last a year for a man of his habits."

"Pyotr Petrovitch, I beg you," said Dounia, "say no more of Mr. Svidriga&#65533;lov. It makes me miserable."

"He has just been to see me," said Raskolnikov, breaking his silence for the first time.

There were exclamations from all, and they all turned to him. Even Pyotr Petrovitch was roused.

"An hour and a half ago, he came in when I was asleep, waked me, and introduced himself," Raskolnikov continued. "He was fairly cheerful and at ease, and quite hopes that we shall become friends. He is particularly anxious, by the way, Dounia, for an interview with you, at which he asked me to assist. He has a proposition to make to you, and he told me about it. He told me, too, that a week before her death Marfa Petrovna left you three thousand roubles in her will, Dounia, and that you can receive the money very shortly."

"Thank God!" cried Pulcheria Alexandrovna, crossing herself. "Pray for her soul, Dounia!"

"It's a fact!" broke from Luzhin.

"Tell us, what more?" Dounia urged Raskolnikov.

"Then he said that he wasn't rich and all the estate was left to his children who are now with an aunt, then that he was staying somewhere not far from me, but where, I don't know, I didn't ask...."

"But what, what does he want to propose to Dounia?" cried Pulcheria Alexandrovna in a fright. "Did he tell you?"

"Yes."

"What was it?"

"I'll tell you afterwards."

Raskolnikov ceased speaking and turned his attention to his tea.

Pyotr Petrovitch looked at his watch.

"I am compelled to keep a business engagement, and so I shall not be in your way," he added with an air of some pique and he began getting up.

"Don't go, Pyotr Petrovitch," said Dounia, "you intended to spend the evening. Besides, you wrote yourself that you wanted to have an explanation with mother."

"Precisely so, Avdotya Romanovna," Pyotr Petrovitch answered impressively, sitting down again, but still holding his hat. "I certainly desired an explanation with you and your honoured mother upon a very important point indeed. But as your brother cannot speak openly in my presence of some proposals of Mr. Svidriga&#65533;lov, I, too, do not desire and am not able to speak openly... in the presence of others... of certain matters of the greatest gravity. Moreover, my most weighty and urgent request has been disregarded...."

Assuming an aggrieved air, Luzhin relapsed into dignified silence.

"Your request that my brother should not be present at our meeting was disregarded solely at my instance," said Dounia. "You wrote that you had been insulted by my brother; I think that this must be explained at once, and you must be reconciled. And if Rodya really has insulted you, then he _should_ and _will_ apologise."

Pyotr Petrovitch took a stronger line.

"There are insults, Avdotya Romanovna, which no goodwill can make us forget. There is a line in everything which it is dangerous to overstep; and when it has been overstepped, there is no return."

"That wasn't what I was speaking of exactly, Pyotr Petrovitch," Dounia interrupted with some impatience. "Please understand that our whole future depends now on whether all this is explained and set right as soon as possible. I tell you frankly at the start that I cannot look at it in any other light, and if you have the least regard for me, all this business must be ended to-day, however hard that may be. I repeat that if my brother is to blame he will ask your forgiveness."

"I am surprised at your putting the question like that," said Luzhin, getting more and more irritated. "Esteeming, and so to say, adoring you, I may at the same time, very well indeed, be able to dislike some member of your family. Though I lay claim to the happiness of your hand, I cannot accept duties incompatible with..."

"Ah, don't be so ready to take offence, Pyotr Petrovitch," Dounia interrupted with feeling, "and be the sensible and generous man I have always considered, and wish to consider, you to be. I've given you a great promise, I am your betrothed. Trust me in this matter and, believe me, I shall be capable of judging impartially. My assuming the part of judge is as much a surprise for my brother as for you. When I insisted on his coming to our interview to-day after your letter, I told him nothing of what I meant to do. Understand that, if you are not reconciled, I must choose between you—it must be either you or he. That is how the question rests on your side and on his. I don't want to be mistaken in my choice, and I must not be. For your sake I must break off with my brother, for my brother's sake I must break off with you. I can find out for certain now whether he is a brother to me, and I want to know it; and of you, whether I am dear to you, whether you esteem me, whether you are the husband for me."

"Avdotya Romanovna," Luzhin declared huffily, "your words are of too much consequence to me; I will say more, they are offensive in view of the position I have the honour to occupy in relation to you. To say nothing of your strange and offensive setting me on a level with an impertinent boy, you admit the possibility of breaking your promise to me. You say 'you or he,' showing thereby of how little consequence I am in your eyes... I cannot let this pass considering the relationship and... the obligations existing between us."

"What!" cried Dounia, flushing. "I set your interest beside all that has hitherto been most precious in my life, what has made up the _whole_ of my life, and here you are offended at my making too _little_ account of you."

Raskolnikov smiled sarcastically, Razumihin fidgeted, but Pyotr Petrovitch did not accept the reproof; on the contrary, at every word he became more persistent and irritable, as though he relished it.

"Love for the future partner of your life, for your husband, ought to outweigh your love for your brother," he pronounced sententiously, "and in any case I cannot be put on the same level.... Although I said so emphatically that I would not speak openly in your brother's presence, nevertheless, I intend now to ask your honoured mother for a necessary explanation on a point of great importance closely affecting my dignity. Your son," he turned to Pulcheria Alexandrovna, "yesterday in the presence of Mr. Razsudkin (or... I think that's it? excuse me I have forgotten your surname," he bowed politely to Razumihin) "insulted me by misrepresenting the idea I expressed to you in a private conversation, drinking coffee, that is, that marriage with a poor girl who has had experience of trouble is more advantageous from the conjugal point of view than with one who has lived in luxury, since it is more profitable for the moral character. Your son intentionally exaggerated the significance of my words and made them ridiculous, accusing me of malicious intentions, and, as far as I could see, relied upon your correspondence with him. I shall consider myself happy, Pulcheria Alexandrovna, if it is possible for you to convince me of an opposite conclusion, and thereby considerately reassure me. Kindly let me know in what terms precisely you repeated my words in your letter to Rodion Romanovitch."

"I don't remember," faltered Pulcheria Alexandrovna. "I repeated them as I understood them. I don't know how Rodya repeated them to you, perhaps he exaggerated."

"He could not have exaggerated them, except at your instigation."

"Pyotr Petrovitch," Pulcheria Alexandrovna declared with dignity, "the proof that Dounia and I did not take your words in a very bad sense is the fact that we are here."

"Good, mother," said Dounia approvingly.

"Then this is my fault again," said Luzhin, aggrieved.

"Well, Pyotr Petrovitch, you keep blaming Rodion, but you yourself have just written what was false about him," Pulcheria Alexandrovna added, gaining courage.

"I don't remember writing anything false."

"You wrote," Raskolnikov said sharply, not turning to Luzhin, "that I gave money yesterday not to the widow of the man who was killed, as was the fact, but to his daughter (whom I had never seen till yesterday). You wrote this to make dissension between me and my family, and for that object added coarse expressions about the conduct of a girl whom you don't know. All that is mean slander."

"Excuse me, sir," said Luzhin, quivering with fury. "I enlarged upon your qualities and conduct in my letter solely in response to your sister's and mother's inquiries, how I found you, and what impression you made on me. As for what you've alluded to in my letter, be so good as to point out one word of falsehood, show, that is, that you didn't throw away your money, and that there are not worthless persons in that family, however unfortunate."

"To my thinking, you, with all your virtues, are not worth the little finger of that unfortunate girl at whom you throw stones."

"Would you go so far then as to let her associate with your mother and sister?"

"I have done so already, if you care to know. I made her sit down to-day with mother and Dounia."

"Rodya!" cried Pulcheria Alexandrovna. Dounia crimsoned, Razumihin knitted his brows. Luzhin smiled with lofty sarcasm.

"You may see for yourself, Avdotya Romanovna," he said, "whether it is possible for us to agree. I hope now that this question is at an end, once and for all. I will withdraw, that I may not hinder the pleasures of family intimacy, and the discussion of secrets." He got up from his chair and took his hat. "But in withdrawing, I venture to request that for the future I may be spared similar meetings, and, so to say, compromises. I appeal particularly to you, honoured Pulcheria Alexandrovna, on this subject, the more as my letter was addressed to you and to no one else."

Pulcheria Alexandrovna was a little offended.

"You seem to think we are completely under your authority, Pyotr Petrovitch. Dounia has told you the reason your desire was disregarded, she had the best intentions. And indeed you write as though you were laying commands upon me. Are we to consider every desire of yours as a command? Let me tell you on the contrary that you ought to show particular delicacy and consideration for us now, because we have thrown up everything, and have come here relying on you, and so we are in any case in a sense in your hands."

"That is not quite true, Pulcheria Alexandrovna, especially at the present moment, when the news has come of Marfa Petrovna's legacy, which seems indeed very apropos, judging from the new tone you take to me," he added sarcastically.

"Judging from that remark, we may certainly presume that you were reckoning on our helplessness," Dounia observed irritably.

"But now in any case I cannot reckon on it, and I particularly desire not to hinder your discussion of the secret proposals of Arkady Ivanovitch Svidriga&#65533;lov, which he has entrusted to your brother and which have, I perceive, a great and possibly a very agreeable interest for you."

"Good heavens!" cried Pulcheria Alexandrovna.

Razumihin could not sit still on his chair.

"Aren't you ashamed now, sister?" asked Raskolnikov.

"I am ashamed, Rodya," said Dounia. "Pyotr Petrovitch, go away," she turned to him, white with anger.

Pyotr Petrovitch had apparently not at all expected such a conclusion. He had too much confidence in himself, in his power and in the helplessness of his victims. He could not believe it even now. He turned pale, and his lips quivered.

"Avdotya Romanovna, if I go out of this door now, after such a dismissal, then, you may reckon on it, I will never come back. Consider what you are doing. My word is not to be shaken."

"What insolence!" cried Dounia, springing up from her seat. "I don't want you to come back again."

"What! So that's how it stands!" cried Luzhin, utterly unable to the last moment to believe in the rupture and so completely thrown out of his reckoning now. "So that's how it stands! But do you know, Avdotya Romanovna, that I might protest?"

"What right have you to speak to her like that?" Pulcheria Alexandrovna intervened hotly. "And what can you protest about? What rights have you? Am I to give my Dounia to a man like you? Go away, leave us altogether! We are to blame for having agreed to a wrong action, and I above all...."

"But you have bound me, Pulcheria Alexandrovna," Luzhin stormed in a frenzy, "by your promise, and now you deny it and... besides... I have been led on account of that into expenses...."

This last complaint was so characteristic of Pyotr Petrovitch, that Raskolnikov, pale with anger and with the effort of restraining it, could not help breaking into laughter. But Pulcheria Alexandrovna was furious.

"Expenses? What expenses? Are you speaking of our trunk? But the conductor brought it for nothing for you. Mercy on us, we have bound you! What are you thinking about, Pyotr Petrovitch, it was you bound us, hand and foot, not we!"

"Enough, mother, no more please," Avdotya Romanovna implored. "Pyotr Petrovitch, do be kind and go!"

"I am going, but one last word," he said, quite unable to control himself. "Your mamma seems to have entirely forgotten that I made up my mind to take you, so to speak, after the gossip of the town had spread all over the district in regard to your reputation. Disregarding public opinion for your sake and reinstating your reputation, I certainly might very well reckon on a fitting return, and might indeed look for gratitude on your part. And my eyes have only now been opened! I see myself that I may have acted very, very recklessly in disregarding the universal verdict...."

"Does the fellow want his head smashed?" cried Razumihin, jumping up.

"You are a mean and spiteful man!" cried Dounia.

"Not a word! Not a movement!" cried Raskolnikov, holding Razumihin back; then going close up to Luzhin, "Kindly leave the room!" he said quietly and distinctly, "and not a word more or..."

Pyotr Petrovitch gazed at him for some seconds with a pale face that worked with anger, then he turned, went out, and rarely has any man carried away in his heart such vindictive hatred as he felt against Raskolnikov. Him, and him alone, he blamed for everything. It is noteworthy that as he went downstairs he still imagined that his case was perhaps not utterly lost, and that, so far as the ladies were concerned, all might "very well indeed" be set right again.

PART 5

CHAPTER 1

The morning that followed the fateful interview with Dounia and her mother brought sobering influences to bear on Pyotr Petrovitch. Intensely unpleasant as it was, he was forced little by little to accept as a fact beyond recall what had seemed to him only the day before fantastic and incredible. The black snake of wounded vanity had been gnawing at his heart all night. When he got out of bed, Pyotr Petrovitch immediately looked in the looking-glass. He was afraid that he had jaundice. However his health seemed unimpaired so far, and looking at his noble, clear-skinned countenance which had grown fattish of late, Pyotr Petrovitch for an instant was positively comforted in the conviction that he would find another bride and, perhaps, even a better one. But coming back to the sense of his present position, he turned aside and spat vigorously, which excited a sarcastic smile in Andrey Semyonovitch Lebeziatnikov; the young friend with whom he was staying. That smile Pyotr Petrovitch noticed, and at once set it down against his young friend's account. He had set down a good many points against him of late. His anger was redoubled when he reflected that he ought not to have told Andrey Semyonovitch about the result of yesterday's interview. That was the second mistake he had made in temper, through impulsiveness and irritability.... Moreover, all that morning one unpleasantness followed another. He even found a hitch awaiting him in his legal case in the senate. He was particularly irritated by the owner of the flat which had been taken in view of his approaching marriage and was being redecorated at his own expense; the owner, a rich German tradesman, would not entertain the idea of breaking the contract which had just been signed and insisted on the full forfeit money, though Pyotr Petrovitch would be giving him back the flat practically redecorated. In the same way the upholsterers refused to return a single rouble of the instalment paid for the furniture purchased but not yet removed to the flat.

"Am I to get married simply for the sake of the furniture?" Pyotr Petrovitch ground his teeth and at the same time once more he had a gleam of desperate hope. "Can all that be really so irrevocably over? Is it no use to make another effort?" The thought of Dounia sent a voluptuous pang through his heart.

He endured anguish at that moment, and if it had been possible to slay Raskolnikov instantly by wishing it, Pyotr Petrovitch would promptly have uttered the wish.

"It was my mistake, too, not to have given them money," he thought, as he returned dejectedly to Lebeziatnikov's room, "and why on earth was I such a Jew? It was false economy! I meant to keep them without a penny so that they should turn to me as their providence, and look at them! foo! If I'd spent some fifteen hundred roubles on them for the trousseau and presents, on knick-knacks, dressing-cases, jewellery, materials, and all that sort of trash from Knopp's and the English shop, my position would have been better and... stronger! They could not have refused me so easily! They are the sort of people that would feel bound to return money and presents if they broke it off; and they would find it hard to do it! And their conscience would prick them: how can we dismiss a man who has hitherto been so generous and delicate?.... H'm! I've made a blunder."

And grinding his teeth again, Pyotr Petrovitch called himself a fool—but not aloud, of course.

He returned home, twice as irritated and angry as before. The preparations for the funeral dinner at Katerina Ivanovna's excited his curiosity as he passed. He had heard about it the day before; he fancied, indeed, that he had been invited, but absorbed in his own cares he had paid no attention. Inquiring of Madame Lippevechsel who was busy laying the table while Katerina Ivanovna was away at the cemetery, he heard that the entertainment was to be a great affair, that all the lodgers had been invited, among them some who had not known the dead man, that even Andrey Semyonovitch Lebeziatnikov was invited in spite of his previous quarrel with Katerina Ivanovna, that he, Pyotr Petrovitch, was not only invited, but was eagerly expected as he was the most important of the lodgers. Amalia Ivanovna herself had been invited with great ceremony in spite of the recent unpleasantness, and so she was very busy with preparations and was taking a positive pleasure in them; she was moreover dressed up to the nines, all in new black silk, and she was proud of it. All this suggested an idea to Pyotr Petrovitch and he went into his room, or rather Lebeziatnikov's, somewhat thoughtful. He had learnt that Raskolnikov was to be one of the guests.

Andrey Semyonovitch had been at home all the morning. The attitude of Pyotr Petrovitch to this gentleman was strange, though perhaps natural. Pyotr Petrovitch had despised and hated him from the day he came to stay with him and at the same time he seemed somewhat afraid of him. He had not come to stay with him on his arrival in Petersburg simply from parsimony, though that had been perhaps his chief object. He had heard of Andrey Semyonovitch, who had once been his ward, as a leading young progressive who was taking an important part in certain interesting circles, the doings of which were a legend in the provinces. It had impressed Pyotr Petrovitch. These powerful omniscient circles who despised everyone and showed everyone up had long inspired in him a peculiar but quite vague alarm. He had not, of course, been able to form even an approximate notion of what they meant. He, like everyone, had heard that there were, especially in Petersburg, progressives of some sort, nihilists and so on, and, like many people, he exaggerated and distorted the significance of those words to an absurd degree. What for many years past he had feared more than anything was _being shown up_ and this was the chief ground for his continual uneasiness at the thought of transferring his business to Petersburg. He was afraid of this as little children are sometimes panic-stricken. Some years before, when he was just entering on his own career, he had come upon two cases in which rather important personages in the province, patrons of his, had been cruelly shown up.

One instance had ended in great scandal for the person attacked and the other had very nearly ended in serious trouble. For this reason Pyotr Petrovitch intended to go into the subject as soon as he reached Petersburg and, if necessary, to anticipate contingencies by seeking the favour of "our younger generation." He relied on Andrey Semyonovitch for this and before his visit to Raskolnikov he had succeeded in picking up some current phrases. He soon discovered that Andrey Semyonovitch was a commonplace simpleton, but that by no means reassured Pyotr Petrovitch. Even if he had been certain that all the progressives were fools like him, it would not have allayed his uneasiness. All the doctrines, the ideas, the systems, with which Andrey Semyonovitch pestered him had no interest for him. He had his own object—he simply wanted to find out at once what was happening _here_. Had these people any power or not? Had he anything to fear from them? Would they expose any enterprise of his? And what precisely was now the object of their attacks? Could he somehow make up to them and get round them if they really were powerful? Was this the thing to do or not? Couldn't he gain something through them? In fact hundreds of questions presented themselves.

Andrey Semyonovitch was an an&#65533;mic, scrofulous little man, with strangely flaxen mutton-chop whiskers of which he was very proud. He was a clerk and had almost always something wrong with his eyes. He was rather soft-hearted, but self-confident and sometimes extremely conceited in speech, which had an absurd effect, incongruous with his little figure. He was one of the lodgers most respected by Amalia Ivanovna, for he did not get drunk and paid regularly for his lodgings. Andrey Semyonovitch really was rather stupid; he attached himself to the cause of progress and "our younger generation" from enthusiasm. He was one of the numerous and varied legion of dullards, of half-animate abortions, conceited, half-educated coxcombs, who attach themselves to the idea most in fashion only to vulgarise it and who caricature every cause they serve, however sincerely.

Though Lebeziatnikov was so good-natured, he, too, was beginning to dislike Pyotr Petrovitch. This happened on both sides unconsciously. However simple Andrey Semyonovitch might be, he began to see that Pyotr Petrovitch was duping him and secretly despising him, and that "he was not the right sort of man." He had tried expounding to him the system of Fourier and the Darwinian theory, but of late Pyotr Petrovitch began to listen too sarcastically and even to be rude. The fact was he had begun instinctively to guess that Lebeziatnikov was not merely a commonplace simpleton, but, perhaps, a liar, too, and that he had no connections of any consequence even in his own circle, but had simply picked things up third-hand; and that very likely he did not even know much about his own work of propaganda, for he was in too great a muddle. A fine person he would be to show anyone up! It must be noted, by the way, that Pyotr Petrovitch had during those ten days eagerly accepted the strangest praise from Andrey Semyonovitch; he had not protested, for instance, when Andrey Semyonovitch belauded him for being ready to contribute to the establishment of the new "commune," or to abstain from christening his future children, or to acquiesce if Dounia were to take a lover a month after marriage, and so on. Pyotr Petrovitch so enjoyed hearing his own praises that he did not disdain even such virtues when they were attributed to him.

Pyotr Petrovitch had had occasion that morning to realise some five-per-cent bonds and now he sat down to the table and counted over bundles of notes. Andrey Semyonovitch who hardly ever had any money walked about the room pretending to himself to look at all those bank notes with indifference and even contempt. Nothing would have convinced Pyotr Petrovitch that Andrey Semyonovitch could really look on the money unmoved, and the latter, on his side, kept thinking bitterly that Pyotr Petrovitch was capable of entertaining such an idea about him and was, perhaps, glad of the opportunity of teasing his young friend by reminding him of his inferiority and the great difference between them.

He found him incredibly inattentive and irritable, though he, Andrey Semyonovitch, began enlarging on his favourite subject, the foundation of a new special "commune." The brief remarks that dropped from Pyotr Petrovitch between the clicking of the beads on the reckoning frame betrayed unmistakable and discourteous irony. But the "humane" Andrey Semyonovitch ascribed Pyotr Petrovitch's ill-humour to his recent breach with Dounia and he was burning with impatience to discourse on that theme. He had something progressive to say on the subject which might console his worthy friend and "could not fail" to promote his development.

"There is some sort of festivity being prepared at that... at the widow's, isn't there?" Pyotr Petrovitch asked suddenly, interrupting Andrey Semyonovitch at the most interesting passage.

"Why, don't you know? Why, I was telling you last night what I think about all such ceremonies. And she invited you too, I heard. You were talking to her yesterday..."

"I should never have expected that beggarly fool would have spent on this feast all the money she got from that other fool, Raskolnikov. I was surprised just now as I came through at the preparations there, the wines! Several people are invited. It's beyond everything!" continued Pyotr Petrovitch, who seemed to have some object in pursuing the conversation. "What? You say I am asked too? When was that? I don't remember. But I shan't go. Why should I? I only said a word to her in passing yesterday of the possibility of her obtaining a year's salary as a destitute widow of a government clerk. I suppose she has invited me on that account, hasn't she? He-he-he!"

"I don't intend to go either," said Lebeziatnikov.

"I should think not, after giving her a thrashing! You might well hesitate, he-he!"

"Who thrashed? Whom?" cried Lebeziatnikov, flustered and blushing.

"Why, you thrashed Katerina Ivanovna a month ago. I heard so yesterday... so that's what your convictions amount to... and the woman question, too, wasn't quite sound, he-he-he!" and Pyotr Petrovitch, as though comforted, went back to clicking his beads.

"It's all slander and nonsense!" cried Lebeziatnikov, who was always afraid of allusions to the subject. "It was not like that at all, it was quite different. You've heard it wrong; it's a libel. I was simply defending myself. She rushed at me first with her nails, she pulled out all my whiskers.... It's permissable for anyone, I should hope, to defend himself and I never allow anyone to use violence to me on principle, for it's an act of despotism. What was I to do? I simply pushed her back."

"He-he-he!" Luzhin went on laughing maliciously.

"You keep on like that because you are out of humour yourself.... But that's nonsense and it has nothing, nothing whatever to do with the woman question! You don't understand; I used to think, indeed, that if women are equal to men in all respects, even in strength (as is maintained now) there ought to be equality in that, too. Of course, I reflected afterwards that such a question ought not really to arise, for there ought not to be fighting and in the future society fighting is unthinkable... and that it would be a queer thing to seek for equality in fighting. I am not so stupid... though, of course, there is fighting... there won't be later, but at present there is... confound it! How muddled one gets with you! It's not on that account that I am not going. I am not going on principle, not to take part in the revolting convention of memorial dinners, that's why! Though, of course, one might go to laugh at it.... I am sorry there won't be any priests at it. I should certainly go if there were."

"Then you would sit down at another man's table and insult it and those who invited you. Eh?"

"Certainly not insult, but protest. I should do it with a good object. I might indirectly assist the cause of enlightenment and propaganda. It's a duty of every man to work for enlightenment and propaganda and the more harshly, perhaps, the better. I might drop a seed, an idea.... And something might grow up from that seed. How should I be insulting them? They might be offended at first, but afterwards they'd see I'd done them a service. You know, Terebyeva (who is in the community now) was blamed because when she left her family and... devoted... herself, she wrote to her father and mother that she wouldn't go on living conventionally and was entering on a free marriage and it was said that that was too harsh, that she might have spared them and have written more kindly. I think that's all nonsense and there's no need of softness; on the contrary, what's wanted is protest. Varents had been married seven years, she abandoned her two children, she told her husband straight out in a letter: 'I have realised that I cannot be happy with you. I can never forgive you that you have deceived me by concealing from me that there is another organisation of society by means of the communities. I have only lately learned it from a great-hearted man to whom I have given myself and with whom I am establishing a community. I speak plainly because I consider it dishonest to deceive you. Do as you think best. Do not hope to get me back, you are too late. I hope you will be happy.' That's how letters like that ought to be written!"

"Is that Terebyeva the one you said had made a third free marriage?"

"No, it's only the second, really! But what if it were the fourth, what if it were the fifteenth, that's all nonsense! And if ever I regretted the death of my father and mother, it is now, and I sometimes think if my parents were living what a protest I would have aimed at them! I would have done something on purpose... I would have shown them! I would have astonished them! I am really sorry there is no one!"

"To surprise! He-he! Well, be that as you will," Pyotr Petrovitch interrupted, "but tell me this; do you know the dead man's daughter, the delicate-looking little thing? It's true what they say about her, isn't it?"

"What of it? I think, that is, it is my own personal conviction that this is the normal condition of women. Why not? I mean, _distinguons_. In our present society it is not altogether normal, because it is compulsory, but in the future society it will be perfectly normal, because it will be voluntary. Even as it is, she was quite right: she was suffering and that was her asset, so to speak, her capital which she had a perfect right to dispose of. Of course, in the future society there will be no need of assets, but her part will have another significance, rational and in harmony with her environment. As to Sofya Semyonovna personally, I regard her action as a vigorous protest against the organisation of society, and I respect her deeply for it; I rejoice indeed when I look at her!"

"I was told that you got her turned out of these lodgings."

Lebeziatnikov was enraged.

"That's another slander," he yelled. "It was not so at all! That was all Katerina Ivanovna's invention, for she did not understand! And I never made love to Sofya Semyonovna! I was simply developing her, entirely disinterestedly, trying to rouse her to protest.... All I wanted was her protest and Sofya Semyonovna could not have remained here anyway!"

"Have you asked her to join your community?"

"You keep on laughing and very inappropriately, allow me to tell you. You don't understand! There is no such r&#65533;le in a community. The community is established that there should be no such r&#65533;les. In a community, such a r&#65533;le is essentially transformed and what is stupid here is sensible there, what, under present conditions, is unnatural becomes perfectly natural in the community. It all depends on the environment. It's all the environment and man himself is nothing. And I am on good terms with Sofya Semyonovna to this day, which is a proof that she never regarded me as having wronged her. I am trying now to attract her to the community, but on quite, quite a different footing. What are you laughing at? We are trying to establish a community of our own, a special one, on a broader basis. We have gone further in our convictions. We reject more! And meanwhile I'm still developing Sofya Semyonovna. She has a beautiful, beautiful character!"

"And you take advantage of her fine character, eh? He-he!"

"No, no! Oh, no! On the contrary."

"Oh, on the contrary! He-he-he! A queer thing to say!"

"Believe me! Why should I disguise it? In fact, I feel it strange myself how timid, chaste and modern she is with me!"

"And you, of course, are developing her... he-he! trying to prove to her that all that modesty is nonsense?"

"Not at all, not at all! How coarsely, how stupidly—excuse me saying so—you misunderstand the word development! Good heavens, how... crude you still are! We are striving for the freedom of women and you have only one idea in your head.... Setting aside the general question of chastity and feminine modesty as useless in themselves and indeed prejudices, I fully accept her chastity with me, because that's for her to decide. Of course if she were to tell me herself that she wanted me, I should think myself very lucky, because I like the girl very much; but as it is, no one has ever treated her more courteously than I, with more respect for her dignity... I wait in hopes, that's all!"

"You had much better make her a present of something. I bet you never thought of that."

"You don't understand, as I've told you already! Of course, she is in such a position, but it's another question. Quite another question! You simply despise her. Seeing a fact which you mistakenly consider deserving of contempt, you refuse to take a humane view of a fellow creature. You don't know what a character she is! I am only sorry that of late she has quite given up reading and borrowing books. I used to lend them to her. I am sorry, too, that with all the energy and resolution in protesting—which she has already shown once—she has little self-reliance, little, so to say, independence, so as to break free from certain prejudices and certain foolish ideas. Yet she thoroughly understands some questions, for instance about kissing of hands, that is, that it's an insult to a woman for a man to kiss her hand, because it's a sign of inequality. We had a debate about it and I described it to her. She listened attentively to an account of the workmen's associations in France, too. Now I am explaining the question of coming into the room in the future society."

"And what's that, pray?"

"We had a debate lately on the question: Has a member of the community the right to enter another member's room, whether man or woman, at any time... and we decided that he has!"

"It might be at an inconvenient moment, he-he!"

Lebeziatnikov was really angry.

"You are always thinking of something unpleasant," he cried with aversion. "Tfoo! How vexed I am that when I was expounding our system, I referred prematurely to the question of personal privacy! It's always a stumbling-block to people like you, they turn it into ridicule before they understand it. And how proud they are of it, too! Tfoo! I've often maintained that that question should not be approached by a novice till he has a firm faith in the system. And tell me, please, what do you find so shameful even in cesspools? I should be the first to be ready to clean out any cesspool you like. And it's not a question of self-sacrifice, it's simply work, honourable, useful work which is as good as any other and much better than the work of a Raphael and a Pushkin, because it is more useful."

"And more honourable, more honourable, he-he-he!"

"What do you mean by 'more honourable'? I don't understand such expressions to describe human activity. 'More honourable,' 'nobler'—all those are old-fashioned prejudices which I reject. Everything which is _of use_ to mankind is honourable. I only understand one word: _useful_! You can snigger as much as you like, but that's so!"

Pyotr Petrovitch laughed heartily. He had finished counting the money and was putting it away. But some of the notes he left on the table. The "cesspool question" had already been a subject of dispute between them. What was absurd was that it made Lebeziatnikov really angry, while it amused Luzhin and at that moment he particularly wanted to anger his young friend.

"It's your ill-luck yesterday that makes you so ill-humoured and annoying," blurted out Lebeziatnikov, who in spite of his "independence" and his "protests" did not venture to oppose Pyotr Petrovitch and still behaved to him with some of the respect habitual in earlier years.

"You'd better tell me this," Pyotr Petrovitch interrupted with haughty displeasure, "can you... or rather are you really friendly enough with that young person to ask her to step in here for a minute? I think they've all come back from the cemetery... I heard the sound of steps... I want to see her, that young person."

"What for?" Lebeziatnikov asked with surprise.

"Oh, I want to. I am leaving here to-day or to-morrow and therefore I wanted to speak to her about... However, you may be present during the interview. It's better you should be, indeed. For there's no knowing what you might imagine."

"I shan't imagine anything. I only asked and, if you've anything to say to her, nothing is easier than to call her in. I'll go directly and you may be sure I won't be in your way."

Five minutes later Lebeziatnikov came in with Sonia. She came in very much surprised and overcome with shyness as usual. She was always shy in such circumstances and was always afraid of new people, she had been as a child and was even more so now.... Pyotr Petrovitch met her "politely and affably," but with a certain shade of bantering familiarity which in his opinion was suitable for a man of his respectability and weight in dealing with a creature so young and so _interesting_ as she. He hastened to "reassure" her and made her sit down facing him at the table. Sonia sat down, looked about her—at Lebeziatnikov, at the notes lying on the table and then again at Pyotr Petrovitch and her eyes remained riveted on him. Lebeziatnikov was moving to the door. Pyotr Petrovitch signed to Sonia to remain seated and stopped Lebeziatnikov.

"Is Raskolnikov in there? Has he come?" he asked him in a whisper.

"Raskolnikov? Yes. Why? Yes, he is there. I saw him just come in.... Why?"

"Well, I particularly beg you to remain here with us and not to leave me alone with this... young woman. I only want a few words with her, but God knows what they may make of it. I shouldn't like Raskolnikov to repeat anything.... You understand what I mean?"

"I understand!" Lebeziatnikov saw the point. "Yes, you are right.... Of course, I am convinced personally that you have no reason to be uneasy, but... still, you are right. Certainly I'll stay. I'll stand here at the window and not be in your way... I think you are right..."

Pyotr Petrovitch returned to the sofa, sat down opposite Sonia, looked attentively at her and assumed an extremely dignified, even severe expression, as much as to say, "don't you make any mistake, madam." Sonia was overwhelmed with embarrassment.

"In the first place, Sofya Semyonovna, will you make my excuses to your respected mamma.... That's right, isn't it? Katerina Ivanovna stands in the place of a mother to you?" Pyotr Petrovitch began with great dignity, though affably.

It was evident that his intentions were friendly.

"Quite so, yes; the place of a mother," Sonia answered, timidly and hurriedly.

"Then will you make my apologies to her? Through inevitable circumstances I am forced to be absent and shall not be at the dinner in spite of your mamma's kind invitation."

"Yes... I'll tell her... at once."

And Sonia hastily jumped up from her seat.

"Wait, that's not all," Pyotr Petrovitch detained her, smiling at her simplicity and ignorance of good manners, "and you know me little, my dear Sofya Semyonovna, if you suppose I would have ventured to trouble a person like you for a matter of so little consequence affecting myself only. I have another object."

Sonia sat down hurriedly. Her eyes rested again for an instant on the grey-and-rainbow-coloured notes that remained on the table, but she quickly looked away and fixed her eyes on Pyotr Petrovitch. She felt it horribly indecorous, especially for _her_, to look at another person's money. She stared at the gold eye-glass which Pyotr Petrovitch held in his left hand and at the massive and extremely handsome ring with a yellow stone on his middle finger. But suddenly she looked away and, not knowing where to turn, ended by staring Pyotr Petrovitch again straight in the face. After a pause of still greater dignity he continued.

"I chanced yesterday in passing to exchange a couple of words with Katerina Ivanovna, poor woman. That was sufficient to enable me to ascertain that she is in a position—preternatural, if one may so express it."

"Yes... preternatural..." Sonia hurriedly assented.

"Or it would be simpler and more comprehensible to say, ill."

"Yes, simpler and more comprehen... yes, ill."

"Quite so. So then from a feeling of humanity and so to speak compassion, I should be glad to be of service to her in any way, foreseeing her unfortunate position. I believe the whole of this poverty-stricken family depends now entirely on you?"

"Allow me to ask," Sonia rose to her feet, "did you say something to her yesterday of the possibility of a pension? Because she told me you had undertaken to get her one. Was that true?"

"Not in the slightest, and indeed it's an absurdity! I merely hinted at her obtaining temporary assistance as the widow of an official who had died in the service—if only she has patronage... but apparently your late parent had not served his full term and had not indeed been in the service at all of late. In fact, if there could be any hope, it would be very ephemeral, because there would be no claim for assistance in that case, far from it.... And she is dreaming of a pension already, he-he-he!... A go-ahead lady!"

"Yes, she is. For she is credulous and good-hearted, and she believes everything from the goodness of her heart and... and... and she is like that... yes... You must excuse her," said Sonia, and again she got up to go.

"But you haven't heard what I have to say."

"No, I haven't heard," muttered Sonia.

"Then sit down." She was terribly confused; she sat down again a third time.

"Seeing her position with her unfortunate little ones, I should be glad, as I have said before, so far as lies in my power, to be of service, that is, so far as is in my power, not more. One might for instance get up a subscription for her, or a lottery, something of the sort, such as is always arranged in such cases by friends or even outsiders desirous of assisting people. It was of that I intended to speak to you; it might be done."

"Yes, yes... God will repay you for it," faltered Sonia, gazing intently at Pyotr Petrovitch.

"It might be, but we will talk of it later. We might begin it to-day, we will talk it over this evening and lay the foundation so to speak. Come to me at seven o'clock. Mr. Lebeziatnikov, I hope, will assist us. But there is one circumstance of which I ought to warn you beforehand and for which I venture to trouble you, Sofya Semyonovna, to come here. In my opinion money cannot be, indeed it's unsafe to put it into Katerina Ivanovna's own hands. The dinner to-day is a proof of that. Though she has not, so to speak, a crust of bread for to-morrow and... well, boots or shoes, or anything; she has bought to-day Jamaica rum, and even, I believe, Madeira and... and coffee. I saw it as I passed through. To-morrow it will all fall upon you again, they won't have a crust of bread. It's absurd, really, and so, to my thinking, a subscription ought to be raised so that the unhappy widow should not know of the money, but only you, for instance. Am I right?"

"I don't know... this is only to-day, once in her life.... She was so anxious to do honour, to celebrate the memory.... And she is very sensible... but just as you think and I shall be very, very... they will all be... and God will reward... and the orphans..."

Sonia burst into tears.

"Very well, then, keep it in mind; and now will you accept for the benefit of your relation the small sum that I am able to spare, from me personally. I am very anxious that my name should not be mentioned in connection with it. Here... having so to speak anxieties of my own, I cannot do more..."

And Pyotr Petrovitch held out to Sonia a ten-rouble note carefully unfolded. Sonia took it, flushed crimson, jumped up, muttered something and began taking leave. Pyotr Petrovitch accompanied her ceremoniously to the door. She got out of the room at last, agitated and distressed, and returned to Katerina Ivanovna, overwhelmed with confusion.

All this time Lebeziatnikov had stood at the window or walked about the room, anxious not to interrupt the conversation; when Sonia had gone he walked up to Pyotr Petrovitch and solemnly held out his hand.

"I heard and _saw_ everything," he said, laying stress on the last verb. "That is honourable, I mean to say, it's humane! You wanted to avoid gratitude, I saw! And although I cannot, I confess, in principle sympathise with private charity, for it not only fails to eradicate the evil but even promotes it, yet I must admit that I saw your action with pleasure—yes, yes, I like it."

"That's all nonsense," muttered Pyotr Petrovitch, somewhat disconcerted, looking carefully at Lebeziatnikov.

"No, it's not nonsense! A man who has suffered distress and annoyance as you did yesterday and who yet can sympathise with the misery of others, such a man... even though he is making a social mistake—is still deserving of respect! I did not expect it indeed of you, Pyotr Petrovitch, especially as according to your ideas... oh, what a drawback your ideas are to you! How distressed you are for instance by your ill-luck yesterday," cried the simple-hearted Lebeziatnikov, who felt a return of affection for Pyotr Petrovitch. "And, what do you want with marriage, with _legal_ marriage, my dear, noble Pyotr Petrovitch? Why do you cling to this _legality_ of marriage? Well, you may beat me if you like, but I am glad, positively glad it hasn't come off, that you are free, that you are not quite lost for humanity.... you see, I've spoken my mind!"

"Because I don't want in your free marriage to be made a fool of and to bring up another man's children, that's why I want legal marriage," Luzhin replied in order to make some answer.

He seemed preoccupied by something.

"Children? You referred to children," Lebeziatnikov started off like a warhorse at the trumpet call. "Children are a social question and a question of first importance, I agree; but the question of children has another solution. Some refuse to have children altogether, because they suggest the institution of the family. We'll speak of children later, but now as to the question of honour, I confess that's my weak point. That horrid, military, Pushkin expression is unthinkable in the dictionary of the future. What does it mean indeed? It's nonsense, there will be no deception in a free marriage! That is only the natural consequence of a legal marriage, so to say, its corrective, a protest. So that indeed it's not humiliating... and if I ever, to suppose an absurdity, were to be legally married, I should be positively glad of it. I should say to my wife: 'My dear, hitherto I have loved you, now I respect you, for you've shown you can protest!' You laugh! That's because you are of incapable of getting away from prejudices. Confound it all! I understand now where the unpleasantness is of being deceived in a legal marriage, but it's simply a despicable consequence of a despicable position in which both are humiliated. When the deception is open, as in a free marriage, then it does not exist, it's unthinkable. Your wife will only prove how she respects you by considering you incapable of opposing her happiness and avenging yourself on her for her new husband. Damn it all! I sometimes dream if I were to be married, pfoo! I mean if I were to marry, legally or not, it's just the same, I should present my wife with a lover if she had not found one for herself. 'My dear,' I should say, 'I love you, but even more than that I desire you to respect me. See!' Am I not right?"

Pyotr Petrovitch sniggered as he listened, but without much merriment. He hardly heard it indeed. He was preoccupied with something else and even Lebeziatnikov at last noticed it. Pyotr Petrovitch seemed excited and rubbed his hands. Lebeziatnikov remembered all this and reflected upon it afterwards.

CHAPTER 2

It would be difficult to explain exactly what could have originated the idea of that senseless dinner in Katerina Ivanovna's disordered brain. Nearly ten of the twenty roubles, given by Raskolnikov for Marmeladov's funeral, were wasted upon it. Possibly Katerina Ivanovna felt obliged to honour the memory of the deceased "suitably," that all the lodgers, and still more Amalia Ivanovna, might know "that he was in no way their inferior, and perhaps very much their superior," and that no one had the right "to turn up his nose at him." Perhaps the chief element was that peculiar "poor man's pride," which compels many poor people to spend their last savings on some traditional social ceremony, simply in order to do "like other people," and not to "be looked down upon." It is very probable, too, that Katerina Ivanovna longed on this occasion, at the moment when she seemed to be abandoned by everyone, to show those "wretched contemptible lodgers" that she knew "how to do things, how to entertain" and that she had been brought up "in a genteel, she might almost say aristocratic colonel's family" and had not been meant for sweeping floors and washing the children's rags at night. Even the poorest and most broken-spirited people are sometimes liable to these paroxysms of pride and vanity which take the form of an irresistible nervous craving. And Katerina Ivanovna was not broken-spirited; she might have been killed by circumstance, but her spirit could not have been broken, that is, she could not have been intimidated, her will could not be crushed. Moreover Sonia had said with good reason that her mind was unhinged. She could not be said to be insane, but for a year past she had been so harassed that her mind might well be overstrained. The later stages of consumption are apt, doctors tell us, to affect the intellect.

There was no great variety of wines, nor was there Madeira; but wine there was. There was vodka, rum and Lisbon wine, all of the poorest quality but in sufficient quantity. Besides the traditional rice and honey, there were three or four dishes, one of which consisted of pancakes, all prepared in Amalia Ivanovna's kitchen. Two samovars were boiling, that tea and punch might be offered after dinner. Katerina Ivanovna had herself seen to purchasing the provisions, with the help of one of the lodgers, an unfortunate little Pole who had somehow been stranded at Madame Lippevechsel's. He promptly put himself at Katerina Ivanovna's disposal and had been all that morning and all the day before running about as fast as his legs could carry him, and very anxious that everyone should be aware of it. For every trifle he ran to Katerina Ivanovna, even hunting her out at the bazaar, at every instant called her "_Pani_." She was heartily sick of him before the end, though she had declared at first that she could not have got on without this "serviceable and magnanimous man." It was one of Katerina Ivanovna's characteristics to paint everyone she met in the most glowing colours. Her praises were so exaggerated as sometimes to be embarrassing; she would invent various circumstances to the credit of her new acquaintance and quite genuinely believe in their reality. Then all of a sudden she would be disillusioned and would rudely and contemptuously repulse the person she had only a few hours before been literally adoring. She was naturally of a gay, lively and peace-loving disposition, but from continual failures and misfortunes she had come to desire so _keenly_ that all should live in peace and joy and should not _dare_ to break the peace, that the slightest jar, the smallest disaster reduced her almost to frenzy, and she would pass in an instant from the brightest hopes and fancies to cursing her fate and raving, and knocking her head against the wall.

Amalia Ivanovna, too, suddenly acquired extraordinary importance in Katerina Ivanovna's eyes and was treated by her with extraordinary respect, probably only because Amalia Ivanovna had thrown herself heart and soul into the preparations. She had undertaken to lay the table, to provide the linen, crockery, etc., and to cook the dishes in her kitchen, and Katerina Ivanovna had left it all in her hands and gone herself to the cemetery. Everything had been well done. Even the table-cloth was nearly clean; the crockery, knives, forks and glasses were, of course, of all shapes and patterns, lent by different lodgers, but the table was properly laid at the time fixed, and Amalia Ivanovna, feeling she had done her work well, had put on a black silk dress and a cap with new mourning ribbons and met the returning party with some pride. This pride, though justifiable, displeased Katerina Ivanovna for some reason: "as though the table could not have been laid except by Amalia Ivanovna!" She disliked the cap with new ribbons, too. "Could she be stuck up, the stupid German, because she was mistress of the house, and had consented as a favour to help her poor lodgers! As a favour! Fancy that! Katerina Ivanovna's father who had been a colonel and almost a governor had sometimes had the table set for forty persons, and then anyone like Amalia Ivanovna, or rather Ludwigovna, would not have been allowed into the kitchen."

Katerina Ivanovna, however, put off expressing her feelings for the time and contented herself with treating her coldly, though she decided inwardly that she would certainly have to put Amalia Ivanovna down and set her in her proper place, for goodness only knew what she was fancying herself. Katerina Ivanovna was irritated too by the fact that hardly any of the lodgers invited had come to the funeral, except the Pole who had just managed to run into the cemetery, while to the memorial dinner the poorest and most insignificant of them had turned up, the wretched creatures, many of them not quite sober. The older and more respectable of them all, as if by common consent, stayed away. Pyotr Petrovitch Luzhin, for instance, who might be said to be the most respectable of all the lodgers, did not appear, though Katerina Ivanovna had the evening before told all the world, that is Amalia Ivanovna, Polenka, Sonia and the Pole, that he was the most generous, noble-hearted man with a large property and vast connections, who had been a friend of her first husband's, and a guest in her father's house, and that he had promised to use all his influence to secure her a considerable pension. It must be noted that when Katerina Ivanovna exalted anyone's connections and fortune, it was without any ulterior motive, quite disinterestedly, for the mere pleasure of adding to the consequence of the person praised. Probably "taking his cue" from Luzhin, "that contemptible wretch Lebeziatnikov had not turned up either. What did he fancy himself? He was only asked out of kindness and because he was sharing the same room with Pyotr Petrovitch and was a friend of his, so that it would have been awkward not to invite him."

Among those who failed to appear were "the genteel lady and her old-maidish daughter," who had only been lodgers in the house for the last fortnight, but had several times complained of the noise and uproar in Katerina Ivanovna's room, especially when Marmeladov had come back drunk. Katerina Ivanovna heard this from Amalia Ivanovna who, quarrelling with Katerina Ivanovna, and threatening to turn the whole family out of doors, had shouted at her that they "were not worth the foot" of the honourable lodgers whom they were disturbing. Katerina Ivanovna determined now to invite this lady and her daughter, "whose foot she was not worth," and who had turned away haughtily when she casually met them, so that they might know that "she was more noble in her thoughts and feelings and did not harbour malice," and might see that she was not accustomed to her way of living. She had proposed to make this clear to them at dinner with allusions to her late father's governorship, and also at the same time to hint that it was exceedingly stupid of them to turn away on meeting her. The fat colonel-major (he was really a discharged officer of low rank) was also absent, but it appeared that he had been "not himself" for the last two days. The party consisted of the Pole, a wretched looking clerk with a spotty face and a greasy coat, who had not a word to say for himself, and smelt abominably, a deaf and almost blind old man who had once been in the post office and who had been from immemorial ages maintained by someone at Amalia Ivanovna's.

A retired clerk of the commissariat department came, too; he was drunk, had a loud and most unseemly laugh and only fancy—was without a waistcoat! One of the visitors sat straight down to the table without even greeting Katerina Ivanovna. Finally one person having no suit appeared in his dressing-gown, but this was too much, and the efforts of Amalia Ivanovna and the Pole succeeded in removing him. The Pole brought with him, however, two other Poles who did not live at Amalia Ivanovna's and whom no one had seen here before. All this irritated Katerina Ivanovna intensely. "For whom had they made all these preparations then?" To make room for the visitors the children had not even been laid for at the table; but the two little ones were sitting on a bench in the furthest corner with their dinner laid on a box, while Polenka as a big girl had to look after them, feed them, and keep their noses wiped like well-bred children's.

Katerina Ivanovna, in fact, could hardly help meeting her guests with increased dignity, and even haughtiness. She stared at some of them with special severity, and loftily invited them to take their seats. Rushing to the conclusion that Amalia Ivanovna must be responsible for those who were absent, she began treating her with extreme nonchalance, which the latter promptly observed and resented. Such a beginning was no good omen for the end. All were seated at last.

Raskolnikov came in almost at the moment of their return from the cemetery. Katerina Ivanovna was greatly delighted to see him, in the first place, because he was the one "educated visitor, and, as everyone knew, was in two years to take a professorship in the university," and secondly because he immediately and respectfully apologised for having been unable to be at the funeral. She positively pounced upon him, and made him sit on her left hand (Amalia Ivanovna was on her right). In spite of her continual anxiety that the dishes should be passed round correctly and that everyone should taste them, in spite of the agonising cough which interrupted her every minute and seemed to have grown worse during the last few days, she hastened to pour out in a half whisper to Raskolnikov all her suppressed feelings and her just indignation at the failure of the dinner, interspersing her remarks with lively and uncontrollable laughter at the expense of her visitors and especially of her landlady.

"It's all that cuckoo's fault! You know whom I mean? Her, her!" Katerina Ivanovna nodded towards the landlady. "Look at her, she's making round eyes, she feels that we are talking about her and can't understand. Pfoo, the owl! Ha-ha! (Cough-cough-cough.) And what does she put on that cap for? (Cough-cough-cough.) Have you noticed that she wants everyone to consider that she is patronising me and doing me an honour by being here? I asked her like a sensible woman to invite people, especially those who knew my late husband, and look at the set of fools she has brought! The sweeps! Look at that one with the spotty face. And those wretched Poles, ha-ha-ha! (Cough-cough-cough.) Not one of them has ever poked his nose in here, I've never set eyes on them. What have they come here for, I ask you? There they sit in a row. Hey, _pan_!" she cried suddenly to one of them, "have you tasted the pancakes? Take some more! Have some beer! Won't you have some vodka? Look, he's jumped up and is making his bows, they must be quite starved, poor things. Never mind, let them eat! They don't make a noise, anyway, though I'm really afraid for our landlady's silver spoons... Amalia Ivanovna!" she addressed her suddenly, almost aloud, "if your spoons should happen to be stolen, I won't be responsible, I warn you! Ha-ha-ha!" She laughed turning to Raskolnikov, and again nodding towards the landlady, in high glee at her sally. "She didn't understand, she didn't understand again! Look how she sits with her mouth open! An owl, a real owl! An owl in new ribbons, ha-ha-ha!"

Here her laugh turned again to an insufferable fit of coughing that lasted five minutes. Drops of perspiration stood out on her forehead and her handkerchief was stained with blood. She showed Raskolnikov the blood in silence, and as soon as she could get her breath began whispering to him again with extreme animation and a hectic flush on her cheeks.

"Do you know, I gave her the most delicate instructions, so to speak, for inviting that lady and her daughter, you understand of whom I am speaking? It needed the utmost delicacy, the greatest nicety, but she has managed things so that that fool, that conceited baggage, that provincial nonentity, simply because she is the widow of a major, and has come to try and get a pension and to fray out her skirts in the government offices, because at fifty she paints her face (everybody knows it)... a creature like that did not think fit to come, and has not even answered the invitation, which the most ordinary good manners required! I can't understand why Pyotr Petrovitch has not come? But where's Sonia? Where has she gone? Ah, there she is at last! what is it, Sonia, where have you been? It's odd that even at your father's funeral you should be so unpunctual. Rodion Romanovitch, make room for her beside you. That's your place, Sonia... take what you like. Have some of the cold entr&#65533;e with jelly, that's the best. They'll bring the pancakes directly. Have they given the children some? Polenka, have you got everything? (Cough-cough-cough.) That's all right. Be a good girl, Lida, and, Kolya, don't fidget with your feet; sit like a little gentleman. What are you saying, Sonia?"

Sonia hastened to give her Pyotr Petrovitch's apologies, trying to speak loud enough for everyone to hear and carefully choosing the most respectful phrases which she attributed to Pyotr Petrovitch. She added that Pyotr Petrovitch had particularly told her to say that, as soon as he possibly could, he would come immediately to discuss _business_ alone with her and to consider what could be done for her, etc., etc.

Sonia knew that this would comfort Katerina Ivanovna, would flatter her and gratify her pride. She sat down beside Raskolnikov; she made him a hurried bow, glancing curiously at him. But for the rest of the time she seemed to avoid looking at him or speaking to him. She seemed absent-minded, though she kept looking at Katerina Ivanovna, trying to please her. Neither she nor Katerina Ivanovna had been able to get mourning; Sonia was wearing dark brown, and Katerina Ivanovna had on her only dress, a dark striped cotton one.

The message from Pyotr Petrovitch was very successful. Listening to Sonia with dignity, Katerina Ivanovna inquired with equal dignity how Pyotr Petrovitch was, then at once whispered almost aloud to Raskolnikov that it certainly would have been strange for a man of Pyotr Petrovitch's position and standing to find himself in such "extraordinary company," in spite of his devotion to her family and his old friendship with her father.

"That's why I am so grateful to you, Rodion Romanovitch, that you have not disdained my hospitality, even in such surroundings," she added almost aloud. "But I am sure that it was only your special affection for my poor husband that has made you keep your promise."

Then once more with pride and dignity she scanned her visitors, and suddenly inquired aloud across the table of the deaf man: "Wouldn't he have some more meat, and had he been given some wine?" The old man made no answer and for a long while could not understand what he was asked, though his neighbours amused themselves by poking and shaking him. He simply gazed about him with his mouth open, which only increased the general mirth.

"What an imbecile! Look, look! Why was he brought? But as to Pyotr Petrovitch, I always had confidence in him," Katerina Ivanovna continued, "and, of course, he is not like..." with an extremely stern face she addressed Amalia Ivanovna so sharply and loudly that the latter was quite disconcerted, "not like your dressed up draggletails whom my father would not have taken as cooks into his kitchen, and my late husband would have done them honour if he had invited them in the goodness of his heart."

"Yes, he was fond of drink, he was fond of it, he did drink!" cried the commissariat clerk, gulping down his twelfth glass of vodka.

"My late husband certainly had that weakness, and everyone knows it," Katerina Ivanovna attacked him at once, "but he was a kind and honourable man, who loved and respected his family. The worst of it was his good nature made him trust all sorts of disreputable people, and he drank with fellows who were not worth the sole of his shoe. Would you believe it, Rodion Romanovitch, they found a gingerbread cock in his pocket; he was dead drunk, but he did not forget the children!"

"A cock? Did you say a cock?" shouted the commissariat clerk.

Katerina Ivanovna did not vouchsafe a reply. She sighed, lost in thought.

"No doubt you think, like everyone, that I was too severe with him," she went on, addressing Raskolnikov. "But that's not so! He respected me, he respected me very much! He was a kind-hearted man! And how sorry I was for him sometimes! He would sit in a corner and look at me, I used to feel so sorry for him, I used to want to be kind to him and then would think to myself: 'Be kind to him and he will drink again,' it was only by severity that you could keep him within bounds."

"Yes, he used to get his hair pulled pretty often," roared the commissariat clerk again, swallowing another glass of vodka.

"Some fools would be the better for a good drubbing, as well as having their hair pulled. I am not talking of my late husband now!" Katerina Ivanovna snapped at him.

The flush on her cheeks grew more and more marked, her chest heaved. In another minute she would have been ready to make a scene. Many of the visitors were sniggering, evidently delighted. They began poking the commissariat clerk and whispering something to him. They were evidently trying to egg him on.

"Allow me to ask what are you alluding to," began the clerk, "that is to say, whose... about whom... did you say just now... But I don't care! That's nonsense! Widow! I forgive you.... Pass!"

And he took another drink of vodka.

Raskolnikov sat in silence, listening with disgust. He only ate from politeness, just tasting the food that Katerina

Ivanovna was continually putting on his plate, to avoid hurting her feelings. He watched Sonia intently. But Sonia became more and more anxious and distressed; she, too, foresaw that the dinner would not end peaceably, and saw with terror Katerina Ivanovna's growing irritation. She knew that she, Sonia, was the chief reason for the 'genteel' ladies' contemptuous treatment of Katerina Ivanovna's invitation. She had heard from Amalia Ivanovna that the mother was positively offended at the invitation and had asked the question: "How could she let her daughter sit down beside _that young person_?" Sonia had a feeling that Katerina Ivanovna had already heard this and an insult to Sonia meant more to Katerina Ivanovna than an insult to herself, her children, or her father, Sonia knew that Katerina Ivanovna would not be satisfied now, "till she had shown those draggletails that they were both..." To make matters worse someone passed Sonia, from the other end of the table, a plate with two hearts pierced with an arrow, cut out of black bread. Katerina Ivanovna flushed crimson and at once said aloud across the table that the man who sent it was "a drunken ass!"

Amalia Ivanovna was foreseeing something amiss, and at the same time deeply wounded by Katerina Ivanovna's haughtiness, and to restore the good-humour of the company and raise herself in their esteem she began, apropos of nothing, telling a story about an acquaintance of hers "Karl from the chemist's," who was driving one night in a cab, and that "the cabman wanted him to kill, and Karl very much begged him not to kill, and wept and clasped hands, and frightened and from fear pierced his heart." Though Katerina Ivanovna smiled, she observed at once that Amalia Ivanovna ought not to tell anecdotes in Russian; the latter was still more offended, and she retorted that her "_Vater aus Berlin_ was a very important man, and always went with his hands in pockets." Katerina Ivanovna could not restrain herself and laughed so much that Amalia Ivanovna lost patience and could scarcely control herself.

"Listen to the owl!" Katerina Ivanovna whispered at once, her good-humour almost restored, "she meant to say he kept his hands in his pockets, but she said he put his hands in people's pockets. (Cough-cough.) And have you noticed, Rodion Romanovitch, that all these Petersburg foreigners, the Germans especially, are all stupider than we! Can you fancy anyone of us telling how 'Karl from the chemist's' 'pierced his heart from fear' and that the idiot, instead of punishing the cabman, 'clasped his hands and wept, and much begged.' Ah, the fool! And you know she fancies it's very touching and does not suspect how stupid she is! To my thinking that drunken commissariat clerk is a great deal cleverer, anyway one can see that he has addled his brains with drink, but you know, these foreigners are always so well behaved and serious.... Look how she sits glaring! She is angry, ha-ha! (Cough-cough-cough.)"

Regaining her good-humour, Katerina Ivanovna began at once telling Raskolnikov that when she had obtained her pension, she intended to open a school for the daughters of gentlemen in her native town T——. This was the first time she had spoken to him of the project, and she launched out into the most alluring details. It suddenly appeared that Katerina Ivanovna had in her hands the very certificate of honour of which Marmeladov had spoken to Raskolnikov in the tavern, when he told him that Katerina Ivanovna, his wife, had danced the shawl dance before the governor and other great personages on leaving school. This certificate of honour was obviously intended now to prove Katerina Ivanovna's right to open a boarding-school; but she had armed herself with it chiefly with the object of overwhelming "those two stuck-up draggletails" if they came to the dinner, and proving incontestably that Katerina Ivanovna was of the most noble, "she might even say aristocratic family, a colonel's daughter and was far superior to certain adventuresses who have been so much to the fore of late." The certificate of honour immediately passed into the hands of the drunken guests, and Katerina Ivanovna did not try to retain it, for it actually contained the statement _en toutes lettres_, that her father was of the rank of a major, and also a companion of an order, so that she really was almost the daughter of a colonel.

Warming up, Katerina Ivanovna proceeded to enlarge on the peaceful and happy life they would lead in T——, on the gymnasium teachers whom she would engage to give lessons in her boarding-school, one a most respectable old Frenchman, one Mangot, who had taught Katerina Ivanovna herself in old days and was still living in T——, and would no doubt teach in her school on moderate terms. Next she spoke of Sonia who would go with her to T—— and help her in all her plans. At this someone at the further end of the table gave a sudden guffaw.

Though Katerina Ivanovna tried to appear to be disdainfully unaware of it, she raised her voice and began at once speaking with conviction of Sonia's undoubted ability to assist her, of "her gentleness, patience, devotion, generosity and good education," tapping Sonia on the cheek and kissing her warmly twice. Sonia flushed crimson, and Katerina Ivanovna suddenly burst into tears, immediately observing that she was "nervous and silly, that she was too much upset, that it was time to finish, and as the dinner was over, it was time to hand round the tea."

At that moment, Amalia Ivanovna, deeply aggrieved at taking no part in the conversation, and not being listened to, made one last effort, and with secret misgivings ventured on an exceedingly deep and weighty observation, that "in the future boarding-school she would have to pay particular attention to _die W&#65533;sche_, and that there certainly must be a good _dame_ to look after the linen, and secondly that the young ladies must not novels at night read."

Katerina Ivanovna, who certainly was upset and very tired, as well as heartily sick of the dinner, at once cut short Amalia Ivanovna, saying "she knew nothing about it and was talking nonsense, that it was the business of the laundry maid, and not of the directress of a high-class boarding-school to look after _die W&#65533;sche_, and as for novel-reading, that was simply rudeness, and she begged her to be silent." Amalia Ivanovna fired up and getting angry observed that she only "meant her good," and that "she had meant her very good," and that "it was long since she had paid her _gold_ for the lodgings."

Katerina Ivanovna at once "set her down," saying that it was a lie to say she wished her good, because only yesterday when her dead husband was lying on the table, she had worried her about the lodgings. To this Amalia Ivanovna very appropriately observed that she had invited those ladies, but "those ladies had not come, because those ladies _are_ ladies and cannot come to a lady who is not a lady." Katerina Ivanovna at once pointed out to her, that as she was a slut she could not judge what made one really a lady. Amalia Ivanovna at once declared that her "_Vater aus Berlin_ was a very, very important man, and both hands in pockets went, and always used to say: 'Poof! poof!'" and she leapt up from the table to represent her father, sticking her hands in her pockets, puffing her cheeks, and uttering vague sounds resembling "poof! poof!" amid loud laughter from all the lodgers, who purposely encouraged Amalia Ivanovna, hoping for a fight.

But this was too much for Katerina Ivanovna, and she at once declared, so that all could hear, that Amalia Ivanovna probably never had a father, but was simply a drunken Petersburg Finn, and had certainly once been a cook and probably something worse. Amalia Ivanovna turned as red as a lobster and squealed that perhaps Katerina Ivanovna never had a father, "but she had a _Vater aus Berlin_ and that he wore a long coat and always said poof-poof-poof!"

Katerina Ivanovna observed contemptuously that all knew what her family was and that on that very certificate of honour it was stated in print that her father was a colonel, while Amalia Ivanovna's father—if she really had one—was probably some Finnish milkman, but that probably she never had a father at all, since it was still uncertain whether her name was Amalia Ivanovna or Amalia Ludwigovna.

At this Amalia Ivanovna, lashed to fury, struck the table with her fist, and shrieked that she was Amalia Ivanovna, and not Ludwigovna, "that her _Vater_ was named Johann and that he was a burgomeister, and that Katerina Ivanovna's

Vater was quite never a burgomeister." Katerina Ivanovna rose from her chair, and with a stern and apparently calm voice (though she was pale and her chest was heaving) observed that "if she dared for one moment to set her contemptible wretch of a father on a level with her papa, she, Katerina Ivanovna, would tear her cap off her head and trample it under foot." Amalia Ivanovna ran about the room, shouting at the top of her voice, that she was mistress of the house and that Katerina Ivanovna should leave the lodgings that minute; then she rushed for some reason to collect the silver spoons from the table. There was a great outcry and uproar, the children began crying. Sonia ran to restrain Katerina Ivanovna; but when Amalia Ivanovna shouted something about "the yellow ticket," Katerina Ivanovna pushed Sonia away, and rushed at the landlady to carry out her threat.

At that minute the door opened, and Pyotr Petrovitch Luzhin appeared on the threshold. He stood scanning the party with severe and vigilant eyes. Katerina Ivanovna rushed to him.

CHAPTER 4

Raskolnikov had been a vigourous and active champion of Sonia against Luzhin, although he had such a load of horror and anguish in his own heart. But having gone through so much in the morning, he found a sort of relief in a change of sensations, apart from the strong personal feeling which impelled him to defend Sonia. He was agitated too, especially at some moments, by the thought of his approaching interview with Sonia: he /had/ to tell her who had killed Lizaveta. He knew the terrible suffering it would be to him and, as it were, brushed away the thought of it. So when he cried as he left Katerina Ivanovna's, "Well, Sofya Semyonovna, we shall see what you'll say now!" he was still superficially excited, still vigourous and defiant from his triumph over Luzhin. But, strange to say, by the time he reached Sonia's lodging, he felt a sudden impotence and fear. He stood still in hesitation at the door, asking himself the strange question: "Must he tell her who killed Lizaveta?" It was a strange question because he felt at the very time not only that he could not help telling her, but also that he could not put off the telling. He did not yet know why it must be so, he only /felt/ it, and the agonising sense of his impotence before the inevitable almost crushed him. To cut short his hesitation and suffering, he quickly opened the door and looked at Sonia from the doorway. She was sitting with her elbows on the table and her face in her hands, but seeing Raskolnikov she got up at once and came to meet him as though she were expecting him.

"What would have become of me but for you?" she said quickly, meeting him in the middle of the room.

Evidently she was in haste to say this to him. It was what she had been waiting for.

Raskolnikov went to the table and sat down on the chair from which she had only just risen. She stood facing him, two steps away, just as she had done the day before.

"Well, Sonia?" he said, and felt that his voice was trembling, "it was all due to 'your social position and the habits associated with it.' Did you understand that just now?"

Her face showed her distress.

"Only don't talk to me as you did yesterday," she interrupted him. "Please don't begin it. There is misery enough without that."

She made haste to smile, afraid that he might not like the reproach.

"I was silly to come away from there. What is happening there now? I wanted to go back directly, but I kept thinking that... you would come."

He told her that Amalia Ivanovna was turning them out of their lodging and that Katerina Ivanovna had run off somewhere "to seek justice."

"My God!" cried Sonia, "let's go at once...."

PART 6

CHAPTER 1

A strange period began for Raskolnikov: it was as though a fog had fallen upon him and wrapped him in a dreary solitude from which there was no escape. Recalling that period long after, he believed that his mind had been clouded at times, and that it had continued so, with intervals, till the final catastrophe. He was convinced that he had been mistaken about many things at that time, for instance as to the date of certain events. Anyway, when he tried later on to piece his recollections together, he learnt a great deal about himself from what other people told him. He had mixed up incidents and had explained events as due to circumstances which existed only in his imagination. At times he was a prey to agonies of morbid uneasiness, amounting sometimes to panic. But he remembered, too, moments, hours, and perhaps whole days, of complete apathy, which came upon him as a reaction from his previous terror and might be compared with the abnormal insensibility, sometimes seen in the dying. He seemed to be trying in that latter stage to escape from a full and clear understanding of his position. Certain essential facts which required immediate consideration were particularly irksome to him. How glad he would have been to be free from some cares, the neglect of which would have threatened him with complete, inevitable ruin.

He was particularly worried about Svidrigaïlov, he might be said to be permanently thinking of Svidrigaïlov. From the time of Svidrigaïlov's too menacing and unmistakable words in Sonia's room at the moment of Katerina Ivanovna's death, the normal working of his mind seemed to break down. But although this new fact caused him extreme uneasiness, Raskolnikov was in no hurry for an explanation of it. At times, finding himself in a solitary and remote part of the town, in some wretched eating-house, sitting alone lost in thought, hardly knowing how he had come there, he suddenly thought of Svidrigaïlov. He recognised suddenly, clearly, and with dismay that he ought at once to come to an understanding with that man and to make what terms he could. Walking outside the city gates one day, he positively fancied that they had fixed a meeting there, that he was waiting for Svidrigaïlov. Another time he woke up before daybreak lying on the ground under some bushes and could not at first understand how he had come there.

But during the two or three days after Katerina Ivanovna's death, he had two or three times met Svidrigaïlov at Sonia's lodging, where he had gone aimlessly for a moment. They exchanged a few words and made no reference to the vital subject, as though they were tacitly agreed not to speak of it for a time.

Katerina Ivanovna's body was still lying in the coffin, Svidrigaïlov was busy making arrangements for the funeral. Sonia too was very busy. At their last meeting Svidrigaïlov informed Raskolnikov that he had made an arrangement, and a very satisfactory one, for Katerina Ivanovna's children; that he had, through certain connections, succeeded in getting hold of certain personages by whose help the three orphans could be at once placed in very suitable institutions; that the money he had settled on them had been of great assistance, as it is much easier to place orphans with some property than destitute ones. He said something too about Sonia and promised to come himself in a day or two to see Raskolnikov, mentioning that "he would like to consult with him, that there were things they must talk over...."

This conversation took place in the passage on the stairs. Svidrigaïlov looked intently at Raskolnikov and suddenly, after a brief pause, dropping his voice, asked: "But how is it, Rodion Romanovitch; you don't seem yourself? You look and you listen, but you don't seem to understand. Cheer up! We'll talk things over; I am only sorry, I've so much to do of my own business and other people's. Ah, Rodion Romanovitch," he added suddenly, "what all men need is fresh air, fresh air... more than anything!"

He moved to one side to make way for the priest and server, who were coming up the stairs. They had come for the requiem service. By Svidrigaïlov's orders it was sung twice a day punctually. Svidrigaïlov went his way. Raskolnikov stood still a moment, thought, and followed the priest into Sonia's room. He stood at the door. They began quietly, slowly and mournfully singing the service. From his childhood the thought of death and the presence of death had something oppressive and mysteriously awful; and it was long since he had heard the requiem service. And there was something else here as well, too awful and disturbing. He looked at the children: they were all kneeling by the coffin; Polenka was weeping. Behind them Sonia prayed, softly and, as it were, timidly weeping.

"These last two days she hasn't said a word to me, she hasn't glanced at me," Raskolnikov thought suddenly. The sunlight was bright in the room; the incense rose in clouds; the priest read, "Give rest, oh Lord...." Raskolnikov stayed all through the service. As he blessed them and took his leave, the priest looked round strangely. After the service, Raskolnikov went up to Sonia. She took both his hands and let her head sink on his shoulder. This slight friendly gesture bewildered Raskolnikov. It seemed strange to him that there was no trace of repugnance, no trace of disgust, no tremor in her hand. It was the furthest limit of self-abnegation, at least so he interpreted it.

CHAPTER 2

He hurried to Svidriga&#65533;lov's. What he had to hope from that man he did not know. But that man had some hidden power over him. Having once recognised this, he could not rest, and now the time had come.

On the way, one question particularly worried him: had Svidriga&#65533;lov been to Porfiry's?

As far as he could judge, he would swear to it, that he had not. He pondered again and again, went over Porfiry's visit; no, he hadn't been, of course he hadn't.

But if he had not been yet, would he go? Meanwhile, for the present he fancied he couldn't. Why? He could not have explained, but if he could, he would not have wasted much thought over it at the moment. It all worried him and at the same time he could not attend to it. Strange to say, none would have believed it perhaps, but he only felt a faint vague anxiety about his immediate future. Another, much more important anxiety tormented him—it concerned himself, but in a different, more vital way. Moreover, he was conscious of immense moral fatigue, though his mind was working better that morning than it had done of late.

And was it worth while, after all that had happened, to contend with these new trivial difficulties? Was it worth while, for instance, to manoeuvre that Svidriga&#65533;lov should not go to Porfiry's? Was it worth while to investigate, to ascertain the facts, to waste time over anyone like Svidriga&#65533;lov?

Oh, how sick he was of it all!

And yet he was hastening to Svidriga&#65533;lov; could he be expecting something _new_ from him, information, or means of escape? Men will catch at straws! Was it destiny or some instinct bringing them together? Perhaps it was only fatigue, despair; perhaps it was not Svidriga&#65533;lov but some other whom he needed, and Svidriga&#65533;lov had simply presented himself by chance. Sonia? But what should he go to Sonia for now? To beg her tears again? He was afraid of Sonia, too. Sonia stood before him as an irrevocable sentence. He must go his own way or hers. At that moment especially he did not feel equal to seeing her. No, would it not be better to try Svidriga&#65533;lov? And he could not help inwardly owning that he had long felt that he must see him for some reason.

But what could they have in common? Their very evil-doing could not be of the same kind. The man, moreover, was very unpleasant, evidently depraved, undoubtedly cunning and deceitful, possibly malignant. Such stories were told about him. It is true he was befriending Katerina Ivanovna's children, but who could tell with what motive and what it meant? The man always had some design, some project.

There was another thought which had been continually hovering of late about Raskolnikov's mind, and causing him great uneasiness. It was so painful that he made distinct efforts to get rid of it. He sometimes thought that Svidriga&#65533;lov was dogging his footsteps. Svidriga&#65533;lov had found out his secret and had had designs on Dounia. What if he had them still? Wasn't it practically certain that he had? And what if, having learnt his secret and so having gained power over him, he were to use it as a weapon against Dounia?

This idea sometimes even tormented his dreams, but it had never presented itself so vividly to him as on his way to Svidriga&#65533;lov. The very thought moved him to gloomy rage. To begin with, this would transform everything, even his own position; he would have at once to confess his secret to Dounia. Would he have to give himself up perhaps to prevent Dounia from taking some rash step? The letter? This morning Dounia had received a letter. From whom could she get letters in Petersburg? Luzhin, perhaps? It's true Razumihin was there to protect her, but Razumihin knew nothing of the position. Perhaps it was his duty to tell Razumihin? He thought of it with repugnance.

In any case he must see Svidriga&#65533;lov as soon as possible, he decided finally. Thank God, the details of the interview were of little consequence, if only he could get at the root of the matter; but if Svidriga&#65533;lov were capable... if he were intriguing against Dounia—then...

Raskolnikov was so exhausted by what he had passed through that month that he could only decide such questions in one way; "then I shall kill him," he thought in cold despair.

A sudden anguish oppressed his heart, he stood still in the middle of the street and began looking about to see where he was and which way he was going. He found himself in X. Prospect, thirty or forty paces from the Hay Market, through which he had come. The whole second storey of the house on the left was used as a tavern. All the windows were wide open; judging from the figures moving at the windows, the rooms were full to overflowing. There were sounds of singing, of clarionet and violin, and the boom of a Turkish drum. He could hear women shrieking. He was about to turn back wondering why he had come to the X. Prospect, when suddenly at one of the end windows he saw Svidriga&#65533;lov, sitting at a tea-table right in the open window with a pipe in his mouth. Raskolnikov was dreadfully taken aback, almost terrified. Svidriga&#65533;lov was silently watching and scrutinising him and, what struck Raskolnikov at once, seemed to be meaning to get up and slip away unobserved. Raskolnikov at once pretended not to have seen him, but to be looking absent-mindedly away, while he watched him out of the corner of his eye. His heart was beating violently. Yet, it was evident that Svidriga&#65533;lov did not want to be seen. He took the pipe out of his mouth and was on the point of concealing himself, but as he got up and moved back his chair, he seemed to have become suddenly aware that Raskolnikov had seen him, and was watching him. What had passed between them was much the same as what happened at their first meeting in Raskolnikov's room. A sly smile came into Svidriga&#65533;lov's face and grew broader and broader. Each knew that he was seen and watched by the other. At last Svidriga&#65533;lov broke into a loud laugh.

"Well, well, come in if you want me; I am here!" he shouted from the window.

Raskolnikov went up into the tavern. He found Svidriga&#65533;lov in a tiny back room, adjoining the saloon in which merchants, clerks and numbers of people of all sorts were drinking tea at twenty little tables to the desperate bawling of a chorus of singers. The click of billiard balls could be heard in the distance. On the table before Svidriga&#65533;lov stood an open bottle and a glass half full of champagne. In the room he found also a boy with a little hand organ, a healthy-looking red-cheeked girl of eighteen, wearing a tucked-up striped skirt, and a Tyrolese hat with ribbons. In spite of the chorus in the other room, she was singing some servants' hall song in a rather husky contralto, to the accompaniment of the organ.

"Come, that's enough," Svidriga&#65533;lov stopped her at Raskolnikov's entrance. The girl at once broke off and stood waiting respectfully. She had sung her guttural rhymes, too, with a serious and respectful expression in her face.

"Hey, Philip, a glass!" shouted Svidriga&#65533;lov.

"I won't drink anything," said Raskolnikov.

"As you like, I didn't mean it for you. Drink, Katia! I don't want anything more to-day, you can go." He poured her out a full glass, and laid down a yellow note.

Katia drank off her glass of wine, as women do, without putting it down, in twenty gulps, took the note and kissed Svidriga&#65533;lov's hand, which he allowed quite seriously. She went out of the room and the boy trailed after her with the organ. Both had been brought in from the street. Svidriga&#65533;lov had not been a week in Petersburg, but everything about him was already, so to speak, on a patriarchal footing; the waiter, Philip, was by now an old friend and very obsequious.

The door leading to the saloon had a lock on it. Svidriga&#65533;lov was at home in this room and perhaps spent whole days in it. The tavern was dirty and wretched, not even second-rate.

"I was going to see you and looking for you," Raskolnikov began, "but I don't know what made me turn from the Hay Market into the X. Prospect just now. I never take this turning. I turn to the right from the Hay Market. And this isn't the way to you. I simply turned and here you are. It is strange!"

"Why don't you say at once 'it's a miracle'?"

"Because it may be only chance."

"Oh, that's the way with all you folk," laughed Svidriga&#65533;lov. "You won't admit it, even if you do inwardly believe it a miracle! Here you say that it may be only chance. And what cowards they all are here, about having an opinion of their own, you can't fancy, Rodion Romanovitch. I don't mean you, you have an opinion of your own and are not afraid to have it. That's how it was you attracted my curiosity."

"Nothing else?"

"Well, that's enough, you know," Svidriga&#65533;lov was obviously exhilarated, but only slightly so, he had not had more than half a glass of wine.

"I fancy you came to see me before you knew that I was capable of having what you call an opinion of my own," observed Raskolnikov.

"Oh, well, it was a different matter. Everyone has his own plans. And apropos of the miracle let me tell you that I think you have been asleep for the last two or three days. I told you of this tavern myself, there is no miracle in your coming straight here. I explained the way myself, told you where it was, and the hours you could find me here. Do you remember?"

"I don't remember," answered Raskolnikov with surprise.

"I believe you. I told you twice. The address has been stamped mechanically on your memory. You turned this way mechanically and yet precisely according to the direction, though you are not aware of it. When I told you then, I hardly hoped you understood me. You give yourself away too much, Rodion Romanovitch. And another thing, I'm convinced there are lots of people in Petersburg who talk to themselves as they walk. This is a town of crazy people. If only we had scientific men, doctors, lawyers and philosophers might make most valuable investigations in Petersburg each in his own line. There are few places where there are so many gloomy, strong and queer influences on the soul of man as in Petersburg. The mere influences of climate mean so much. And it's the administrative centre of all Russia and its character must be reflected on the whole country. But that is neither here nor there now. The point is that I have several times watched you. You walk out of your house—holding your head high—twenty paces from home you let it sink, and fold your hands behind your back. You look and evidently see nothing before nor beside you. At last you begin moving your lips and talking to yourself, and sometimes you wave one hand and declaim, and at last stand still in the middle of the road. That's not at all the thing. Someone may be watching you besides me, and it won't do you any good. It's nothing really to do with me and I can't cure you, but, of course, you understand me."

"Do you know that I am being followed?" asked Raskolnikov, looking inquisitively at him.

"No, I know nothing about it," said Svidriga&#65533;lov, seeming surprised.

"Well, then, let us leave me alone," Raskolnikov muttered, frowning.

"Very good, let us leave you alone."

"You had better tell me, if you come here to drink, and directed me twice to come here to you, why did you hide, and try to get away just now when I looked at the window from the street? I saw it."

"He-he! And why was it you lay on your sofa with closed eyes and pretended to be asleep, though you were wide awake while I stood in your doorway? I saw it."

"I may have had... reasons. You know that yourself."

"And I may have had my reasons, though you don't know them."

Raskolnikov dropped his right elbow on the table, leaned his chin in the fingers of his right hand, and stared intently at Svidriga&#65533;lov. For a full minute he scrutinised his face, which had impressed him before. It was a strange face, like a mask; white and red, with bright red lips, with a flaxen beard, and still thick flaxen hair. His eyes were somehow too blue and their expression somehow too heavy and fixed. There was something awfully unpleasant in that handsome face, which looked so wonderfully young for his age. Svidriga&#65533;lov was smartly dressed in light summer clothes and was particularly dainty in his linen. He wore a huge ring with a precious stone in it.

"Have I got to bother myself about you, too, now?" said Raskolnikov suddenly, coming with nervous impatience straight to the point. "Even though perhaps you are the most dangerous man if you care to injure me, I don't want to put myself out any more. I will show you at once that I don't prize myself as you probably think I do. I've come to tell you at once that if you keep to your former intentions with regard to my sister and if you think to derive any benefit in that direction from what has been discovered of late, I will kill you before you get me locked up. You can reckon on my word. You know that I can keep it. And in the second place if you want to tell me anything—for I keep fancying all this time that you have something to tell me—make haste and tell it, for time is precious and very likely it will soon be too late."

"Why in such haste?" asked Svidriga&#65533;lov, looking at him curiously.

"Everyonc has his plans," Raskolnikov answered gloomily and impatiently.

"You urged me yourself to frankness just now, and at the first question you refuse to answer," Svidriga&#65533;lov observed with a smile. "You keep fancying that I have aims of my own and so you look at me with suspicion. Of course it's perfectly natural in your position. But though I should like to be friends with you, I shan't trouble myself to convince you of the contrary. The game isn't worth the candle and I wasn't intending to talk to you about anything special."

"What did you want me, for, then? It was you who came hanging about me."

"Why, simply as an interesting subject for observation. I liked the fantastic nature of your position—that's what it was! Besides you are the brother of a person who greatly interested me, and from that person I had in the past heard a very great deal about you, from which I gathered that you had a great influence over her; isn't that enough? Ha-ha-ha! Still I must admit that your question is rather complex, and is difficult for me to answer. Here, you, for instance, have come to me not only for a definite object, but for the sake of hearing something new. Isn't that so? Isn't that so?" persisted Svidriga&#65533;lov with a sly smile. "Well, can't you fancy then that I, too, on my way here in the train was reckoning on you, on your telling me something new, and on my making some profit out of you! You see what rich men we are!"

"What profit could you make?"

"How can I tell you? How do I know? You see in what a tavern I spend all my time and it's my enjoyment, that's to say it's no great enjoyment, but one must sit somewhere; that poor Katia now—you saw her?... If only I had been a glutton now, a club gourmand, but you see I can eat this."

He pointed to a little table in the corner where the remnants of a terrible-looking beef-steak and potatoes lay on a tin dish.

"Have you dined, by the way? I've had something and want nothing more. I don't drink, for instance, at all. Except for champagne I never touch anything, and not more than a glass of that all the evening, and even that is enough to make my head ache. I ordered it just now to wind myself up, for I am just going off somewhere and you see me in a peculiar state of mind. That was why I hid myself just now like a schoolboy, for I was afraid you would hinder me. But I believe," he pulled out his watch, "I can spend an hour with you. It's half-past four now. If only I'd been something, a landowner, a father, a cavalry officer, a photographer, a journalist... I am nothing, no specialty, and sometimes I am positively bored. I really thought you would tell me something new."

"But what are you, and why have you come here?"

"What am I? You know, a gentleman, I served for two years in the cavalry, then I knocked about here in Petersburg, then I married Marfa Petrovna and lived in the country. There you have my biography!"

"You are a gambler, I believe?"

"No, a poor sort of gambler. A card-sharper—not a gambler."

"You have been a card-sharper then?"

"Yes, I've been a card-sharper too."

"Didn't you get thrashed sometimes?"

"It did happen. Why?"

"Why, you might have challenged them... altogether it must have been lively."

"I won't contradict you, and besides I am no hand at philosophy. I confess that I hastened here for the sake of the women."

"As soon as you buried Marfa Petrovna?"

"Quite so," Svidriga&#65533;lov smiled with engaging candour. "What of it? You seem to find something wrong in my speaking like that about women?"

"You ask whether I find anything wrong in vice?"

"Vice! Oh, that's what you are after! But I'll answer you in order, first about women in general; you know I am fond of talking. Tell me, what should I restrain myself for? Why should I give up women, since I have a passion for them? It's an occupation, anyway."

"So you hope for nothing here but vice?"

"Oh, very well, for vice then. You insist on its being vice. But anyway I like a direct question. In this vice at least there is something permanent, founded indeed upon nature and not dependent on fantasy, something present in the blood like an ever-burning ember, for ever setting one on fire and, maybe, not to be quickly extinguished, even with years. You'll agree it's an occupation of a sort."

"That's nothing to rejoice at, it's a disease and a dangerous one."

"Oh, that's what you think, is it! I agree, that it is a disease like everything that exceeds moderation. And, of course, in this one must exceed moderation. But in the first place, everybody does so in one way or another, and in the second place, of course, one ought to be moderate and prudent, however mean it may be, but what am I to do? If I hadn't this, I might have to shoot myself. I am ready to admit that a decent man ought to put up with being bored, but yet..."

"And could you shoot yourself?"

"Oh, come!" Svidriga&#65533;lov parried with disgust. "Please don't speak of it," he added hurriedly and with none of the bragging tone he had shown in all the previous conversation. His face quite changed. "I admit it's an unpardonable weakness, but I can't help it. I am afraid of death and I dislike its being talked of. Do you know that I am to a certain extent a mystic?"

"Ah, the apparitions of Marfa Petrovna! Do they still go on visiting you?"

"Oh, don't talk of them; there have been no more in Petersburg, confound them!" he cried with an air of irritation. "Let's rather talk of that... though... H'm! I have not much time, and can't stay long with you, it's a pity! I should have found plenty to tell you."

"What's your engagement, a woman?"

"Yes, a woman, a casual incident.... No, that's not what I want to talk of."

"And the hideousness, the filthiness of all your surroundings, doesn't that affect you? Have you lost the strength to stop yourself?"

"And do you pretend to strength, too? He-he-he! You surprised me just now, Rodion Romanovitch, though I knew beforehand it would be so. You preach to me about vice and &#65533;sthetics! You—a Schiller, you—an idealist! Of course that's all as it should be and it would be surprising if it were not so, yet it is strange in reality.... Ah, what a pity I have no time, for you're a most interesting type! And, by-the-way, are you fond of Schiller? I am awfully fond of him."

"But what a braggart you are," Raskolnikov said with some disgust.

"Upon my word, I am not," answered Svidriga&#65533;lov laughing. "However, I won't dispute it, let me be a braggart, why not brag, if it hurts no one? I spent seven years in the country with Marfa Petrovna, so now when I come across an intelligent person like you—intelligent and highly interesting—I am simply glad to talk and, besides, I've drunk that half-glass of champagne and it's gone to my head a little. And besides, there's a certain fact that has wound me up tremendously, but about that I... will keep quiet. Where are you off to?" he asked in alarm.

Raskolnikov had begun getting up. He felt oppressed and stifled and, as it were, ill at ease at having come here. He felt convinced that Svidriga&#65533;lov was the most worthless scoundrel on the face of the earth.

"A-ach! Sit down, stay a little!" Svidriga&#65533;lov begged. "Let them bring you some tea, anyway. Stay a little, I won't talk nonsense, about myself, I mean. I'll tell you something. If you like I'll tell you how a woman tried 'to save' me, as you would call it? It will be an answer to your first question indeed, for the woman was your sister. May I tell you? It will help to spend the time."

"Tell me, but I trust that you..."

"Oh, don't be uneasy. Besides, even in a worthless low fellow like me, Avdotya Romanovna can only excite the deepest respect."

CHAPTER 4

"You know perhaps—yes, I told you myself," began Svidriga&#65533;lov, "that I was in the debtors' prison here, for an immense sum, and had not any expectation of being able to pay it. There's no need to go into particulars how Marfa Petrovna bought me out; do you know to what a point of insanity a woman can sometimes love? She was an honest woman, and very sensible, although completely uneducated. Would you believe that this honest and jealous woman, after many scenes of hysterics and reproaches, condescended to enter into a kind of contract with me which she kept throughout our married life? She was considerably older than I, and besides, she always kept a clove or something in her mouth. There was so much swinishness in my soul and honesty too, of a sort, as to tell her straight out that I couldn't be absolutely faithful to her.

This confession drove her to frenzy, but yet she seems in a way to have liked my brutal frankness. She thought it showed I was unwilling to deceive her if I warned her like this beforehand and for a jealous woman, you know, that's the first consideration. After many tears an unwritten contract was drawn up between us: first, that I would never leave Marfa Petrovna and would always be her husband; secondly, that I would never absent myself without her permission; thirdly, that I would never set up a permanent mistress; fourthly, in return for this, Marfa Petrovna gave me a free hand with the maidservants, but only with her secret knowledge; fifthly, God forbid my falling in love with a woman of our class; sixthly, in case I—which God forbid—should be visited by a great serious passion I was bound to reveal it to Marfa Petrovna. On this last score, however, Marfa Petrovna was fairly at ease. She was a sensible woman and so she could not help looking upon me as a dissolute profligate incapable of real love.

But a sensible woman and a jealous woman are two very different things, and that's where the trouble came in. But to judge some people impartially we must renounce certain preconceived opinions and our habitual attitude to the ordinary people about us. I have reason to have faith in your judgment rather than in anyone's. Perhaps you have already heard a great deal that was ridiculous and absurd about Marfa Petrovna. She certainly had some very ridiculous ways, but I tell you frankly that I feel really sorry for the innumerable woes of which I was the cause. Well, and that's enough, I think, by way of a decorous _oraison fun&#65533;bre_ for the most tender wife of a most tender husband. When we quarrelled, I usually held my tongue and did not irritate her and that gentlemanly conduct rarely failed to attain its object, it influenced her, it pleased her, indeed. These were times when she was positively proud of me. But your sister she couldn't put up with, anyway. And however she came to risk taking such a beautiful creature into her house as a governess. My explanation is that Marfa Petrovna was an ardent and impressionable woman and simply fell in love herself—literally fell in love—with your sister. Well, little wonder—look at Avdotya Romanovna! I saw the danger at the first glance and what do you think, I resolved not to look at her even.

But Avdotya Romanovna herself made the first step, would you believe it? Would you believe it too that Marfa Petrovna was positively angry with me at first for my persistent silence about your sister, for my careless reception of her continual adoring praises of Avdotya Romanovna. I don't know what it was she wanted! Well, of course, Marfa Petrovna told Avdotya Romanovna every detail about me. She had the unfortunate habit of telling literally everyone all our family secrets and continually complaining of me; how could she fail to confide in such a delightful new friend? I expect they talked of nothing else but me and no doubt Avdotya Romanovna heard all those dark mysterious rumours that were current about me.... I don't mind betting that you too have heard something of the sort already?"

"I have. Luzhin charged you with having caused the death of a child. Is that true?"

"Don't refer to those vulgar tales, I beg," said Svidriga&#65533;lov with disgust and annoyance. "If you insist on wanting to know about all that idiocy, I will tell you one day, but now..."

"I was told too about some footman of yours in the country whom you treated badly."

"I beg you to drop the subject," Svidriga&#65533;lov interrupted again with obvious impatience.

"Was that the footman who came to you after death to fill your pipe?... you told me about it yourself." Raskolnikov felt more and more irritated.

Svidriga&#65533;lov looked at him attentively and Raskolnikov fancied he caught a flash of spiteful mockery in that look. But Svidriga&#65533;lov restrained himself and answered very civilly:

"Yes, it was. I see that you, too, are extremely interested and shall feel it my duty to satisfy your curiosity at the first opportunity. Upon my soul! I see that I really might pass for a romantic figure with some people. Judge how grateful I must be to Marfa Petrovna for having repeated to Avdotya Romanovna such mysterious and interesting gossip about me. I dare not guess what impression it made on her, but in any case it worked in my interests. With all Avdotya Romanovna's natural aversion and in spite of my invariably gloomy and repellent aspect—she did at least feel pity for me, pity for a lost soul.

And if once a girl's heart is moved to _pity_, it's more dangerous than anything. She is bound to want to 'save him,' to bring him to his senses, and lift him up and draw him to nobler aims, and restore him to new life and usefulness—well, we all know how far such dreams can go. I saw at once that the bird was flying into the cage of herself. And I too made ready. I think you are frowning, Rodion Romanovitch? There's no need. As you know, it all ended in smoke. (Hang it all, what a lot I am drinking!) Do you know, I always, from the very beginning, regretted that it wasn't your sister's fate to be born in the second or third century A.D., as the daughter of a reigning prince or some governor or pro-consul in Asia Minor.

She would undoubtedly have been one of those who would endure martyrdom and would have smiled when they branded her bosom with hot pincers. And she would have gone to it of herself. And in the fourth or fifth century she would have walked away into the Egyptian desert and would have stayed there thirty years living on roots and ecstasies and visions. She is simply thirsting to face some torture for someone, and if she can't get her torture, she'll throw herself out of a window. I've heard something of a Mr. Razumihin—he's said to be a sensible fellow; his surname suggests it, indeed. He's probably a divinity student. Well, he'd better look after your sister! I believe I understand her, and I am proud of it. But at the beginning of an acquaintance, as you know, one is apt to be more heedless and stupid.

One doesn't see clearly. Hang it all, why is she so handsome? It's not my fault. In fact, it began on my side with a most irresistible physical desire. Avdotya Romanovna is awfully chaste, incredibly and phenomenally so. Take note, I tell you this about your sister as a fact. She is almost morbidly chaste, in spite of her broad intelligence, and it will stand in her way. There happened to be a girl in the house then, Parasha, a black-eyed wench, whom I had never seen before—she had just come from another village—very pretty, but incredibly stupid: she burst into tears, wailed so that she could be heard all over the place and caused scandal. One day after dinner Avdotya Romanovna followed me into an avenue in the garden and with flashing eyes _insisted_ on my leaving poor Parasha alone. It was almost our first conversation by ourselves. I, of course, was only too pleased to obey her wishes, tried to appear disconcerted, embarrassed, in fact played my part not badly.

Then came interviews, mysterious conversations, exhortations, entreaties, supplications, even tears—would you believe it, even tears? Think what the passion for propaganda will bring some girls to! I, of course, threw it all on my destiny, posed as hungering and thirsting for light, and finally resorted to the most powerful weapon in the subjection of the female heart, a weapon which never fails one. It's the well-known resource—flattery. Nothing in the world is harder than speaking the truth and nothing easier than flattery. If there's the hundredth part of a false note in speaking the truth, it leads to a discord, and that leads to trouble. But if all, to the last note, is false in flattery, it is just as agreeable, and is heard not without satisfaction. It may be a coarse satisfaction, but still a satisfaction. And however coarse the flattery, at least half will be sure to seem true.

That's so for all stages of development and classes of society. A vestal virgin might be seduced by flattery. I can never remember without laughter how I once seduced a lady who was devoted to her husband, her children, and her principles. What fun it was and how little trouble! And the lady really had principles—of her own, anyway.

All my tactics lay in simply being utterly annihilated and prostrate before her purity. I flattered her shamelessly, and as soon as I succeeded in getting a pressure of the hand, even a glance from her, I would reproach myself for having snatched it by force, and would declare that she had resisted, so that I could never have gained anything but for my being so unprincipled. I maintained that she was so innocent that she could not foresee my treachery, and yielded to me unconsciously, unawares, and so on.

In fact, I triumphed, while my lady remained firmly convinced that she was innocent, chaste, and faithful to all her duties and obligations and had succumbed quite by accident. And how angry she was with me when I explained to her at last that it was my sincere conviction that she was just as eager as I. Poor Marfa Petrovna was awfully weak on the side of flattery, and if I had only cared to, I might have had all her property settled on me during her lifetime. (I am drinking an awful lot of wine now and talking too much.) I hope you won't be angry if I mention now that I was beginning to produce the same effect on Avdotya Romanovna. But I was stupid and impatient and spoiled it all.

Avdotya Romanovna had several times—and one time in particular—been greatly displeased by the expression of my eyes, would you believe it? There was sometimes a light in them which frightened her and grew stronger and stronger and more unguarded till it was hateful to her. No need to go into detail, but we parted. There I acted stupidly again. I fell to jeering in the coarsest way at all such propaganda and efforts to convert me; Parasha came on to the scene again, and not she alone; in fact there was a tremendous to-do. Ah, Rodion Romanovitch, if you could only see how your sister's eyes can flash sometimes! Never mind my being drunk at this moment and having had a whole glass of wine. I am speaking the truth.

I assure you that this glance has haunted my dreams; the very rustle of her dress was more than I could stand at last.

I really began to think that I might become epileptic. I could never have believed that I could be moved to such a frenzy. It was essential, indeed, to be reconciled, but by then it was impossible. And imagine what I did then! To what a pitch of stupidity a man can be brought by frenzy! Never undertake anything in a frenzy, Rodion Romanovitch. I reflected that Avdotya Romanovna was after all a beggar (ach, excuse me, that's not the word... but does it matter if it expresses the meaning?), that she lived by her work, that she had her mother and you to keep (ach, hang it, you are frowning again), and I resolved to offer her all my money—thirty thousand roubles I could have realised then—if she would run away with me here, to Petersburg.

Of course I should have vowed eternal love, rapture, and so on. Do you know, I was so wild about her at that time that if she had told me to poison Marfa Petrovna or to cut her throat and to marry herself, it would have been done at once! But it ended in the catastrophe of which you know already. You can fancy how frantic I was when I heard that Marfa Petrovna had got hold of that scoundrelly attorney, Luzhin, and had almost made a match between them—which would really have been just the same thing as I was proposing. Wouldn't it? Wouldn't it? I notice that you've begun to be very attentive... you interesting young man...."

Svidriga&#65533;lov struck the table with his fist impatiently. He was flushed. Raskolnikov saw clearly that the glass or glass and a half of champagne that he had sipped almost unconsciously was affecting him—and he resolved to take advantage of the opportunity. He felt very suspicious of Svidriga&#65533;lov.

"Well, after what you have said, I am fully convinced that you have come to Petersburg with designs on my sister," he said directly to Svidriga&#65533;lov, in order to irritate him further.

"Oh, nonsense," said Svidriga&#65533;lov, seeming to rouse himself. "Why, I told you... besides your sister can't endure me."

"Yes, I am certain that she can't, but that's not the point."

"Are you so sure that she can't?" Svidriga&#65533;lov screwed up his eyes and smiled mockingly. "You are right, she doesn't love me, but you can never be sure of what has passed between husband and wife or lover and mistress. There's always a little corner which remains a secret to the world and is only known to those two. Will you answer for it that Avdotya Romanovna regarded me with aversion?"

"From some words you've dropped, I notice that you still have designs—and of course evil ones—on Dounia and mean to carry them out promptly."

"What, have I dropped words like that?" Svidriga&#65533;lov asked in na&#65533;ve dismay, taking not the slightest notice of the epithet bestowed on his designs.

"Why, you are dropping them even now. Why are you so frightened? What are you so afraid of now?"

"Me—afraid? Afraid of you? You have rather to be afraid of me, _cher ami_. But what nonsense.... I've drunk too much though, I see that. I was almost saying too much again. Damn the wine! Hi! there, water!"

He snatched up the champagne bottle and flung it without ceremony out of the window. Philip brought the water.

"That's all nonsense!" said Svidriga&#65533;lov, wetting a towel and putting it to his head. "But I can answer you in one word and annihilate all your suspicions. Do you know that I am going to get married?"

"You told me so before."

"Did I? I've forgotten. But I couldn't have told you so for certain for I had not even seen my betrothed; I only meant to. But now I really have a betrothed and it's a settled thing, and if it weren't that I have business that can't be put off, I would have taken you to see them at once, for I should like to ask your advice. Ach, hang it, only ten minutes left! See, look at the watch. But I must tell you, for it's an interesting story, my marriage, in its own way. Where are you off to? Going again?"

"No, I'm not going away now."

"Not at all? We shall see. I'll take you there, I'll show you my betrothed, only not now. For you'll soon have to be off. You have to go to the right and I to the left. Do you know that Madame Resslich, the woman I am lodging with now, eh? I know what you're thinking, that she's the woman whose girl they say drowned herself in the winter. Come, are you listening? She arranged it all for me. You're bored, she said, you want something to fill up your time. For, you know, I am a gloomy, depressed person. Do you think I'm light-hearted? No, I'm gloomy. I do no harm, but sit in a corner without speaking a word for three days at a time. And that Resslich is a sly hussy, I tell you. I know what she has got in her mind; she thinks I shall get sick of it, abandon my wife and depart, and she'll get hold of her and make a profit out of her—in our class, of course, or higher. She told me the father was a broken-down retired official, who has been sitting in a chair for the last three years with his legs paralysed. The mamma, she said, was a sensible woman.

There is a son serving in the provinces, but he doesn't help; there is a daughter, who is married, but she doesn't visit them. And they've two little nephews on their hands, as though their own children were not enough, and they've taken from school their youngest daughter, a girl who'll be sixteen in another month, so that then she can be married. She was for me. We went there. How funny it was! I present myself—a landowner, a widower, of a well-known name, with connections, with a fortune. What if I am fifty and she is not sixteen? Who thinks of that? But it's fascinating, isn't it? It is fascinating, ha-ha! You should have seen how I talked to the papa and mamma. It was worth paying to have seen me at that moment. She comes in, curtseys, you can fancy, still in a short frock—an unopened bud! Flushing like a sunset—she had been told, no doubt. I don't know how you feel about female faces, but to my mind these sixteen years, these childish eyes, shyness and tears of bashfulness are better than beauty; and she is a perfect little picture, too.

Fair hair in little curls, like a lamb's, full little rosy lips, tiny feet, a charmer!... Well, we made friends. I told them I was in a hurry owing to domestic circumstances, and the next day, that is the day before yesterday, we were betrothed. When I go now I take her on my knee at once and keep her there.... Well, she flushes like a sunset and I kiss her every minute. Her mamma of course impresses on her that this is her husband and that this must be so. It's simply delicious! The present betrothed condition is perhaps better than marriage. Here you have what is called _la nature et la v&#65533;rit&#65533;_, ha-ha! I've talked to her twice, she is far from a fool. Sometimes she steals a look at me that positively scorches me. Her face is like Raphael's Madonna. You know, the Sistine Madonna's face has something fantastic in it, the face of mournful religious ecstasy. Haven't you noticed it? Well, she's something in that line.

The day after we'd been betrothed, I bought her presents to the value of fifteen hundred roubles—a set of diamonds and another of pearls and a silver dressing-case as large as this, with all sorts of things in it, so that even my Madonna's face glowed. I sat her on my knee, yesterday, and I suppose rather too unceremoniously—she flushed crimson and the tears started, but she didn't want to show it. We were left alone, she suddenly flung herself on my neck (for the first time of her own accord), put her little arms round me, kissed me, and vowed that she would be an obedient, faithful, and good wife, would make me happy, would devote all her life, every minute of her life, would sacrifice everything, everything, and that all she asks in return is my _respect_, and that she wants 'nothing, nothing more from me, no presents.' You'll admit that to hear such a confession, alone, from an angel of sixteen in a muslin frock, with little curls, with a flush of maiden shyness in her cheeks and tears of enthusiasm in her eyes is rather fascinating! Isn't it fascinating? It's worth paying for, isn't it? Well... listen, we'll go to see my betrothed, only not just now!"

"The fact is this monstrous difference in age and development excites your sensuality! Will you really make such a marriage?"

"Why, of course. Everyone thinks of himself, and he lives most gaily who knows best how to deceive himself. Ha-ha! But why are you so keen about virtue? Have mercy on me, my good friend. I am a sinful man. Ha-ha-ha!"

"But you have provided for the children of Katerina Ivanovna. Though... though you had your own reasons.... I understand it all now."

"I am always fond of children, very fond of them," laughed Svidriga&#65533;lov. "I can tell you one curious instance of it. The first day I came here I visited various haunts, after seven years I simply rushed at them. You probably notice that I am not in a hurry to renew acquaintance with my old friends. I shall do without them as long as I can. Do you know, when I was with Marfa Petrovna in the country, I was haunted by the thought of these places where anyone who knows his way about can find a great deal. Yes, upon my soul! The peasants have vodka, the educated young people, shut out from activity, waste themselves in impossible dreams and visions and are crippled by theories; Jews have sprung up and are amassing money, and all the rest give themselves up to debauchery.

From the first hour the town reeked of its familiar odours. I chanced to be in a frightful den—I like my dens dirty—it was a dance, so called, and there was a _cancan_ such as I never saw in my day. Yes, there you have progress. All of a sudden I saw a little girl of thirteen, nicely dressed, dancing with a specialist in that line, with another one _vis-&#65533;-vis_. Her mother was sitting on a chair by the wall. You can't fancy what a _cancan_ that was! The girl was ashamed, blushed, at last felt insulted, and began to cry. Her partner seized her and began whirling her round and performing before her; everyone laughed and—I like your public, even the _cancan_ public—

they laughed and shouted, 'Serves her right—serves her right! Shouldn't bring children!' Well, it's not my business whether that consoling reflection was logical or not. I at once fixed on my plan, sat down by the mother, and began by saying that I too was a stranger and that people here were ill-bred and that they couldn't distinguish decent folks and treat them with respect, gave her to understand that I had plenty of money, offered to take them home in my carriage. I took them home and got to know them.

They were lodging in a miserable little hole and had only just arrived from the country. She told me that she and her daughter could only regard my acquaintance as an honour. I found out that they had nothing of their own and had come to town upon some legal business. I proffered my services and money. I learnt that they had gone to the dancing saloon by mistake, believing that it was a genuine dancing class. I offered to assist in the young girl's education in French and dancing. My offer was accepted with enthusiasm as an honour—and we are still friendly.... If you like, we'll go and see them, only not just now."

"Stop! Enough of your vile, nasty anecdotes, depraved vile, sensual man!"

"Schiller, you are a regular Schiller! _O la vertu va-t-elle se nicher?_ But you know I shall tell you these things on purpose, for the pleasure of hearing your outcries!"

"I dare say. I can see I am ridiculous myself," muttered Raskolnikov angrily.

Svidriga&#65533;lov laughed heartily; finally he called Philip, paid his bill, and began getting up.

"I say, but I am drunk, _assez caus&#65533;_," he said. "It's been a pleasure."

"I should rather think it must be a pleasure!" cried Raskolnikov, getting up. "No doubt it is a pleasure for a worn-out profligate to describe such adventures with a monstrous project of the same sort in his mind—especially under such circumstances and to such a man as me.... It's stimulating!"

"Well, if you come to that," Svidriga&#65533;lov answered, scrutinising Raskolnikov with some surprise, "if you come to that, you are a thorough cynic yourself. You've plenty to make you so, anyway. You can understand a great deal... and you can do a great deal too. But enough. I sincerely regret not having had more talk with you, but I shan't lose sight of you.... Only wait a bit."

Svidriga&#65533;lov walked out of the restaurant. Raskolnikov walked out after him. Svidriga&#65533;lov was not however very drunk, the wine had affected him for a moment, but it was passing off every minute. He was preoccupied with something of importance and was frowning. He was apparently excited and uneasy in anticipation of something. His manner to Raskolnikov had changed during the last few minutes, and he was ruder and more sneering every moment. Raskolnikov noticed all this, and he too was uneasy. He became very suspicious of Svidriga&#65533;lov and resolved to follow him.

They came out on to the pavement.

"You go to the right, and I to the left, or if you like, the other way. Only _adieu, mon plaisir_, may we meet again."

And he walked to the right towards the Hay Market.

CHAPTER 7

The same day, about seven o'clock in the evening, Raskolnikov was on his way to his mother's and sister's lodging—the lodging in Bakaleyev's house which Razumihin had found for them. The stairs went up from the street. Raskolnikov walked with lagging steps, as though still hesitating whether to go or not. But nothing would have turned him back: his decision was taken.

"Besides, it doesn't matter, they still know nothing," he thought, "and they are used to thinking of me as eccentric."

He was appallingly dressed: his clothes torn and dirty, soaked with a night's rain. His face was almost distorted from fatigue, exposure, the inward conflict that had lasted for twenty-four hours. He had spent all the previous night alone, God knows where. But anyway he had reached a decision.

He knocked at the door which was opened by his mother. Dounia was not at home. Even the servant happened to be out. At first Pulcheria Alexandrovna was speechless with joy and surprise; then she took him by the hand and drew him into the room.

"Here you are!" she began, faltering with joy. "Don't be angry with me, Rodya, for welcoming you so foolishly with tears: I am laughing not crying. Did you think I was crying? No, I am delighted, but I've got into such a stupid habit of shedding tears. I've been like that ever since your father's death. I cry for anything. Sit down, dear boy, you must be tired; I see you are. Ah, how muddy you are."

CHAPTER 8

When he went into Sonia's room, it was already getting dark. All day Sonia had been waiting for him in terrible anxiety. Dounia had been waiting with her. She had come to her that morning, remembering Svidrigaïlov's words that Sonia knew. We will not describe the conversation and tears of the two girls, and how friendly they became. Dounia gained one comfort at least from that interview, that her brother would not be alone. He had gone to her, Sonia, first with his confession; he had gone to her for human fellowship when he needed it; she would go with him wherever fate might send him. Dounia did not ask, but she knew it was so. She looked at Sonia almost with reverence and at first almost embarrassed her by it. Sonia was almost on the point of tears. She felt herself, on the contrary, hardly worthy to look at Dounia. Dounia's gracious image when she had bowed to her so attentively and respectfully at their first meeting in Raskolnikov's room had remained in her mind as one of the fairest visions of her life.

Dounia at last became impatient and, leaving Sonia, went to her brother's room to await him there; she kept thinking that he would come there first. When she had gone, Sonia began to be tortured by the dread of his committing suicide, and Dounia too feared it. But they had spent the day trying to persuade each other that that could not be, and both were less anxious while they were together. As soon as they parted, each thought of nothing else. Sonia remembered how Svidrigaïlov had said to her the day before that Raskolnikov had two alternatives—Siberia or... Besides she knew his vanity, his pride and his lack of faith.

"Is it possible that he has nothing but cowardice and fear of death to make him live?" she thought at last in despair.

Meanwhile the sun was setting. Sonia was standing in dejection, looking intently out of the window, but from it she could see nothing but the unwhitewashed blank wall of the next house. At last when she began to feel sure of his death—he walked into the room.

She gave a cry of joy, but looking carefully into his face she turned pale.

"Yes," said Raskolnikov, smiling. "I have come for your cross, Sonia. It was you told me to go to the cross-roads; why is it you are frightened now it's come to that?"

Sonia gazed at him astonished. His tone seemed strange to her; a cold shiver ran over her, but in a moment she guessed that the tone and the words were a mask. He spoke to her looking away, as though to avoid meeting her eyes.

"You see, Sonia, I've decided that it will be better so. There is one fact.... But it's a long story and there's no need to discuss it. But do you know what angers me? It annoys me that all those stupid brutish faces will be gaping at me directly, pestering me with their stupid questions, which I shall have to answer—they'll point their fingers at me.... Tfoo! You know I am not going to Porfiry, I am sick of him. I'd rather go to my friend, the Explosive Lieutenant; how I shall surprise him, what a sensation I shall make! But I must be cooler; I've become too irritable of late. You know I was nearly shaking my fist at my sister just now, because she turned to take a last look at me. It's a brutal state to be in! Ah! what am I coming to! Well, where are the crosses?"

He seemed hardly to know what he was doing. He could not stay still or concentrate his attention on anything; his ideas seemed to gallop after one another, he talked incoherently, his hands trembled slightly.

Without a word Sonia took out of the drawer two crosses, one of cypress wood and one of copper. She made the sign of the cross over herself and over him, and put the wooden cross on his neck.

"It's the symbol of my taking up the cross," he laughed. "As though I had not suffered much till now! The wooden cross, that is the peasant one; the copper one, that is Lizaveta's—you will wear yourself, show me! So she had it on... at that moment? I remember two things like these too, a silver one and a little ikon. I threw them back on the old woman's neck. Those would be appropriate now, really, those are what I ought to put on now.... But I am talking nonsense and forgetting what matters; I'm somehow forgetful.... You see I have come to warn you, Sonia, so that you might know... that's all—that's all I came for. But I thought I had more to say. You wanted me to go yourself. Well, now I am going to prison and you'll have your wish. Well, what are you crying for? You too? Don't. Leave off! Oh, how I hate it all!"

But his feeling was stirred; his heart ached, as he looked at her. "Why is she grieving too?" he thought to himself. "What am I to her? Why does she weep? Why is she looking after me, like my mother or Dounia? She'll be my nurse."

Bibliography

A Gentle Creature and Other Stories, 1995.

Belye Notschi, 1848 - White Nights (trans. by Alan Myers) - Vaaleat yöt (suom. Eila Salminen) - films: 1934, dir. by Vera Stroyeva and Grigory Roshal; *Le notti bianche* 1957.

Bloom, Harold, ed. *Fyodor Dostoevsky's* Crime and Punishment. New York: Chelsea House Publishers, 1988.

Djadushkyn Son, 1859 - Uncle's Dream - Vanhan ruhtinaan rakkaus (suom. Juhani Konkka).

Dostoevsky's Occasional Writings, 1997.

Great Short Stories of Fyodor Dostoevsky, 1968.

Grossman, Leonid Petrovich. *Dostoevsky: A Biography*. Trans. Mary Mackler. Indianapolis: Bobbs-Merrill Co., 1975.

Magarshack, David. *Dostoevsky*. New York: Harcourt, Brace & World, 1963.

Miller, Robin Feuer, ed. *Critical Essays on Dostoevsky*. Boston: G. K. Hall, 1986.

Polnoe Sobranie Khudozhestvennykh Proizvedenii, 1926-30 (13 vols.).

Selo Stephanchikovo I Yego Obitateli, 1859 - Friend Of The Family (trans. by Constance Garnett) / The Village Of Stepanchikovo And Its Inhabitants (trans. by Ignat Avsey) - Narri kartanon valtiaana (suom. Juhani Konkka, myös Markku Lahtela 1972).

Sekirin, Peter, ed. *The Dostoevsky Archive: Firsthand Accounts of the Novelist from Contemporaries' Memoirs and Rare Periodicals*. Jefferson, NC: McFarland & Co., 1997.

Terras, Victor. *Reading Dostoevsky*. Madison: University of Wisconsin Press, 1998.

Tuten, Frederic. *Dostoyevsky's* Crime and Punishment. New York: Monarch Press, 1966.

Uncle's Dream and Other Stories, 1989 (trans. by David McDuff).

Unizhennyye I Oskorblyonnyye, 1861 - The Insulted And Injured (trans. by Constance Garnett).

Zapiski Iz Podpolya, 1864 - Notes From Underground (trans. by Constance Garnett) - Kellariloukko (suom. Valto Kallama) / Kirjoituksia kellarista (suom. Esa Adrian).

Zimnie Zametki Na Letnikh Vpechatleniiakh, 1863 - Summer Impressions (trans. by Kyril FitzLyon).